Collected Papers on Trajectory Equifinality Approach

By
TATSUYA SATO

Chitose Press

Recommendation for
Collected Papers on Trajectory Equifinality Approach

This book is an important work in contemporary science, since it overcomes the historical limitations in psychology that have been hindering the science for half a century – the notion or "random sampling" and its corollary – "evidence based science." The contributions in this book show how the new direction in understanding human ways of living – looking respectfully into the basic processes of human creation of personally meaningful life courses. This new direction brings the historical perspective into the center of psychological science – a synthesis that is long awaited.

Jaan Valsiner
Niels Bohr Professor of Cultural Psychology
Aalborg University, Denmark

Preface

This booklet consists of some papers on the Trajectory Equifinality Approach (TEA). These papers have appeared in journals and book chapters for more than the past decade. From them, readers can understand how TEA itself has transformed over the years. Although readers might get confused, this transformation indicates further transformation may occur in the future, and I sincerely hope that new readers promote such a future-oriented transformation of TEA. TEA is a kind of frame-game, like Linux. Therefore, you can use it with no permission *with reference* and create new ideas on TEA.

The Trajectory Equifinality Approach (TEA) has a definite birthday: January 25, 2004. About a decade ago, I welcomed Jaan Valsiner of Clark University, USA (now of Aalborg University in Denmark) as an invited professor of Ritsumeikan University, Kyoto, Japan, where we held a symposium on cultural psychology. I presented my research on pocket money using a basic idea of equifinality in developmental phenomena, after Valsiner (2001b, 2003a). Immediately following this symposium, Professor Valsiner proposed that I write a chapter on TEM. He then decided to transform the symposium on cultural psychology at Beijing, and a presentation concerning TEM was given on the psychology stage on August 12, 2004 (Sato, Yasuda et al., 2004).

Ten years after the first chapter on TEA was written (Valsiner & Sato, 2006), the first English language book on TEA, *Making the future* (Sato et al., 2016), appeared. Colleagues from different countries (i.e., Colombia, Estonia, Denmark, and Switzerland) contributed to the book. I am thrilled that TEA has become a common "methodology" used worldwide in cultural psychology. I am also glad this booklet (of collected papers) will help researchers who have an interest in describing *the process of* human life course.

Papers collected within this booklet have their own history. Many people have made direct and indirect contributions to the papers collected herein. I am deeply

Preface

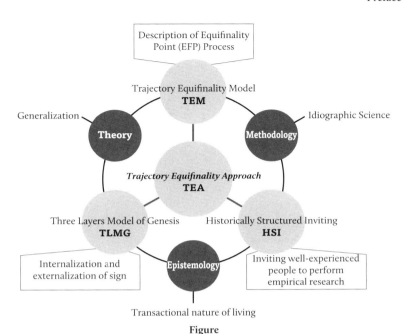

Figure

grateful to all my coauthors. Without their ideas, inspiration, and support, this booklet may have never appeared.

This publication was supported by Ritsumeikan University Program for Promotion of Academic Publication.

January 1, 2017

Tatsuya Sato, Ph.D.

Contents

Part 1
Chronogenesis
Introduction to TEM

Chapter 1
Time in Life and Life in Time
Between Experiencing and Accounting

1. Introduction: The experience of time   *3*

2. "Lived time" and "clock time," are they creating harmony?   *5*

    2.1. "Lived time" and "clock time"   *5*

    2.2. Lifetime, life course and life cycle   *6*

    2.3. Time without life   *7*

    2.4. Toward the notion of chronogenesis   *9*

3. Chronogenesis in understanding human cultural lives   *9*

    3.1. Chronogenesis   *10*

    3.2. *Zeit* and *Stunde*   *11*

    3.3. Harmony between place and time: Chronotope and its meaning   *11*

    3.4. From the "arrow of time" to the "broom of time"   *13*

    3.5. Genetic logic for chronogenesis as a transformation of structures   *15*

4. Conclusion: New methodology for "time-conscious psychology"   *17*

Contents

Part 2
Emergence of TEM

Chapter 2
Minding Money
How Understanding of Value is Culturally Promoted

1. Introduction   *23*

2. Money and psychology   *25*

   2.1. Cultural psychology and the functions of money   *26*

   2.2. Is money a thing?   *27*

3. Children and the "magic of money"   *28*

4. Lessons from the *Money and Child* research project   *29*

   4.1. The *Money and Child* research project   *29*

   4.2. Avoiding the cultural attribution error   *31*

5. Strategies of giving and a receiving pocket money: Case study – Korean girl X   *31*

6. Methodological elaboration of the case: From time line model to Trajectory and Equifinality Model   *34*

7. Theoretical considerations   *37*

8. Open-systemic view of child and money   *40*

9. General conclusions   *41*

Chapter 3
Development, Change or Transformation
How can Psychology Conceive and Depict Professional Identify Construction?

1. Implication of HSS and TEM   *45*

   1.1. An ordinary analogue   *46*

   1.2. Human beings are not a soup   *46*

2. The importance of the notion of trajectories   *49*

3. EFP and OPP in Kullasepp's paper   *51*

4. Dialogical self and its transforming process   *52*

5. Psychology students' experience: Japanese students today   *54*

6. Toward the study of three levels of trajectories   *55*

Chapter 4
Beyond Dichotomy   *57*
Towards Creative Synthesis

1. On sampling and generalization   *58*

   1.1. The notion of "control"   *59*

   1.2. Where is conceptual problem?   *60*

2. On the neo-Galtonian research paradigm and the inference revolution   *61*

3. On the situation of psychology in Japan   *63*

4. Japanese psychology after World War II   *64*

5. Beyond dichotomy and toward a creative synthesis   *65*

6. Concluding remarks   *68*

Part 3
Development of TEM

Chapter 5
Sampling Reconsidered   *73*
Idiographic Science and the Analyses of Personal Life Trajectories

1. Two ways to generalized knowledge   *74*

   1.1. The trajectories of Idiographic Science (IS) and Classifying Science (CS)   *74*

   1.2. Creating norms: The child becomes a classificatory object   *78*

2. What is a sample?   *80*

   2.1. The meaning of "population"   *81*

   2.2. Logic of generalization based on the homogeneity assumption   *82*

   2.3. The notion of sampling in the natural sciences   *83*

   2.4. Sampling in the behavioral sciences   *84*

3. Sampling and statistical theories   *85*

   3.1. Steps in sampling   *87*

   3.2. Changing the axiomatic base: Historicity of life courses   *88*

Contents

    3.3. Types of sampling   *89*

    3.4. Sampling in socio-cultural psychology   *91*

    3.5. Generalization – Knowing about what? Population or generic models?   *93*

    3.6. Development as a process: Constructing histories   *95*

  4. Socio-cultural experiences on the trajectories of living   *96*

  5. A new philosophy of method: HSS (Historically Structured Sampling)   *98*

    5.1. Trajectory Equifinality Model (TEM)-based on HSS   *99*

    5.2. Examples of HSS: Three studies that explicate the TEM   *101*

  6. Conclusion: Re-thinking sampling and re-building theories   *110*

Chapter 6

Depicting the Dynamics of Living the Life   *113*
The Trajectory Equifinality Model

  1. Obstacles in treating the dynamics of the living in psychology and sociology   *115*

    1.1. Life course studies and the notion of life trajectory   *117*

    1.2. Can Structural Equation Models (SEM) reflect the dynamism of development?   *118*

    1.3. Assigning numbers – creating static properties – and scale types   *119*

    1.4. The person-situation debate, and beyond   *120*

  2. Rethinking the rating scale: Toward the new views of trajectory   *123*

  3. Considering trajectories-in-the-making   *126*

    3.1. TEM: Making the past, creating the future   *126*

    3.2. Basic notions of TEM   *128*

    3.3. Empirical studies for depicting dynamics with TEM   *132*

    3.4. Focusing on the dynamics in the personal decision making   *136*

  4. General conclusions   *140*

Chapter 7

The Authentic Culture of Living Well   *143*
Pathways to Psychological Well-Being

  1. How Trajectory Equifinality Model (TEM) deals with Life with Illness (LWI)   *145*

  2. Illness trajectory framework from nursing rsearch and medical sociology   *146*

    2.1. Historical context of ethnography: The archeology of anthropologies   *146*

vii

2.2. Life ethnography   *148*

2.3. Illness trajectory model   *150*

2.4. Life trajectories for the person with illness   *153*

3. Lessons from life of intractable and/or chronic disease and notion of finality: Uncertainty and genesis of multifinality   *155*

3.1. The patients' life of intractable and/or chronic disease   *155*

3.2. Frame of transition process of pathogenesis of intractable and/or chronic disease   *157*

4. Quality of life and beyond   *160*

4.1. On measurement of "quality of life"   *160*

4.2. Equifinality for the person with chronic disease and/or progressive disease   *161*

4.3. The person as a co-investigator in research   *163*

5. Theoretical implications   *164*

5.1. Epigenesis is not necessary for multifinality   *164*

5.2. Multifinality from the perspective of life with illness   *165*

5.3. Multifinality as a spatial extension of finality   *167*

6. Concluding remarks   *168*

7. Future directions   *169*

Appendix

Appendix 1

Historically Structured Sampling (HSS)   *173*

How can Psychology's Methodology Become Tuned in to the Reality of the Historical Nature of Cultural Psychology?

1. Historically Structured Sampling as a new innovation   *174*

1.1. The varieties of sampling   *174*

1.2. Culture as a problem for the social sciences   *176*

2. Design failures: "Blind spots" of "random" sampling   *177*

3. Why has the sample-to-population line of generalization survived?   *181*

3.1. The self-constructed limitation of the social sciences   *182*

4. Sampling in case of non-independent phenomena   *182*

Contents

    4.1. Systemic view: Axiomatic acceptance of interdependence   *184*

5. Historically Structured Sampling (HSS): Selection by histories   *184*

    5.1. Equifinality   *185*

    5.2. Obligatory passage points in the Trajectory Equifinality Model   *187*

    5.3. Obligatory Passage Points (OPP)   *188*

    5.4. The practice of sampling: HSS   *189*

6. Possible applications of HSS in research practices   *191*

7. How trajectories are made: The landscape model   *193*

8. Examples of empirical projects where HSS could be appropriate   *194*

    8.1. Re-considering ontogeny of tactile contact   *199*

    8.2. Same event – different personal experiences   *201*

    8.3. An example at the micro-genetic level   *203*

9. Culture and personal life trajectories   *204*

10. General conclusion   *207*

Appendix 2

Brief Practice for Using Trajectory Equifinality Model (TEM)   *211*
As a General Tool for Understanding the Human Life Course within Irreversible Time

    1. Research using TEM: Simple practice on TEM   *213*

    2. Steps in using TEM for single case example   *214*

    3. Toward a saturation of TEM: The second EFP   *216*

References   *219*

Index   *237*

Acknowledgments

Chapter 1: Sato, T., & Valsiner, J. (2010). Time in life and life in time: Between experiencing and accounting. *Ritsumeikan Journal of Human Sciences*, **20**, 79-92. Reproduced by permission of authors.

Chapter 2: Sato, T. (2011). Minding money: How understanding of value is cuturally promoted. *Integrative Psychological & Behavioural Science*, **45**, 116-131. Reproduced by permission of Springer.

Chapter 3: Sato, T. (2006). Development, change or transformation: How can psychology conceive and depict professional identify construction? *European Journal of School Psychology*, **4**(2), 321-334. Reproduced by permission of Firera & Liuzzo.

Chapter 4: Sato, T., Watanabe, Y., & Omi, Y. (2007). Beyond dichotomy: Towards creative synthesis. *Integrative Psychological & Behavioral Science*, **41**, 50-59. Reproduced by permission of Springer.

Chapter 5: Sato, T., Yasuda, Y., Kido, A., Arakawa, A., Mizoguchi, H., & Valsiner, J. (2007). Sampling reconsidered: Idiographic science and the analyses of personal life trajectories. In J. Valsiner & A. Rosa (Eds.), *The Cambridge handbook of sociocultural psychology* (pp. 82-106). New York: Cambridge University Press. Reproduced by permission of Cambridge University Press.

Chapter 6: Sato, T., Hidaka, T., & Fukuda, M. (2009). Depicting the dynamics of living the life: The Trajectory Equifinality Model. In J. Valsiner, P. C. M. Molenaar, M. C. D. P. Lyra & N. Chaudhary (Eds.), *Dynamic process methodology in the social and developmental sciences* (pp. 217-240). New York: Springer. Reproduced by permission of Springer.

Chapter 7: Sato, T., Fukuda, M., Hidaka, T., Kido, A., Nishida, M., & Akasaka, M. (2012). The authentic culture of living well: Pathways to psychological well-being. In J. Valsiner (Ed.), *The Oxford handbook of culture and psychology* (pp. 1078-1092). New York: Oxford University Press. Reproduced by permission of Oxford University

Press.

Appendix 1: Valsiner, J., & Sato, T. (2006). Historically Structured Sampling (HSS): How can psychology's methodology become tuned in to the reality of the historical nature of cultural psychology? In J. Straub, D. Weidemann, C. Kölbl & B. Zielke (Eds.), *Pursuit of meaning: Advances in cultural and cross-cultural psychology* (pp. 215-251). Bielefeld: Transcript. Reproduced by permission of transcript Verlag.

All chapters are slightly modified for this booklet.

Appendix 2: Newly written for this booklet.

Part 1

Chronogenesis
Introduction to TEM

Chapter 1

Time in Life and Life in Time

Between Experiencing and Accounting

Abstract

Time operates on human lives in two ways – as an inherent duration that is inevitably blended with irreversible experiencing, and as an abstract quality on which different marker events create the possibility of making time into a measurable commodity. We propose an investigation of how the two time perspectives are transforming each other – chronogenesis – and to provide both phenomenological illustrations and cultural psychological methodology of such transformations. HSS, TEM and TLMG are introduced as promising paradigm for a new methodology in cultural psychology.

Keywords

Genesis, Chronogenesis, Duration, Transformation, Trajectory Equifinality Model (TEM)

1. Introduction: The experience of time

Everyone agrees that happy times of the pleasurable kind seem to pass faster than stressful times. When we are in a deep sleep and then wake up, we feel the time as if it had been a moment. We fall asleep instantly – and eight hours later when we wake up, it seems to us as if just a short time has passed. On the other hand, an insomniac – a person who is continuously struggling with habitual sleeplessness – suffers what feels like a long time every night before the transition to sleep. Time

Part 1   CHRONOGENESIS

sometimes "flies" and at other times "drags" – as all of us know. There is a deeply subjective flow involved in living-within-time. Imagine that you decided – or were asked to – do five-hundred push-ups. This is a difficult experience for nearly everyone. You start and then cannot count anymore. You feel that this simple torture is never-ending. It is another kind of pervasive time experience. You cannot go back to the state you were before you embarked on the path to the five-hundred push-ups. You function in pervasive and irreversible time. This corresponds to the suffering of terminally ill patients. Though pleasurable and distressful experiences are both pervasive, feeling relaxed might correspond to an extension of space feeling. In fact, Bergson (1907/1945), in his work "*L'évolution, correlate détente* (i.e. relaxation) to extension, or *créatrice*." Therefore, distress might correspond to convergence of time.

According to Bergson, time is persistent – it is part of everything we do – even our experience of "doing nothing"[1] takes place within time. It is within each biological, psychological, and social event – inseparable from all the growing systems. Pervasive, but irreversible time is experienced during listening to harmonious music. Or, imagine yourself sprawled on the ground and looking up at the sky, when a cloud comes floating in from out of your range of vision, you experience pervasive and irreversible time. Then, it starts to rain! You wonder if you should get up or not. Rupture occurs, and options emerge. You should decide to get up or not.

Yet aside from living-within-time, there is also the clock time. For contrast, we call "non-lived" time, such as "objective" time, "clock time." "Clock time" is based on some basic unit of time. Any measurement of time depends on a procedure that focuses on astronomic and/or physical phenomena for constructing the unit of time. The waxing and waning of the moon and the length of the shadow caused by sunlight are used for creating the calendar and/or clock. Water and sand are also used as indices of homogeneous continuing time. Today, oscillations of physical processes are used for precisely tuning the clock.

Chapter 1   Time in Life and Life in Time

2. "Lived time" and "clock time," are they creating harmony?

2.1. "Lived time" and "clock time"

Mizuki & Minami (2010) have shown how school children prefer to walk narrow and devious back streets − rather than walk on the sidewalk of the main street. Children prefer back streets, because they can see flowers, encounter insects and animals and enjoy *Michikusa* with friends. *Michikusa* literally means "grass by the side of the road," but in the vernacular, it refers to dilly-dallying, as a horse would dilly-dally by stopping to eat the grass. Examples of *Michikusa* are many: a sword battle using parasols, playing with cats and so on. Some children even do homework by studying nature on the street.

However, the pleasures of *Michikusa* for children irritate mothers and teachers. Or, maybe the adults' irritation with children is a *Michikusa* experience for them − who no longer feel the immediate pleasure of encountering a new insect on the street. Even as the street is narrow, the story is wider − we are all enjoying *Michikusa* on our way, in our lives − we enjoy being within our time. And, all our social worlds are expecting us to be "on time" for one objective or another. Thus, we can find that there might be a decarage between time in vivid living or "lived time," and "clock time" that depends on the movement of clock's hands.

Can "lived time" and "clock time" be synthesized into one? And would there be universal harmony of time? Yet, that would require that social institutions stop using "measured time" and/or "counting time" as a social organizing feature. Can that happen? Living in time entails social cohesion − there are "times of prosperity," and "times of economic depression." Young people who decide to get married plan a wedding "high time" (German − *Hochzeit*) − to experience the transition in their irreversible life experience. They cannot reverse that event by "taking it back" − they can only move forward to the end of their marriage in another transition in time − death or divorce. According to Lewin (1939), "Persons of all ages are influenced by the manner in which they see the future, that is by their expectations, fears and hopes ..."

Part 1   CHRONOGENESIS

(Lewin, 1939, p. 878). Because Lewin suggested that time-related actions depend on a person's age, we need to consider a longer time scale than the *Michikusa* time scale. Children enjoying their *Michikusa* have rather a short time perspective of a day after school. However, we usually have a longer time perspective and represent time in various ways. Next, let's consider a longer time scale, such as the life time.

2.2. Lifetime, life course and life cycle

At first glance – the meaning of lifetime is simple – it ranges from birth to death. Yet if we start thinking about human culture, the question becomes fuzzy. Why consider a lifetime as starting at birth – rather than from the moment a pregnant woman feels the movement of the foetus, or the father-to-be delivers the much needed sperm into the vagina? Does a stillborn child have a – before birth?

Furthermore – who determines the limits of a lifetime? As the irreversible time flows without our noticing it, it is the setting of time limits (*Terminierung*) that makes time perceivable phenomena and emerge in the context of specific time-marking events. The doctor performing an abortion is introducing such a marker event into the life course of a woman. The military general sending young soldiers to a heroic battle from which nobody returns, creates a rupture not only in the lives of the to-be-dead soldiers, but also in the historical account of a lost battle. An insurance company that insures an old person by some expected estimate of how many more years that person might live – a marker that is deeply discomforting to the person who does not appreciate such a chronicle of the death foretold. Here, we can see that deciding and/or inferring with the end of life creates non-lived time and these are principally destructive. On the other hand, some regard the end of a person's life as a part of an eternal cycle.

As Müller & Giesbrecht (2006) emphasized that both Rudolph (2006) and Yamada & Kato (2006) were critical of a linear, homogeneous and unidimensional model of time. From their different perspectives, both formulated alternative conceptions of time. Rudolph (2006) proposed a mathematical model of psychological time ("full time") that is inhomogeneous and "one-dimensional only in a global

Chapter 1   Time in Life and Life in Time

sense." Yamada & Kato (2006) suggested multiple and coexisting views of time, even if they were somewhat contradictory. They also suggested that the Generative Life Cycle Model (GLCM) that described temporal phenomena from a subjective perspective. The GLCM is process oriented rather than goal-oriented, with a perspective that is "free" from an individualistic point of view, so that dying is represented as a meaningful transition in a reversible spiral of time (Hood, 2006).

Last – but not least – the meaning of a lifetime can transcend the actual biological birth and death periods. The long-dead ancestors are "alive" in the ritual mythologies of the living. The recently dead spouse is very much "alive" for the partner who is alive and visits the grave (Josephs, 1998). Children can be killed – for the reason of their connection with very much alive "malevolent spirits" – or everything can be done to honor children who are alive and keep them safely alive, because of their connection with "benevolent spirits." Social practices – such as the Yoruba (one of the major ethnic groups in Nigeria) moving from twin infanticide to twin honouring implies a period of uncertainty within the cultural meaning systems (Valsiner, 2001b, p.187). Among the Yoruba, the practice of twin infanticide has been transformed into that of twin adoption. Today, the birth of twins is a predestined event that is to be regarded as a lucky omen. Since twins are a special gift from God (Chappel, 1974). But the historically prior state of affairs in treating twin birth among the Yoruba was that of obligatory infanticide of twins. This was transformed through some members of the Yoruba society who lived in exile – innovation comes on the margins.

2.3. Time without life

Next, we focus on an even longer time scale, or cosmic time, which is far beyond the history of *Homo sapiens*. The cosmic time is not experienced by any person. In fact it would be mind-boggling for ordinary humans to consider time as a measure of cosmic distances.

For example, the star Mizar/Alcor shown by the arrow in Figure 1.1 is a double star – a visible combination of two stars. People with good visual acuity may at times see two stars next to each other in the location indicated by the arrow in Figure 1.1.

Part 1   CHRONOGENESIS

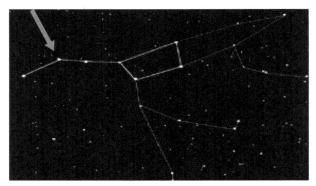

Figure 1.1. The double star Mizar/Alcor in the constellation Ursa Major

There are indeed two stars – and both of them are dual (consist of two stars orbiting each other) – yet they are not as they seem to the naked eye. Mizar is 78 light years from us, Alcor – 81. It takes light 78 years (of our Earth's time) from Mizar to arrive onto our *retina* at the moment of looking at the star. To add to that contrast – the light from Alcor has taken 3 more years – yet arrives on our retina at the same moment as we look at both of them. What is an instant perception of a star for us, is the result of moving celestial bodies where time is equally important – yet there is no subjective perceiver of time moments. Stars and galaxies emerge, develop, and become extinct – with time irreversibly. Yet there is no reflexivity involved – no thinking substance has so far been discovered among the celestial bodies other than on Earth, so far.

In 1927, Edwin Hubble first observed that light from distant galaxies is red shifted and that galaxies are moving farther and farther away from us. It means the universe is expanding. If we take the expansion process backward, the universe must have begun its expansion sometime, somewhere. Astronomers call this event the Big Bang. And astronomers estimate that it took it approximately 15 billion years to grow to the present size for our universe. Big Bang theory – expanding universe theory – ever covers the period before the bang. The theory posits that the bang was when time started. But, once it started – how does it continue? It is unfeasible to think that time was created by the Big Bang at an instant – before it there was no time, and

Chapter 1   Time in Life and Life in Time

after it – time miraculously emerged as a given dimension within which the cosmos has existed ever since. The events that were started by the Big Bang must create, or invent time as a form of organizational bricolage.

2.4. Toward the notion of chronogenesis

Thus far, we have considered the relationship between time and life at various levels. Conflicts between the lived time and the clock time, *Michikusa*. Time and human life; Life course and/or cycle. Time far beyond the history of *Homo sapience*; the light from the double star. Such discussions depend on the existence of time. Is time a premise for human life? If we could throw away time as a premise, the dichotomy between clock time and lived time should also be thrown away.

Let us re-consider the Japanese concept of *Michikusa*. Every school-child is fond of *Michikusa*, but no mother is. While the mother worries – where is my child? The child lives in a person's all-involving personal time (*durée*). The child takes the time to enjoy the moment – and is "late" for school or home. The mother – or the teacher – lives in a control-dominated "clock time" world. They define what "being late" means ("you are late for the 8.00 am class today!"). And the child answers – "Yes, but I saw a beautiful rainbow on my way to school." For the child, there exists no "being late" ... just "being." The "just being" is actually eternal becoming – creation of novelty. James Mark Baldwin (1906) called it persistent imitation – imitation of what we see in ways that go beyond what we see. We create new ways of looking at the world, we behave in new ways, and we seek out experiences that we find meaningful – as solid bases for "where we are" as well as situations for new adventures.

3. Chronogenesis in understanding human cultural lives

Continuing *Michikusa* is just being and is also the accumulation of the constant decision making what to do within irreversible time. Here we can see the core of CHRONOGENESIS. Time emerges with just being and continuous decision.

Part 1   CHRONOGENESIS

3.1. Chronogenesis

We feel it is time to establish the centrality of chronogenesis in the understanding of human cultural lives. Chronogenesis is the cultural invention of time in all of its forms – repetitive (clock, time unit measurements), indicative (the "snow rabbit" and its implications in Figure 1.2), existential ("lifetime" as seen through social representations – Yamada & Kato, 2006), or an abstract formal (Rudolph, 2006). Time is irreversible – both in its role, in all processes of emergence (symmetry-breaking – Prigogine's irreversible thermodynamics), and in our personal-cultural construction of it. The latter constructions are cultural means – semiotic devices – in organizing our lives.

Irreversibility of time makes the phenomena of becoming possible. Driesch (1914) explained the notion of becoming as follows.

> At one moment I "have" this consciously, at another I have that, and then again I have something else, and so on. This is the so-called stream of consciousness. But there is nothing like a stream quite immediately given to me: on the contrary, my having consciously is always a "now", or better still, it is entirely unrelated to time. I have this immediately object, this contents which I have consciously there can be distinguished a very peculiar class of that may be called signs; and these *signs*, which are had in a now, mean "not now but then (*i.e.* earlier)", and they may even mean "earlier than". (Driesch, 1914, p. 191)

According to Driesch, signs are very important for becoming and then for genesis. Here psychological science could find a way to consider the processes of emergence – yet in its present state of affairs psychology is very far from creating an adequate theory of emergence. The statistical orthodoxy it suffered in the recent past (Gigerenzer et al., 1989; Toomela, 2008) blocks its innovative capacities. Likewise, the norm of study of samples (Valsiner & Sato, 2006) – rather than individual cases over time – has limited the handling by psychology of its phenomena. Wilhelm Roux, who created *Entwicklungsmechanik* ("mechanics of development" or genesis), defined genesis as a visible process of variety. Even though the biological proof of Roux's

Chapter 1   Time in Life and Life in Time

insist was denied by Driesch's famous sea urchin experiment, Roux's theoretical ground is useful for the theory of development.

3.2. *Zeit* and *Stunde*

In German,[2] there are two basic words to present time. One is *Zeit* (time in general) and the other is *Stunde* (hour). *Zeit* is a general term for irreversible and pervasive time. *Stunde* is a unit – representing distinguishable and measurable time. It is not marked by irreversibility – one can talk and think of hours (*Stunde*) as if these are entities, consider them measures of work (e.g., "35 hour workweek"). In contrast, the irreversible time is marked by distinctions that fit under the German term *Terminierung* – creating specific time points (markers) on the irreversible timeline.[3] A *Stunde* is one of the abstractions from the process of *Terminierung* – alongside with many others (day, season, lifetime, light year, etc.). When *Terminierung* is created by any process that reflects upon irreversibility – usually the human thinking – then accounts of time emerge. This is what we call chronogenesis – the emergence of signs that mark time (moments, periods, quality, etc.) by the person in dialogue within oneself under the pressures of the eternal flow of the irreversible time.

Our story of chronogenesis builds on the synthesis in Bergson's philosophy of time and James Mark Baldwin's "genetic logic" (Valsiner, 2008, 2009). Bergson professed time is occupied by space when the word "measurement" is used. The notion of "measurement" by the beginning of the 20th century had taken on a mechanistic form – largely by the focus of spatial measurements (e.g., the etalon of a meter). Psychology needs to reverse our way of thinking about the relationship between time and space, that is, chronotope. All living beings live in concrete space, thus, chronogenesis occur neither in vacuum nor abstract space.

3.3. Harmony between place and time: Chronotope and its meaning

Time should never be regarded as space. If we said "measurement of time," the notion of space would invade the notion of time. Therefore, to escape from such danger, we should pay attention to the concept of chronotope and its example.

Part 1   CHRONOGENESIS

Chronotope comes from the Greek words for time (χρόνος) and space (τόπος). Thus, the word "chronotope" can be literally translated as "time-space." This is a term taken over by Mikhail Bakhtin from 1920s science (Einstein's theory of relativity) to describe the manner in which literature represents time and space (Bakhtin, 1984, 1986). Chronotope is defined as "the interrelation between time and space." For Bakhtin, the notion of chronotope was a tool for the critiques of historical literature, this notion helps psychologists to integrate the concept of time and space with the real person. We easily forget the simple fact that each person's life is itself irreplaceable and life should be respected from the viewpoint of chronotope. For example, Morioka (2008) focused on the relationship between the client and the therapist, which occur in irreplaceable time and space and he called it the "therapeutic chronotope."

Actually, the life of humans is not dominated by clock-time. Japanese farmers need time perspectives and it does not depend on the calendar. In Japan, melting of snow tells farmers the timing is right for planting the rice crop. Such a moment entails their creation of the time-to-be (and does) – *chronogenesis*. Farmers never start planting on just the same day of the calendar (for example May first every year). Planting depends on the climate. The farmers have the wisdom to know the good timing (Figure 1.2) for planting – generalizing from their seasonal experience.

Beginning to plant on the same day every year does not promise a good harvest. We can say that signs of future perspectives guide the farmer's plan for planting. Here is one example that the planting of rice by farmers in Japan is guided by a constructed sign.

Can you find the rabbit on the right photo in Figure 1.2. The mountain in winter seen on the left photo is fully covered by snow. Time passes. The snow that remains on the mountain in the right photo takes on the form of a "rabbit." Farmers call this shape, "*YUKI USAGI*" (*Yuki* means snow and *Usagi* means rabbit). Farmers also call this rabbit "*TANEMAKI USAGI*" (seed-planting rabbit), because it represents the climate favorable for planting and informs the proper temperature for the start of spring rice cropping. More importantly, it makes farmers expect the autumn harvest.

Chapter 1   Time in Life and Life in Time

Figure 1.2. The snow-scape of Mt. AZUMA KOFUJI in Fukushima Prefecture in Japan

Whenever rice farmers see the snow rabbit, they start the planting. In other word, after seeing the rabbit, the rice cropping starts.[4]

Each place has its own timing for starting based on the chronotope. Cronotope is regarded as the genesis of time, chronogenesis.

3.4. From the "arrow of time" to the "broom of time"

The asymmetry of the future and the past (Figure 1.3) creates a situation in which the traditional ("objective time" model based) notion of the "arrow of time" does not fit. The future is rich in potential courses of events, whereas the past is characterized by uni-linearity – in our "objective" retrospect. Aleksander Anisov (2005) has suggested the use of a new metaphor – "the broom of time" (Figure 1.3).

Since the future is constantly in the process of becoming the past, movement towards the "new present" (to become past) entails losing the features of possible future trajectories (loss of predicates in terms of logic). In Figure 1.3 this amounts to ignoring "branches" of the possible future as the singular present course is being created. Once this has happened the (by now) present becomes immediate past – with the loss of the "branches" crystallized. According to Anisov,

> The mentioned removal of ignored branches is of great importance for an adequate understanding of the phenomenon of the past. Earnest historians come to a conclusion that *history does not allow of subjunctive mood*. Any argument about what would have happened if dinosaurs did not exist, if Napoleon was killed in his youth, or if Lenin was arrested in 1917 by czar's authorities, – contain no scientific meaning and may not have any. The

Part 1   CHRONOGENESIS

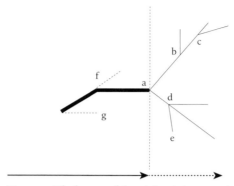

Figure 1.3. The broom of time (after Anisov, 2001)

offered axioms of time order precisely express this specific aspect. The past has no valid alternatives even given that sometime back certain past meta-moments contained the listed events in the zone of real possible future. The essence of the issue is in the impossibility to return back to such meta-moments. (Anisov, 2005, p. 81)

Thus, the branches f and g in Figure 1.3 would be inaccessible from the point of view of temporal logic. A century before him, his predecessor in the effort to build logic of development, Baldwin (1906) commented on the issue of how to study development:

> that series of events is truly genetic [developmental] which cannot be constructed before it has happened, and which cannot be exhausted backwards, after it has happened. (Baldwin, 1906, p. 21)

What seemed an agnostic or nihilistic statement hundred years ago makes sense in conjunction with temporal logic as it had developed in the second half of the 20th century. Overcoming the institutional habits of "mainstream" psychology, to "predict" different separated "variables" over time as the "study of development" becomes obvious when one moves from an axiomatic system of time as a moving

Chapter 1   Time in Life and Life in Time

event-organizer between past and future to empirical investigations. Any develop-
mentally oriented science requires the establishment of its own concise theoretically
elaborated and phenomenological research methodology, in which the qualitative
and dynamic features of the phenomena are preserved in the data. The methodology
used in "mainstream" psychology is incapable of producing adequate knowledge
about development (For elaboration of this point see Smedslund (1995a), Toomela
(2007, 2008, 2009), Valsiner & Rosa (2007a)). The axioms of "mainstream" psychology exclude the focus on development – hence psychology has been blind to the
notion of "qualitative transformation" in lived time. Genesis needs time and form
changes, and therefore, transformation occurs within time, its principle is qualitative
(not quantitative).

3.5. Genetic logic for chronogenesis as a transformation of structures

There are very few logical systems that belong to the category of logic of emergence – a formal rule system by which something comes from nothing – or from
something else (e.g., Herbst, 1995). James Mark Baldwin's "genetic logic" (Baldwin,
1906, 1908a, 1908b) was one such a system, providing rules of thought about emerging phenomena. Baldwin tried to phrase a general philosophy of development in
terms of logic. It was a schema-based logic of apprehension – its main issue was
to formalize the move from the present to a possible future (apprehending of the
future). The future is being apprehended through the present, on the basis of generalizations from past materials. The uncertainty of the apprehensive process is the
birthplace for construction of meanings in the present, facing the future with some
illusion of determinacy (Valsiner, 2002, 2009). Baldwin's focus makes the irreversible
time as the core of his "genetic logic."

Any conceptualization of time is based on an abstraction that differentiates time
from things and processes that occur in time (Wieland, 1985). However, if time is inevitably bound with things and process, how can we differentiate them? There is no
pure time, as there is no pure space. It is the notion of transformation that makes it
possible to understand life within time. Central to understanding development is the

Part 1   CHRONOGENESIS

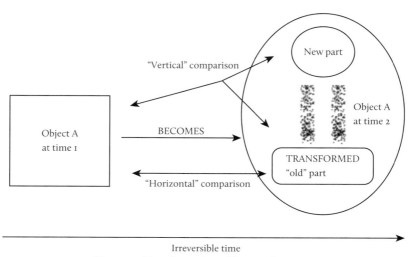

Figure 1.4. **Transformation of form** (Valsiner, 2001b)

notion of transformation (Valsiner & Connolly, 2003a). Here we should not regard that transformation occurs *along with* time. Transformation is a time-inclusive concept – as the transforming organism accomplishes its development through time. Transform implies changing of form, i.e., some form of the previous kind turns into a new form (Sato et al., 2009).

It involves moving towards the future on the basis of the web of the real and potential trajectories of the past (Figure 1.4). Here we need a methodology for describing the transformation (Valsiner, 2001b) and/or the broom of time (Anisov, 2001).

Bergson's notion of adaptation does not mean that the environment "molds" or "shapes" the organism. Instead, the environment triggers the emergence of new forms – biological and symbolic alike (Valsiner, 2004). In sum – in the case of creative adaptation, the organizational forms that emerge in adaptation go beyond the "fit with" the present state of the survival conditions, and set the basis for facing the challenges of possible future demands.

Bergson's notion of becoming on the material of human personality was expressed in his characteristic ways:

Chapter 1   Time in Life and Life in Time

Our personality, which is being built up at each instant with its accumulated experience changes without ceasing. By changing it prevents any state, although superficially identical with another, from forever repeating it in its very depth [*En changeant, elle empêche ur état, fût-il identique à lui-même en surface, de se répéter jamais en profondeur*]. That is why our duration is irreversible. We could not live over again a single moment, for we should have to begin by effacing the memory of all [*souvenir de tout*] that had followed. (Bergson, 1911, p. 8; French versions inserted from Bergson, 1907/1945, p. 23)

In a dynamic universe of a chronogenetic kind, time cannot operate as an independently given. It can be eventually abstracted as a static entity by the mind that attempts to create stability – yet it is merely a generalized illusion.

Bergson's notion of duration is such a pure duration and it is the form that the succession of our conscious states assumes when our ego lets itself live, when it refrains from separating its present state from its former states (Bergson, 1907/1945, translation, p. 100).

4. Conclusion: New methodology for "time-conscious psychology"

Psychologists have principally disregard the notion of time, because abstract and timeless "true and universal knowledge" should be the objective of this academic discipline. Yet psychologists need to consider the notion of time – differently from how they have treated it, only as an extrinsic and independent factor in research. Here, in psychology, not "lived time" but "clock time" is regarded as the important scale for understanding psychological mechanisms. Experimental psychologists use reaction time based on the clock time to infer the internal mechanisms of memory and/or other cognitive processes. Developmental psychologists use the chronological age as the external scale for understanding the maturity and/or declination of the function of an organism.

Part 1   CHRONOGENESIS

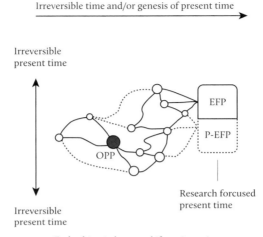

Each white circle means bifurcation point.
Black circle means obligatory passage point.
P-EFP is the polarized equifinality point.

Figure 1.5. Trajectory Equifinality Model

Therefore, if we want to reach to treat "lived time" in psychology, we need a new methodology. We have invented a new methodology for describing human life within irreversible time known as TEM (Trajectory Equifinality Model; In English, Valsiner & Sato, 2006; Sato, Yasuda et al., 2007; Sato et al., 2009; In Japanese, Sato, 2009). One of the important notions in TEM is "Equifinality Points (EFP)" and the other is "Bifurcation Points (BFP)." Both notions are inevitable for describing the diversity of trajectory, and, if not, causal and linear trajectory (= straight line) stays behind. In Figure 1.5, each white circle represents BFPs and one of the circles is blackened because it represents the Obligatory Passage Points (OPP).

A person at each BFP looks toward the future and makes a choice. At such a point, time emerges and transformation occurs. As mentioned above, ancient Greeks had two words for time, chronos (χρόνος) and kairos (καιρός). Whereas the former refers to chronological or sequential time, the latter signifies a time in between, a moment of an undetermined period of time, in which something special happens. Whereas chronos is quantitative, kairos has a qualitative nature (Freier, 2006).

Chapter 1   Time in Life and Life in Time

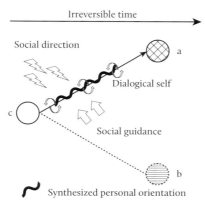

Figure 1.6. The making of the future: BFP as the point of transformation and brooming time

Therefore, BFP is the very point that needs to be described as human experiences in lived time within irreversible time.

What would happen at the BFP?

We can see in Figure 1.6 the two opposite powers that are in conflict between social direction and social guidance. Each person is supposed to have his/her original orientation to EFP. It is called, "Synthesized Personal Orientation (SPO)" and SPO reflects the fluctuated orientation and open-systemic nature of human being within irreversible time (Sato et al., 2009). A person proceeds with his or her orientation as an open system (which means that the orientation is not internally derived) and struggles to realize own orientation against the Social Directions (SD) with the support of Social Guidance (SG) supplied by intimate social relationships. Therefore, we could define time in BFP as the time of kairos within irreversible time (time of duration).

TEM can depict the two different modes of time, "*kairos*" and "*durée*." Chronogenesis in our life occurs at a decisive point in peaceful and/or mundane life. Even as our social life in modern times might be controlled by "clock time," our life ought to be considered as embedded in the time of *durée* and something happen at the time of *kairos*. TEM as a new methodology in psychology makes it possible to describe and

Part 1   CHRONOGENESIS

understand life in irreversible time with chronogenesis.

Notes

1) It is important not to forget that "nothing" is not the absence of all experience, but a special experience of feeling nothingness. Human beings cannot literally "do nothing" – if they live in complete sensory isolation their minds create something out of such "nothing" – hallucinations.

2) Why select German – rather than any other language (Swahili, Chinese, Hindi, or Latvian) for elaborating the example here? It may be a historical artifact that psychology as a science emerged from philosophy in the Occident under the dominant role of the German language (and history). To understand that past – and to extend its implications to generalized knowledge applicable to our globalized world, tracing key concepts of philosophy and psychology to their German heritage is useful. Interestingly there are two words in Japanese language, Jikan (時間) and Jikoku (時刻). "Kan (間)" in Jikan (時間) is the duration, and 間 is pronounced as "Kan" and "Ma" in Japanese, thus Jikan seems to correspond to *Zeit* in German. On the other hand,"Koku (刻)" in Jikoku (時刻) means "ticking down" so this word seems to correspond to *Stunde.*"

3) The roots of *Terminierung* go back to Latin – *terminare* – meaning "to finish." It can be seen as the act of introducing "terminating points" for various events onto the non-marked flow of irreversible time.

4) It is different from the mode of workers demonstration. Modern factory workers gather and call on the same calendar day (May first). Even if they could fight with the capitalists, they are ruled by the system of "Modern time." It reminds us of a famous movie.

Part 2
Emergence of TEM

Chapter 2

Minding Money

How Understanding of Value is Culturally Promoted

Abstract

Adding to the issues of cognitive economics (Cortés & Londoño, 2009) and the social psychology of "shadow economics" (Salvatore et al., 2009), the carrier of economic exchanges, money, plays a key role in children's socialization in different societies. Money given to children, "pocket money," is a negotiated settlement between children's social demands and those of their parents. I analyze such negotiations here on the basis of a concrete case of a Korean family in which the provision of pocket money given the child was inconsistent over time. The results indicate the social ecology of money use, in both children and their parents, sets the stage for value construction of the meaning of money.

Keywords

Money, Value, Open systems, Trajectory Equifinality Model (TEM), Cultural psychology, Sign, Social norm

1. Introduction

This chapter builds on the basic concepts outlined in Cortés & Londoño (2009) and aims to analyze how money becomes a semiotic device by means of which we are able to mediate the relations between the demands from both the social system and the family system. This takes place within the process development of social bonding in human relations. Money is not a neutral tool; it is rather a device mediating social

Part 2   EMERGENCE OF TEM

relationships, which vary from formal deals between people who buy and sell commodities to the very deep intimate relations between lovers and family members.

What is money? It is currency. Yet this leads us to ask: what is currency? Although it may seem that such a question is mainly a problem for economists, once we look carefully at how people manage money, it turns out that this can also be seen as a question that can be addressed through psychology. Money mediates possession and exchanges in market- and exchange- based societies. It can help children realize some of their desires. These could include such things as buying books and/or manga, playing video games at an arcade, eating sweets and so on; children's desires vary due to cultural and historical context, as well as the economic status of their country. This issue should be of interest to both economists and psychologists, but it has not received much attention, especially in the field of economics.

Today, one of the most influential schools in economics is the neo-classical school (Cortés & Londoño, 2009; Yamamoto & Takahashi, 2007). According to Uzawa (1989), this school has two basic premises. First, each individual can use or exchange the scarce resources, such as goods and services, which he or she possesses in the way in which he or she desires, following his or her subjective value criteria (utility). Second, the fundamental economic agent that comprises the economics is the abstract *Homo economicus*, and each individual acts rationally based on subjective value criteria, which are expressed by his or her preference. So from the viewpoint of the neo-classical school, *Homo economicus* seems to be regarded as a rational utility maximizer. That means human beings take actions rationally in order to maximize utility. In general, psychologists tend to disagree with a statement that classifies human beings as "rational." Salvatore et al. (2009) discussed the issue of underground economies and insisted that economic phenomena should be regarded not as products of rational choice making but as communicative acts, since they are acts that attempt to create meaning.

One of the functions of money is unambiguously linked to liberalization of exchange, and this means money inherently constitutes a relation-free exchange system. Yet this freedom is constrained. Yamamoto & Pian (2000) pointed out that

Chapter 2   Minding Money

money possesses a kind of magic. In that sense using money gives children the ability "to become magicians." However, referring to money as "magic" creates a variety of connotations. Money has an abstract power of exchange. In an exchange, the value of money derives from trust. But on the other hand, money creates restrictions. Imagine you are engaging in collage therapy, and in front of you there are many papers second-hand calendars, and 10,000-yen (about 85 USD in December 2016) notes Would you tear up the paper money? Would you use it as ordinary paper? It's rather difficult to imagine how a person would make a collage out of money. Money is made of a tangible substance, be it cowry shells, pieces of gold, or paper, but it has symbolic power. Before we recognize it as money, making a collage of currency from a foreign country would be easy, so we might not hesitate to use foreign bills in a collage. Yet most people would not find it so easy to destroy this paper once it had been recognized as money from a foreign country. Money seems to possess a magic power.

2. Money and psychology

Although the question of how money enters into a child's world is an interesting subject for investigation, there has been little developmental psychology research devoted to this area. There have been two lines of research investigating the relationship between children and money in psychology. The first one is based on the Piagetian framework and looks at issues such as children's understanding of the socio-economic system connected with money as an element of social cognition (Berti & Bombi, 1988; Strauss, 1952, etc.). The other line of research has studied the developmental process involved in the acquisition of basic concepts of economics, such as lack, value, opportunity cost, and cost and benefit (Kourilsky & Graff, 1986; Schug, 1983). These studies tended to underestimate the importance of the economic activities that are embedded in the everyday lives of children. Through these activities, children are expected to learn to control desires, participate in consumer society, and acquire the skills necessary to live in the society in which they are being raised.

Part 2   EMERGENCE OF TEM

In what ways does money pervade the live of children? In most cases, children can never get the amount of money they would like to have and cannot buy everything that they desire. Various customs, rules, social norms, and even restrictions exist governing the acquisition and use of money, and children have to follow these rules and customs when they use money. It is appropriate to say that the manner in which they should use money is influenced by their household economic situation as well as by the national economic situation. Moreover, a cultural context, such as the way that personal relationships are constructed, may also influence the ways in which money changes hands between parents and children (Yamamoto et al., 2003).

2.1. Cultural psychology and the functions of money

In recent years we have seen the growth of a new integrative sub-discipline in psychology, cultural psychology (Cole, 1996; Valsiner, 2001b). How can cultural psychology fulfill its promises to unite the study of processes, not products, and of socialization and cognition? There is an increasing movement towards the study of complex daily contexts, and here we investigate one of these contexts, the allocation of money from parents to children, in order to outline new methodological possibilities.

Cultural psychology focuses on individuals and their participation in social institutions. The individual case, which is studied as an integrated system interacting with its environment, is the basis for all scientific data in psychology (Valsiner, 2003a). Culture should be viewed as a process (rather than an entity). Thus, cultural psychology is developmental at its core, and cultural psychologists study an individual, regardless of age, as a developing system within a developing social context. Therefore, cultural psychology belongs to the field of general psychology as a basic science, while cross-cultural psychology is a branch of differential psychology. The two are complementary to each other (Valsiner, 2003a). Cultural psychology aims to be a basic science and to create general knowledge about culture in the context of psychological processes. It is through the generalized application of abstract knowledge that psychology at as a field of study becomes applicable for specific purposes within a society (Valsiner, 2005).

2.2. Is money a thing?

Obviously, money is not a mere "thing." Although it may be made of metal, paper, stones or shells, money has a power that cannot be reduced to the substance of its materials. Signs (Cole, 1996), social norms (Sherif, 1936) and social representations (Valsiner, 2003a) contribute to make the concept of money a complicated psychological system as a whole. So this system of money consists of powerful objects that are suited for investigation through cultural psychology.

From the viewpoint of the market economy, money is neutral in the following two senses: it can be exchanged for any equivalent, and it exists outside any specific human relationships other than that of exchange (Yamamoto & Takahashi, 2007). However, in the real world, the neutrality of money cannot be simplified in this manner. This can be seen in the case of pocket money (allowances). As pocket money is a transfer within the human relationships in an intra-family context, parents sometimes restrict the usage of this money. The allowance that parents give to children carries with it many connotations, so money is not a neutral "thing" but is a *semiotic means* to an end.

In many cases, allowances are examples of one-way transfers within a family. The money transferred *inside* the family (parents –> children) is then used *outside* of the family. In this transfer, money also is related to social norms in regards to its use. Usually, adults, for example parents and teachers, place some restrictions on the use of this money. They might assume that a friend could influence their children to use the money in a "bad" way. The definition of "badness" depends on the cultural context, therefore money is essentially a cultural construction.

More importantly, money can be believed in as it might foretell, or guarantee, one's future. If children have and save money, they believe they will be able get the objects they want in future when they want them. Young children might not need to receive an allowance on a periodic schedule (e.g., once a week, because they do not always need money and/or dislike managing money). In this way receiving pocket

Part 2   EMERGENCE OF TEM

money fosters a child's perspective on his or her future. If a child gets pocket money from his or her mother on Monday, he/she could use it arbitrarily, i.e., immediately to buy sweets, to buy brand-new comics, or even to save. In contrast, adults believe in the long-term accumulation of money, which should retain its value as long as the economy or society does not collapse.

3. Children and the "magic of money"

From the viewpoint of children, money acquires meaning due to the social circumstances, mediated by others, surrounding it. Babies do not have any innate sense of money. Therefore before acquiring the meaning of money, babies may try to eat coins and/or easily tear an expensive bill into pieces. These actions might make their parents astonished. In line with Yamamoto & Pian (2000), "a magic stick" can never exist as a "child's thing," unless it is given over to them by adults, especially by parents. In this sense, learning how to use money is a communicative act (Salvatore et al., 2009) taking place between adults and children.

So, how do children learn how to use such a "magic stick"? Children are surrounded by various goods and products (their environmental setting) from the very beginning of their lives. As all these things are given to them by others, children do not get these things by themselves. Thus, exchange is not needed, and to children money does not represent power. But, as they grow up, it becomes harder and harder for children to be satisfied with only what they are given. For a variety of reasons, children begin to want act independently when they purchase things. Although in the discussion of this topic, it is very important for us to be sensitive to its limitations. The above might be true for children in a family living in a modern consumer society. The situation may be much different for children growing up in a non-developed society. Children raised without families or living on their own in non-developed societies might themselves have to earn money to survive. This type of relationship between children and money in non-developed societies is outside the scope of this chapter.

However, in modern consumer-based societies, learning how to use money is an essential developmental task for children. The task of learning how to use money seems to be built on the own experience of exchange and possession. For instance, children need to be trained how to shop effectively, especially children who may have difficulty using money. For example, training in the use of money is included in education for mentally handicapped children (Aeschleman & Schladenhauffen, 1984; Nozoe et al., 2004). In another example, children, aged 2 to 8, living in a foster care home in Japan, named *Jido Yogo Shisetsu*, receive an allowance. This money is budgeted by the Japanese national government, with support from local authorities. Both cases reflect the fact that the allocation and spending of money by children is an issue that society takes seriously. So, research into the use of money by children should also be conducted in the fields of educational psychology and/or clinical psychology.

Money is embedded in a wider cultural context in which meaning is acquired through developing relationships and continuing communication with others. This view seems to conflict with the perspective that emphasizes the usage of money as an exchange activity that is a product of rational choice. To address money issue from our perspective, the author will present two types of analysis. First, analysis of events related to the giving and receiving of pocket money and second analysis of changing social relations which alter the meaning of money for the individual. The first analysis resulted in the developing the new methodology of qualitative psychology called TEM (Trajectory and Equifinality Model; Valsiner & Sato, 2006; Sato, Yasuda et al., 2007; Sato et al., 2009), TEM would be precisely explained later.

4. Lessons from the *Money and Child* research project

4.1. The *Money and Child* research project

The example in this chapter comes from one of our studies from the *Money and Child* research project, which was conducted in China, Korea, Japan and

Part 2   EMERGENCE OF TEM

Vietnam since 2002 (Yamamoto & Pian, 2000; Yamamoto et al., 2003; Oh et al., 2005; Yamamoto & Takahashi, 2007). This project is not a traditional cross-cultural study. The intent is not to compare samples from four different countries. We have looked at similar variations in individual cases, which overlap, and through these cases we have sought greater understanding of human nature and our social institutions and culture. Large differences in human nature tend to be easily attributed to definitive factors such as national character and/or a race, yet delicate differences are useful when considering relations between humans and the society in which they live. Our research objective is to clarify the concrete interpersonal relationship structure embedded in culture through analysis of real-world situations involving children and the use of money. The four countries in which our subjects live have a similar cultural background, for example, they all use or have in the past used Chinese characters in their writing systems, and they all belong to the so-called Confucian cultural sphere. These four countries are parts of a culturally and historically homogeneous area. Regardless of whether the residents of these countries would all concur; Korea, Vietnam, and Japan are sometimes regarded as satellite states of China. And of course, even contemporary China itself is not truly a homogeneous state. All said, these four countries could be regarded as sharing some elements of their value systems and philosophical outlook.

School-aged children in many countries, including European countries, the U.S., and eastern Asian countries such as China, Korea, and Japan receive pocket money in various ways. This pocket money could be regarded as payment for household chores or it may simply be seen as an entitlement given by the parents. The money may be given for the purpose of purchasing needed items (Furnham, 1999), or as a regular resource for not yet specified needs. From the parents' perspective, when, whether, how, and what to give as pocket money are all possible issues of concern. As there are many issues involved, there is no single method for handling the issue of a child's allowance. The connotations tied to this pocket money are ambiguous, and this therefore may reflect the complexity of life and human relationships.

4.2. Avoiding the cultural attribution error

We must take care that we do not fall into the trap of the *cultural attribution error* in which researchers are more likely to observe a "new" phenomenon when studying individuals in a foreign country than in their own society. In these cases, they tend to attribute the cause of a "newly discovered" phenomenon to a stable factor such as national character and/or race, while in reality these explanatory terms are inventions of the researchers themselves. We always should be conscious that not only our subjects, but also we as researchers are products of our own cultures.

How can we escape from the trap? Heterogeneity (or diversity) is the key. Diversity should be an element of both the research team and the research methods. First, a research group should ideally be composed of researchers from various countries and ethnic backgrounds and therefore be able to discuss the phenomena in the study from various viewpoints. Second, research must take place using a triangulation of methods, thus multi-method approaches including observations, interviews, and questionnaires are needed.

5. Strategies of giving and a receiving pocket money: Case study — Korean girl X

Both Japanese and Korean researchers are able to point to many differences in the social structures in Korea and Japan. One of the most remarkable difference in social relationships is that of socially prescribed sharing with other children (*Ogori* in Japanese). It is true that Japanese children sometimes share their money or other wealth with their peers, but Japanese adults, e.g., teachers and parents, do not evaluate *Ogori* positively. Korean children, however, are guided towards sharing wealth with each other and this has a role in regulating peer group relationships (Oh, 2005; Oh et al., 2005).

A case study from interviews with Korean mother-child dyad is presented here. We pay special attention to one mother-child dyad in Korea on the starting and stop-

Part 2   EMERGENCE OF TEM

ping of regular allowance (i.e., periodical-fixed-amount; e.g., once a week or once a month).

X is a girl with who lives with her parents and brother in Seoul. At the time of being interviewed for this study, she was an elementary school fifth-grader. Once she had been given a regular, periodically fixed amount of pocket money (PM) from her parents, but that practice was suddenly suspended when she was interviewed.

The background of her situation concerning pocket money is as follows. First of all, X's mother had never received pocket money from her parents during her child-hood, so the mother never intended to give pocket money to her child. Then, the child X asked the mother to give her a regular allowance, because *a few of* X's friends got started to receive PM. The mother decided to start to give her girl a periodical PM for training her to manage money. This PM practice seemed to be based on child's desire. However, after receiving a regular allowance, X didn't manage own money well, she neither used nor saved her own money. Sometimes money was left on her writing desk. Her mother became upset at this and finally decided to stop giving her a fixed allowance. X didn't contest her mother's decision. Instead of receiving money regularly, X asked her mother for a small amount of money anytime she needed it. Then X's mother could selectively give money to her daughter when X asked for it. Though sometimes X's requests were rejected, this system seemed to be comfortable for X.

A few months later X asked her mother to resume giving her a fixed allowance, because *MANY* of her friends had started to get it. Children in Korea tend to treat each other and share sweets (Oh et al., 2005), many friends' receiving pocket money also means mutual treating and sharing circle might be activated. Joining treating and sharing circle needs to pay money for friends arbitrary time, so X needs to pre-pare some kind of "disposable personal income" whenever she played with friends. The mother didn't accept to her daughter's request immediately, because her daugh-ter once gave up receiving a fixed allowance. So she only planned to resume the reg-ular allowance in the near future. We can see the timeline of the dyad's interaction in Figure 2.1. The central arrow is the timeline. This arrow divide this dyad into two

Chapter 2 Minding Money

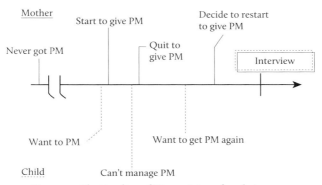

Figure 2.1. The timeline of X's receiving of pocket money

parts, a mother and a child.

Regarding Figure 2.1, I would like to consider the factors that inhibit or promote the transfer of PM separately.

The promoting factors are:

- *A FEW OF* X's friends get PM from their parents and the child needs to be equal.
- X's mother decides to give PM for some kind of discipline (managing money in modern consumer society)
- *MANY* friends get PM from their parents and the child needs to prepare money for sharing foods (*Ogori*).

The inhibiting factors for giving PM are:

- X's mother's experience (never received pocket money as child)
- X's failure to manage her pocket money

Simply speaking, we can find that both promoting and inhibiting factors derived from different parts (a mother or a child). What we need to understand here is all promoting and inhibiting factors are embedded in their living situations. And there situations are construed historically and culturally.

The question here is "Were receiving regular PM for the first time and restarting of PM money similar experiences for X?" If not, how do you explain such phenome-

Part 2   EMERGENCE OF TEM

non? The result for X seems to be similar; it means just getting money periodically. But the connotation of getting PM might not be same. The first time, she wanted to get PM because she wanted to do what others did. From the perspective of a child X, getting PM just meant to have a mean for exchange. She could not imagine the responsibility of getting PM (for example, saving). On the other hand, restarting PM in near future in this case was facilitated different motivation of X. Getting a regular allowance is needed to share foods with friends frequently. It means children including X always prepare money to buy whenever they needs. Korean children are embedded in such a sharing system and the turn of buying is not strictly decided. Change of motivation for getting PM is not due to the passage of time, but it is a result of the transformation of the life world of children.

There is no clear-cut (i.e., discrete) set of stages in the child's acquisition of pocket money. It is not a linear growth system, but it is a struggle over time. The back ground of this process will be mentioned later in new methodological scheme.

6. Methodological elaboration of the case: From time line model to Trajectory and Equifinality Model

The Equifinality process model (Trajectory and Equifinality Model; TEM), which focuses on the convergence and divergence of the courses of events, can be applied to the story of X's pocket money with its various starts and stops. If an appropriate theory does not exist for a study, any empirical data, samples or case studies done in the course of research have little value. Using the Equifinality process model would help us to understand both the process in which X received PM and the larger implication of a single case such as this. The concept of equifinality originated in the general system model proposed by von Bertalanffy (1968), and it means that the same and/or a similar final state may be reached from different initial conditions and in different ways. He preferred equifinality better than "goal," because the notion of equifinality does not represent a termination point.

Chapter 2   Minding Money

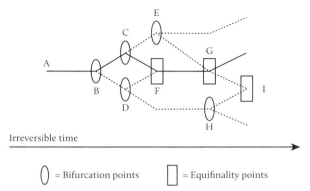

= Bifurcation points   = Equifinality points

Figure 2.2. Equifinality in development (modified after Valsiner, 2001b)

We can imagine the diverse trajectories. These include bifurcation points and equifinality points. Equifinality is a general property of open systems (von Bertalanffy, 1968).

In Figure 2.2, ellipses indicate the critical junctions when moving in a certain direction and are called Bifurcation Points (BFP). Rectangles indicate the points where the trajectories of different directions may converge and are called Equifinality Points (EFP). Solid lines indicate an actualized course of development (which is non-linear) dotted lines indicate the appropriate alternative routes that could have been taken by the given organism (but were not).

Let's apply X's case to Equifinality process model. How can we depict the process of X's experience within the irreversible time?

When our research team met X, she was supposed to be at G. Here, B = occasionally receiving money from her mother, C = receiving a fixed allowance, D = receiving no pocket money, E = earning money by herself, F and G = receiving pocket money temporarily, I = receiving a fixed allowance. X was once at point C, but is now at point G moving to point I. Both F and G imply that X is receiving money temporarily, but the desire and attitude toward receiving PM are slightly changing as time passes (Figure 2.3).

In the case of this example in Korea, the cultural system of sharing sweets with

Part 2 EMERGENCE OF TEM

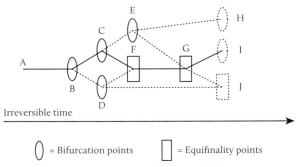

Figure 2.3. Trajectory and Equifinality Model for receiving PM

peers is important. The girl's friends began to receive pocket money regularly, and this not only means that these friends can buy some of the products they desire, be they accessories or candy, but it also means that her friends could treat their peers to snacks or small meals when the turn for them to treat the other members of the social circle comes. In general, this system is mutually beneficial; children in this type of social circle are likely to be under peer expectation that they also should receive money in order to participate in the mutual treating of others in the group. This is what X confronted after her mother discontinued her allowance. Currently the situation has changed, and therefore her relationship with friends has been transformed. Thus, X's receiving of a fixed allowance means that she is able to function comfortably within her circle of friends. For X, PM is not simply disposable income. She needed PM because she wanted to treat her friends to sweets or small meals when she felt that this was required.

From the perspective of X's mother, this situation is not unwelcome, because the occasional giving of pocket money to her child is slightly inconvenient. But a more important reason for the regular allowance is to facilitate her daughter in joining a social circle. By giving her daughter pocket money, X's mother wanted to help her daughter join and maintain her status in her circle of friends. Here, neither the developmental stage of the child nor the mother's experience determined the management of the daughter's allowance. Nevertheless, the relationships between children and the culture in which these relationships are embedded have influenced the system of allowance of pocket money. We find that mutual or catalyzed relationships surround the use of money and interpersonal relationships in the daily lives of children.

7. Theoretical considerations

Pocket money might be defined as "cash for day-to-day spending on personal and/or incidental expenses." This doesn't include expenses for fundamental survival. The study of pocket money focuses on the developmental transformation of the mediating function of money in human relationships, and attempts to reveal this developmental transformation of relationships with others and of sociality from a new perspective (Takeo et al., 2009). From the perspective of a child who would represent an "open system," the Korean girl didn't repeat the categories of receiving and rejecting pocket money as simple opposite actions.

In the case of X, initially, she accepted receiving PM as a fixed allowance, then she gave up receiving PM. Then X would begin to receive a periodical allowance, because of the need to be a part of a peer relationship group that included the mutual give and take of paying for food and candy. Such a process is not one of "trial and error" that disregards the time in which these events occurred. Rejecting and receiving should not be interpreted as simple opposite actions (being alternately turned on and off) as Figure 2.4 shows.

During the initial period during which girl X received pocket money on a periodic fixed basis, the child herself couldn't manage the money. Because, the influence of the mother on the child as a system might be of relative importance, and a mother-child bond is so strong at this time in a child's development, the daughter willingly gave up the right to receive a regular allocation of money. Though, subsequently the situation changed. MANY of X's friends started to get pocket money regularly. In Korea, this would mean that the system in which friends are expected to mutually

Part 2   EMERGENCE OF TEM

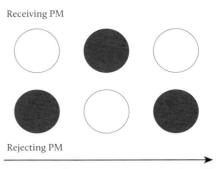

Figure 2.4. "On" and "off" – receiving/rejecting of PM (black = "off")

share wealth had been initiated. According to the research conducted by our group, this system cannot be a unidirectional phenomenon. At one occasion a member of the group members would buy sweets for all the other members and at the next occasion another member would be expected to do the same. This system represents a way to construct and maintain peer relationships between children in Korea. Therefore, for children, money is an important semiotic mediation tool. We can see this in the case of X, as she wanted to receive PM again. Her friends' receiving PM had an effect on X and influenced her to negotiate with her mother.

How can we depict this transformation? If we want to describe the transformation process itself, a scheme representing two kinds of comparisons might be useful. When development is taking place, two kinds of comparisons are possible across developmental time (Valsiner, 2001b, pp. 26-27). Both vertical and horizontal comparisons are needed (Figure 2.5). Within irreversible time, the same object (organism A) is converted from one form to another. The emergent form entails differentiation and hierarchical integration. Here the object at time 1 would change qualitatively over the course represented in Figure 2.5.

Such transformation cannot be "measurable," since it cannot be reduced to elementary quantities. Here we need a qualitative method to understand the development that takes place within irreversible time. TEM in Figure 2.3 could depict X's fluctuating development process as trajectories (both real and possible) within

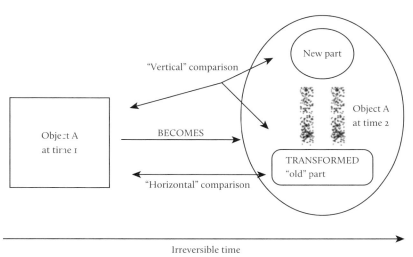

Figure 2.5. Horizontal and vertical comparisons in cultural psychology (Valsiner 2001b)

irreversible time. This introduces the difficult challenge of how to express an open system and its transformation.

The notion of equifinality in the TEM derives from Hans Driesch's philosophy of potentials, which was outlined at the beginning of the 20th century. Driesch regarded all biological organisms, including human beings, as open systems. An open system is characterized by the principle of equifinality. The human psychological structure functions likewise as an open system not as closed system, as Sato, Yasuda et al. (2007) emphasized. Thus there is no point in depicting the fluctuating process of receiving - rejecting - receiving PM as the result of the interaction of closed systems, which could include "measurable" quantities. An interactive system consisting of a mother and child cannot be considered closed.

This is the reason why a new view on the process might be needed. The concept of TEM depends on the notion of an open system and it successfully depicts the enduring process and never-ending process of human experience. Such a theory could be represented as "bird's eye view," but for closer scrutiny we would actually need something closer to a fly-on-the-wall perspective. In the Korean case covered here,

Part 2   EMERGENCE OF TEM

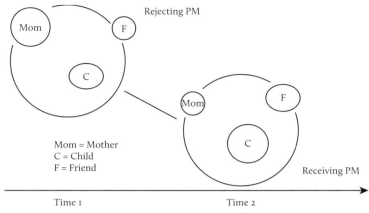

Figure 2.6. Transformation of the social network involved in decisions about pocket money

both the mother and child underwent continual transformation. The two-dimensional comparison in Figure 2.6 is the ideal type of model for depicting the transformation of an object, so this model itself should be transformed, because this type of comparison is a task for researchers. Here we should try to present a new type of graph.

8. Open-systemic view of child and money

This figure mainly views children as an open system. In X's case, at time 1 in Figure 2.6, the practice of PM was initiated by child's simple desire to get money to buy stuff. From the X (child)'s position, the desire for PM was not very strong, and the management of PM was not worth the cost in effort for her. A non-fixed temporal PM was enough for the mother-child dyad at that time. This was comfortable for both mother and child at time 1. However, the X as an open system gradually transforms. The part of the system (open) represented by the child's peers gradually emerged. What the most important is the change (transformation) of peer relationship, which is led by *MANY* members of the group receiving pocket money. The peer relationship of Korean children is mediated by this system of mutual sharing, and children are easily initiated into the system once it begins to operate in a peer group. As a result, at time 2, X became eager to receive a fixed allowance of PM. Pocket money is key to interaction in the local children's "society." Therefore it can be surmised that X might at this point be willing to manage her own pocket money.

9. General conclusions

... the present is half past and half to come. (Peirce, 1892/1923, p. 219)

The diversity in the course of a life (life trajectory) needs to be viewed through the framework of equifinality, and then the concept of equifinality leads us the notion of an open system. Both equifinality and open systems inevitably show that we travel on trajectories (multilinearity). These three notions affect each other. Any economic phenomenon is at the same time a communicative act as it is contingent to sense-making (Salvatore et al., 2009).

Receiving pocket money (PM) periodically and managing it reflect a transformation occurring on the ontogenetic level. But in achieving such status, many things must happen on both the meso- and micro- genetic level. If we could depict such a process, we would understand the real epigenetic process of cultural development. Cultural psychology is not a collection of local developments, but an integrative explanatory mode of human development within time and place. So it provides a general framework for understanding development in a cultural context.

The issue of receiving regular pocket money cannot be explained through the perspective that views the usage of money as a rational choice and exchange activity. Receiving pocket money should be considered as a part of a broader dynamic process of a child's ecological setting, mother-child interaction, managing money by herself, buying various goods, and relationship building with friends. A process of

Part 2   EMERGENCE OF TEM

sense-making (Salvatore et al., 2009) that in turn shapes and is shaped by the activity it is interwoven with. First, the benefit of asking one's mother for money as needs arise and the cost of managing money overwhelm the convenience of readiness for expense at any time. However, time goes by, and the situation changes. The burden of asking for money occasionally emerges because of transformations in the child's relationship with his/her friends and then he/she needs money frequently in this social context. This process is based on the development of social relationships and these relationships are also embedded in the cultural-historical context of the country or society in which the child lives.

The Korean girl X in this study simply acted in the manner that she saw fit, based on the factors surrounding her at a given moment. We should not interpret her decision as either a "trial and error" process or a "fail then succeed" process. Furthermore, we should not interpret her decisions as always being rational. We should not postulate the girl X made her choices based on the perspective pay-off matrix at each decision point. These three interpretations regard the girl as closedsystem and miss the transformation process of the girl who is the emerging subject. A process-based semiotic approach that focuses on sense-making (Cortés & Londoño, 2009) is needed. Under the ambiguity perspective on decision making, decisions are themselves the means for construction of meaning and interpretation of reality. Decisions would serve for development of meaning, and this development would be the main activity in decision making (March, 1994).

Last but not least, as mentioned earlier, I would like to contrast our views with the rational choice approach. The family in our case wishes to belong to and to integrate with Korean culture. The money in this case is not used to fulfill consumer desires through the purchase of goods. But this does not mean that culture operates in a onesided and deterministic way upon human behavior. The culture itself continuously emerges in the process of sense-making in the family, in this case giving and receiving pocket money. It is not from the perspective of economics but from the angle of cultural psychology that we can begin to understand the phenomenon of money and how it is embedded in cultural sense-making. Through the use of new TEM methodology, genetic cultural psychology investigating human development can contribute to the study of the multiple facets of money in human lives and societies. TEM can treat the dynamic process of decision making as a process involving ambiguity and uncertainty. The Equifinality process model (Trajectory and Equifinality Model) was created to explain X's case. Since that time this model has evolved, and it is now called Trajectory Equifinality Model (TEM; Valsiner & Sato, 2006; Sato, Yasuda et al., 2007). Even though TEM has only a brief methodological history (Sato et al., 2009), it can help us to explain the shortcomings of the rational choice approach and bring into the open the advantages of the semiotic view more systematically and in a more "linear" manner. In short, in order to place this study in the wider field of research, the TEM emphasizes the originality and benefits of the semiotic view and acts as a frame for the empirical part of this chapter.

Acknowledgments
The author is grateful to the international research team for "Pocket money and chi - dren in East Asia" – Yamamoto, T. (Project leader), Takahashi, N., Pian, C., Oh, S., Takeo K., Choi, S. J., Kim, S. J., Zhou, N., Houng, P. M., and Hoa, X.

Related websites
http://www.psy.ritsumei.ac.jp/~satot/diarybox/Val/VAL04/Index.html

Chapter 3

Development, Change or Transformation

How can Psychology Conceive and Depict Professional Identify Construction?

Abstract

Kullasepp (2006) discusses the construction of professional identify from the viewpoint of dialogical processes of the self. Both identify formation and psychology education may be related to this paper. Kullasepp defines the self as an open-system – and as is known – every open-system operates by the principles of equifinality. For her study, Kullasepp adopted the framework of Trajectory Equifinality Model (TEM – Valsiner & Sato, 2006; Sato, Yasuda et al., 2007) in addition to the model of dialogical self (Hermans, 2001). Here I try to take a brief look at the TEM, and then discuss the construction of self as psychologists in college students. Lastly, similar situation of psychology students in Japan is introduced.

Keywords

Trajectory Equifinality Model (TEM), Historically Structured Sampling (HSS), Dialogical self, Professional identify construction

1. Implication of HSS and TEM

As Kullasepp (2006) pointed out, Historically Structured Sampling (HSS) and Trajectory Equifinality Model (TEM) brings to psychology the notion of history, and emphasizes the idea of equifinality: similar states can be attained through a number

Part 2   EMERGENCE OF TEM

of different ways. Methodologically speaking, equifinality is a good point to look at if we focus on the open systems. It is a principle for sampling. Sampling is an inevitable operation in any research project. Any research effort – unless it analyzes the whole realm of the given phenomenon – requires some way of sampling (Valsiner & Sato, 2006). Random sampling is highly recommended in psychology discipline. The rationale says that "random sampling" is needed because individual human beings are not homogeneous. If research objects were supposed to be homogeneous, an arbitrary sampling would be enough to go on psychological studies.

1.1. An ordinary analogue

Let's think of cooking. Imagine you tried to make a soup. After adding salt, you would have a taste of soup to detect its saltiness. In such a situation, you never taste all of soup. Instead of devouring all the half-made soup in the pot, you only take a sip to taste. For avoiding mistakes, all of the soup in the pot should be homogeneous. So you need to give the soup a few stirs. If you were a cook – and were convinced that the soup is homogeneous – only one sip is enough for tasting. Homogeneity guarantees the representativeness – a sip of stands adequately for the whole pot-ful of the liquid-in-the-making. In such a situation, you can take a sip anywhere from stockpot.

But if you were an eater and/or not convinced with homogeneity, things would be different. You would insist that a cooker should try to taste many portions of soup, if possible – by a rule you call "random." You want to make sure your information from portion tasted first are the same as the ones tasted last – allowing you to assume that all of the soup is as you taste it.

1.2. Human beings are not a soup

Any selection of human is not from a soup. It is absurd to presume that researcher ensures equal taste of "soup of subjects." What we can only do is balancing. Not stirring human being to acquire homogeneity. Actually, the random sampling is recommended to neutralize the unexpected effect to outcome, i.e., to reduce statistical error. Each sample is not regarded as an irreplaceable individual. Sample is the

Chapter 3 Development, Change or Transformation

representative data of population in many disciplines of social sciences including psychology (We know perception study never need random sampling). The random sampling used by social science including psychology samples not just a few people. Random sampling might need a representative set of subject so that it could infer parameters of population. This methodology focuses on persons just because they have variables. Each person is described by numerical values on variables. For example, one researcher has interests in a relationship between personality traits and subjective happiness, five traits' scores and subjective happiness score are enough for study. So each person is described by such scores. This tendency is more strong in North American psychological thought than in German – Austrian one (For a comparison between two thought, see Toomela (2007)). As Danziger (1997) pointed out, North American psychological methodology tend to place a person as a bunch of many relatively independent "variables."

And – most importantly – the observed variables are only used for inferring the parameter of population. Living persons as a whole are disregarded. But if homogeneity is not presumed in human being to study, there is an alternative option. Open system has a process of interaction with the outer world and it depends on outside factors (von Bertalanffy, 1968). So the human being as research sample is compared to not human being as a unity but is compared to between each of the states that its development has reached. Here the "state" means the psychological condition and/or events of human being on which researchers focus to search. Infertility treatment (Yasuda, 2005, 2006), anxiety for future, identity formation, graduation, marriage and so on. We call such state as Equifinality Points (EFP). Equifinality point is a state to reach from the one viewpoint, and from another viewpoint. Again we can say that EFP is a point on which researchers focus to study. Actually, the notion of equifinality has begun to be paid attention in life course developmental psychology (e.g., Baltes et al., 1999).

The EFP in the TEM is a final state and also a start point to later life, English word "commencement" is a good example of EFP. Because commencement means "graduation ceremony" and originally means "start point." So EFP is a convergent

Part 2   EMERGENCE OF TEM

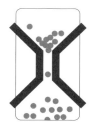

Figure 3.1. A sandglass

point which almost research participants' experience. And EFP is a research focus in which the researcher has interest. Though equifinality is the originally a biological notion, Sato, Yasuda et al. (2007) regarded EFP as socio-cultural experience in life course. Equifinality is the similar end states to which many different ways may exist to arrive. So, the notion of trajectories is inseparable from the notion of equifinality. Equifinality inevitably involves trajectories and vice versa. Of course, after EFP, the life courses continue and have various directions.

Thus – one more notion is needed – multifinality. For thinking about the notion of multifinality, let's imagine a sandglass (Figure 3.1).

In a sandglass, sand slides and should pass through its central hole. Getting through the neck of the sandglass, sands scatter wide range. Not only one point, but many possible points. In next figure, trajectory before EFP is past history and TEM can depict virtual trajectory (dotted lines). On the other hand, trajectory after EFP is not occurred. And there should be various finality points in the life (Figure 3.2).

Multifinality is depicted by such states (H, I in Figure 3.2). Our sampling method should reflect both real life courses and researchers' research questions.

Our contemporary psychology looks upon human psyche as social in its ontogeny and constructive in its microgenesis (Valsiner, 2000). Thus, psychology is necessarily a historical science. We call this new methodology as Historically Structured Sampling (HSS). The notion of HSS entails a radical move from other accepted methods of sampling – random sampling being the most glorified – to a version of non-random sampling of individual cases. HSS presumes that the definitive data base for any scientific generalization in developmental and cultural psychology is a

Chapter 3　Development, Change or Transformation

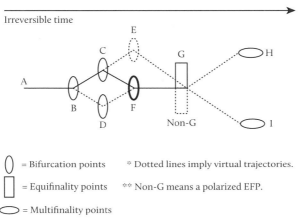

Figure 3.2. Bifurcation, equifinality and multifinality on TEM

single case (rather than a sample), from which generalization of knowledge is possible (and testable on other single cases – Valsiner, 2003a). This is in contrast to the usual sample population generalization in which the systemic nature of the single case is irreversibly lost in the process of generalization. HSS is a method of sampling individual cases based on their previous (up-to-now) life course histories analyzed as a series of bifurcation points. It makes possible to contrast individuals who have arrived at the present state (equifinality point) through vastly different life course trajectories. The notion of equifinality is in the limelight of developmental psychology.

2. The importance of the notion of trajectories

The notion of trajectories doesn't mean simple multi-linearity. Some kind of developmental psychology, such as life course psychology, begins to attend the notion of trajectory. In these studies, trajectory is based on positive data of actual subjects and means multi-tracks. These tracks never inter-twist. However, trajectories in TEM imply rather vast meanings. Trajectories are both real and virtual. Trajectory means complicated and nested ways – each of which connects at a bifurcation point.

Part 2　EMERGENCE OF TEM

Logical possibility and other's life course can construct the trajectories as a model.

Modern psychology is an a-historical discipline. Even in the longitudinal study of developmental psychology, the time is only the point, not duration. Time is not regarded as flow. Average of data is taken seriously and data of each point is lined by psychologists. In this way, psychologists think they can depict the developmental course of stability and/or change and infer the underlying mechanism. Here individual is abstracted and tend to be considered less serious. Jointing the dots of average score doesn't mean to take diversity of human life seriously. Average score deny the diversity. So, each individual trajectory of life should be depicted as itself. So, next step is to explain the method for delineating the life courses. Here, irreversibility of time doesn't mean measurable and one-dimensional time. The essence of "irreversibility of time" is its pervasiveness.

Developmental psychology ought not to pursue the causal relationship. In stead of the nomothetic view, the idiographic view should be adopted to describe the variation and possibility of individual lives. Constructing the model is the way to describe the lives without a cause-and-effect sequence of events. This way of modeling might leads to describe the possible worlds (Bruner, 1986). One person can never choose multiple options at one time and at one place. And even if trajectories are described and perceived, a person couldn't choose freely any possible trajectory. In such a case, we need a notion of Obligatory Passage Points (OPP) and/or social directions (Valsiner, 2001b; Kido, 2006).

For example, before World War II, Japanese women couldn't enter a university, so couldn't earn a degree. Social trends prevented women to receive higher education. Actually, almost children of both gender only studied at the elementary school before World War II in Japan. After primary school, there was a bifurcation point. After finishing six years of compulsory education, children (and their parents) chose the options to go to middle schools, girls' advanced schools, vocational schools or higher elementary schools. Even though females could perceive all four courses at this bifurcation point, females could only go girls' advanced schools. And universities didn't allow entering the person on this track. This means females couldn't enter

Chapter 3   Development, Change or Transformation

the university. Social Direction (SD) works. In this case "girls' advanced school" is an Obligatory Passage Point (OPP) for females and social direction strongly suggested girls not to get an academic course. Interestingly enough, universities of foreign countries such as U.S. opened the door to foreign females without strict certification, so some Japanese females entered and graduated universities and a few women could earn Ph.D. degree at graduate schools in the pre-war period of Japan. We can find one of glorious figures in the history of psychology. Ms. Tsuruko Arai (1886-1915) entered graduate school of Columbia University and was supervised by Edward L. Thorndike. She could earn Ph.D. Degree in 1912. Fortunately enough she got married at the very same day of earning her degree and she changed her family name as Haraguchi. She published some books and articles in both U.S. and Japan (In English; Arai, 1912), but unfortunately she died in 1915 at the age of 30. Arai/Haraguchi's story taught us an alternative option seemed to be fruitful for Japanese females in the pre-war period. And she could not know at that time that so many female students can study psychology in Estonia!

3. EFP and OPP in Kullasepp's paper

Kullasepp's sampling is based on the notion of Historically Structured Sampling (HSS) (Valsiner & Sato, 2006). She chose the psychology students at the university of Estonia (n = 23; 2 men and 21 women). She set a period of socialization as EFP. In this period, students would get the psychological meaning system and their everyday representation was influenced by disciplinary meaning system. Phase 1 (baseline) of the study was done nine months after the start of the academic year, when the participants took part in interviews and filled out questionnaires. In this article, EFP and OPP seem to be a little ambiguous. Though a period of socialization may be regarded as EFP first, the graduation is regarded as an EFP in latter part. Setting the EFP depends on research questions, and research questions would transform through research. This would inevitably occur. So, the first step EFP for sampling and

Part 2　EMERGENCE OF TEM

the last step EFP for writing papers maybe different. In longitudinal study, EFP may transform more. It's inevitable research process so that the researcher might obtain a better research question. And a good research question contributes both theory and practice.

We proposed the notion of Polarized EFP, P-EFP (Valsiner & Sato, 2006) and it means the complementary class of researcher's interest – "if I am interested in X, the contrast is with the imaginary non-X." So, dropping out from professional socialization and/or graduation would be depicted, even if there were no students such as this in the cohort in reality.

4. Dialogical self and its transforming process

Kullasepp (2006) insists that the present perspective on identity is developmental and dialogical. The Dialogical Self Theory (Hermans, 2001, 2002) is an important trend within the socio-cultural perspective. People's ordinary life is embedded in real context and one sometimes binds oneself to hard situation. In such situations, people struggle to change themselves. According to Kullasepp, "AS-IF" construction is effective to transform self so that the distancing from here-and-now setting might create dialogicality within self-system and might lead to re-organization in there. Taking the other's position as imaginary self, in stead of here-and-now I-position, doesn't mean one imagine the pipe dream and fantasy. Other's position also is embedded in real life situation. There are realistic constraints in other's position. And I-positions emerge over time. So, Dialogical self is intrinsically dynamic and I-positions transforms always.

For the professional self, realistic restrictions lead to limitation of information. It's difficult for younger adolescence to gather sufficient information of professions. This limitation creates the information gaps. In addition to such limitation, there is a tendency for individuals to seek consistency among their thoughts. This is what Cognitive Dissonance Theory developed by Leon Festinger (1957) teaches us. One

Chapter 3   Development, Change or Transformation

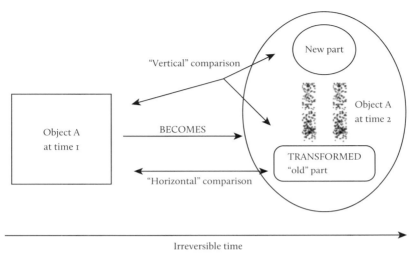

Figure 3.3. **Transformation within irreversible time** (Valsiner, 2001b)

doesn't want to access contradicting information. So, gaps are on the increase. The notion "psychologists as a profession" may be one of such gap-widening professional.

After entering the psychology course, self-construction process is not assumed to be simple. To understand such process, one should choose samples by appropriate methodology. According to Historically Structured Sampling (HSS) (Valsiner & Sato, 2006), Kullasepp asked all students of psychology course in university of Estonia to participate. 20 participants were interviewed several times so that their process of professional identity formation and its transformation might be understood. How could we imagine the transformation process?

Figure 3.3 was originally intended to explain the two types of comparison in cultural psychology (Valsiner, 2001b). But it also presents us a good imaginary scheme of transformation within irreversible time. In this Figure, object A at time 1 (left square) becomes an ellipse including a roundish rectangle and a small ellipse. The former implies the transformed "old" rectangle and the latter demonstrates a new generated part. So a simple comparison such as vertical one could never grasp the transformation. Before entering university, students had had some kinds of profes-

Part 2   EMERGENCE OF TEM

sional identity and it transformed after entering psychology course within irreversible time. University curriculum supply largely knowledge and skills of psychology. Experiences in university changed students' knowledge on psychology. As Table 2 in Kullasepp (2006) showed, students used "before-now" pair to explain the change (i.e., they often said "before ..., but now ..."). This comparison focuses on the intra-individual differences. But these differences shouldn't be understood as a uni-dimensional change. A simple increasing of the quantity of knowledge induces such differences. It is not quantitative change but transformation. And there are trajectories to same equifinality point of identify formation.

The university as a social institution frames experiences, contributes to development of the sense of self through social interactions, narrative thinking and processes of transformation. We hope that Phase 2 (Spring, 2006) data may reveal the trajectories of professional identity formation.

5. Psychology students' experience: Japanese students today

In Japan, the situation is similar to that of Estonia. Psychology is currently one of the most popular subjects in undergraduate level. Some people are attracted to psychology because they believe it will help them to understand themselves, and the others are attracted to clinical practical aspects. Higashi et al. (1994) investigated undergraduate students in various faculties of universities in Japan. Using a 15-item questionnaire on the image of psychology, three factors were extracted by factor analysis on the data. Factor 1 consisted of 7 items such as "psychology tell us to detect others personality" and "psychology tell us the way of mind reading." This factor was therefore named "naive image of efficiency of psychology." Factor 2 was named "interest to psychology" and factor 3 was named "non-scientific aspect of psychology." Factor 3 consisted of items such as "psychology is related to a fortune-telling" "Blood type can explain one's personality" (I'm afraid non East-Asian readers would feel strange to this item).

Chapter 3　Development, Change or Transformation

The comparison between freshmen (1st grade students) and more than 2nd year students in psychology course is interest. The first grade psychology students appear high factor score on the factor 1 and 2, while low score on the factor 3. So the first grade students of psychology believe that psychology is efficient to daily life and has interest in psychology and don't believe psychology is not science. Second year and later-years students score of factor 1 decrease so socialization in psychology discipline make them to throw away the naive belief in the sufficiency of psychology. But a slightly ironically – they appear on the factor 2 to score less high than the first grade students (though maintain the interest itself). Higashi et al. (1994)'s study implies that the situation of psychology students in Japan is similar to Kullasepp's Estonian psychology students. But there is one of notable differences. The number of university has increased after the World War II, so almost half population of same age high school students enter undergraduate courses in Japan. So, learning at course never link to students' job directly. Almost psychology students get non-psychological jobs.

Last, but not least, in addition to high school students, officers and workers in Japan also want to enter undergraduate course. At the bifurcation point of the end of a high school, half of people chose the way to work. But, in a few decades, some of them decide to return to university to study more. Psychology is one of the popular subjects for such students. We can see here the alternative trajectory emerges to study psychology.

6. Toward the study of three levels of trajectories

The diversity of trajectories is not regarded as deviations from an assumed norm. Trajectory doesn't mean "error." In statistic study, calculating mean scores and standard deviations is static understanding of variation of individual lives. The score of mean is index of "TRUE VALUE." Trajectories ought not to be understood as variation of single "true" trajectory. Trajectories are process and trajectories in TEM can imply the decision making and possible world. In addition, depicting TEM would

Part 2   EMERGENCE OF TEM

make us to notify possible options and alternative life ways. This is the very characteristics of this methodology and may connect to other concepts such as Jerome
Bruner's possible world (Bruner, 1986) and Amartya Sen's capability. The Novel prize
winner Amartya Sen (1999) argues that capability deprivation is a better measure of
poverty than low income. Capability deprivation should be regarded as deprivation
from sufficient chances or occasions to live.

Not only for understanding the life history, the TEM is useful to understand
the three levels of the process on the irreversible time; i.e., history, life course development and decision making. Three levels of organization of phenomena at which
HSS is applicable are:

1. macro-genetic level: history of a society or social group, or institution
2. meso-genetic level: human individual life course development (ontogeny)
3. micro-genetic level: decision making in semiotically over-determined everyday life situations.

For example, we try to depict the trajectory of the course work system in psychology. It was Edward B. Titchener who dominated as a constructing the system
of basic experimental course in psychology. His standard four-volume textbook
containing both teachers' manuals and students' tutorials had vast influences many
university psychology courses. This course work system has continued for long time.
How has it continue so long time? It's interesting, because if all students only suffered from such course works, they couldn't be continued. Perhaps, some kinds of
essence of course work encourage psychology students. And this course work system
makes influence to each student in all over the world.

Acknowledgements

I am grateful to Jaan Valsiner for kind support on an earlier version of this manu-
script. And I also wish to express my gratitude to Jaan for frequent, stimulating and help-
ful discussions at his Worcester apartment with coffee and his home-made kidney stew.
This chapter was supported by a Grant-in-Aid for Scientific Research (B) (No. 16330138)
provided by Japan Society for Promotion of Science.

Chapter 4

Beyond Dichotomy

Towards Creative Synthesis

Abstract

There are two ways for overcoming limitations of methods used in psychology, as Toomela (2007) points out. These are inventing new methods of research, and looking back into the history of methodological thought for new ideas. Though he limited the former as if it is a quantitative area and he declared to take the latter path, his paper actually advocates the need to create new methodology for understanding the human psyche through historical approach. We discuss problems of sampling and generalization in that context, and suggest a new way to creative synthesis through elaboration of qualitative methodologies. To us this direction constitutes an updated version of the German – Austrian methodology exactly as Toomela suggests.

Keywords

Qualitative methodology, North American thought, German – Austrian thought, History of methodological thought, Sampling

There were two psychologies in the pre-World War II era. We may also call the two schools as *the German – Austrian thought and North American thought* – merely for the sake of convenience. Geographical distribution is of secondary importance when the focus is on the qualities of ideas. Before discussing, a brief look at both Watson's (1934) and Toomela's (2007) claims is convenient (see Table 4.1).

Part 2   EMERGENCE OF TEM

Table 4.1. Watson's and Toomela's contrast of the two psychologies

Number	German – Austrian psychological thinking; Watson's (1934)	Contemporary mainstream methodological principles; Toomela's (2007)
1	German psychology was more interested in qualitative descriptions than in objective scores	Objective scores without qualitative descriptions
2	German psychology was more interested in psychological rather than in physical controls	Limiting description of experimental conditions to physical controls
3	German psychology was predominantly concerned with wholes and relationships	Fragments without whole and relationships
4	German psychology showed more concern about understanding a single case than the probabilities in a group	Probabilities in a group without additional case studies
5	German psychology saw individual trait differences as consequences of more basic type differences	Individual trait differences isolated from more basic (*Weltanschauung*) type differences
6	German psychology was more concerned with insight than with prediction	Prediction without insight
7	German psychology was more systematic	Nonsystematic approach to research and theory-building
8	German psychology was more interested in thinking than in the accumulation of facts	Accumulation of facts without (complex) thinking

1. On sampling and generalization

An issue which is not focused upon by Watson is the concept of generalization which should be reexamined. In other words, what almost of all psychological findings basically depend on is the production of mean scores, standard deviation and Pearson's (or other) correlation coefficients. This is theoretically problematic. Especially dangerous the excessive trust on the average scores and sheer weight of sample numbers since it could distort many psychologists' view of generalization (Omi & Kawano, 1994). The sample-to-population generalization trajectory is limited in its knowledge construction power because of its hidden assumption of the average (or prototypic) phenotype allowing us to infer the causality for its population. This assumption is untenable (Valsiner, 1984, 1986c).

1.1. The notion of "control"

Controlling the unrelated factors involved in a study is one of the important issues. In area of lower psychological functions such as sensation and perception, controlling the experimental variable (stimulus) does work well. The experimental procedure is set up so as to preemptively block the impacts of secondary variables. But in area of higher psychological functions such as cognitive or social functions operating under the guidance of persons' intentions, the situation is different.

American psychologists inevitably face to this problem, because American society is presented as a "melting pot." Right after establishing the role of empiricism (also called "evidence-based" science) in social psychology, psychologists were a bit too optimistic about removal of secondary variables, even though the control of exogenous variables is difficult. Statistical procedures are usually utilized for such tasks – yet the reality value of such uses is never proven.

The way of random sampling was suggested to solve this problem. Yet it just reminds us of a sip from "the melting pot" of some textured – yet believed to be homogeneous-soup. Though this strategy might make psychologists comfortable, it remains superficial. We should paraphrase the famous saying – "there is no use crying over spilt milk" – "there is no use being satisfied by sampling from a 'melting pot'." Human beings should not be regarded as units of a homogeneous whole.

Chauvinism of the dominance of random sampling is problematic. Such chauvinism has the ammunition to fire at the "bad mannered jobs" of researchers who use single subjects, or small samples that cannot but be selected through existing access channels. Actually, even though not so many psychological studies use random sampling, it is usually overlooked that the "randomness" of the "random sample" is there mostly by belief in mechanical "selection of participants." Participants who can – but decide not to – participate in the study cannot be "randomly sampled" by the

Part 2   EMERGENCE OF TEM

researchers' nonbinding will and administrative command systems.

Based on the statistical mindset, the idea of random sampling in the past appeared to be an important method to resolve the problems of sampling. But we should say that random sampling is not a creative solution but a compromise. Superficial peace was declared between "measurement-" and phenomena-oriented groups of psychologists, and a quantitative alliance – between experimenters and questionnaire/survey users – emerged.

1.2. Where is conceptual problem?

Random sampling might need a representative set of subjects so that it could infer parameters of population (Sato, 2007). This methodology focuses on persons just because they are assumed to consist of a selected variety of features labeled "variables." We must say this assumption is preposterous. Just think – is psychology the discipline for a population – or do we study of human beings? Historically speaking, psychology is a rather new discipline that was set to study the mental states of the human beings. What we habitually call "populations" are mere aggregates of organisms – they have no mental states of their own.

The stream of German – Austrian psychological thought has never needed the notion of population. Already Immanuel Kant declared the impossibility of empirical psychology as a science at the end of the eighteenth century. In his preface to *Metaphysical foundations of natural science* (Kant, 1786), Kant examined the question of whether empirical psychology could ever achieve a scientific status (Hatfield, 1992). He answered "no," because both mathematics and experiment should not be applied to the object of empirical psychology. However many of his successors struggled with that verdict – and constructed a new science. It was the mental state or functioning that psychologists focused upon. In it, sensation was regarded as important because it was an interface of outer world and inner world of a person. The efforts by Ernst H. Weber, Gustav T. Fechner, Wilhelm Wundt, and Hermann Ebbinghaus were in the line of such intellectual quest. Sensation, perception and memory – these were the themes of earlier psychology – and the notion of population was never needed there.

Chapter 4   Beyond Dichotomy

On the other hand, the population-based understanding of human mental state is related intensely with the view of human being as a bunch of variables. In such a view, each person is described by numerical values on variables. And the result is described by numerical scores. To make matters worse, psychologists sometimes use the notion of "error." Of course, the score of parameter has an error – in the context of the "law of large numbers." Yet the talk about "error" presumes the axiomatic acceptance of its opposite – "the truth." As a socially and/or statistically accepted rule, the average score is regarded as the best inference of "true value." An average score of sample is a parameter of population. Here the parameter means predicting the unknown "true score" of a population. Hence the notion of population is conceptually needed to find "the true value." However, here is the qualitative leap – the "true value" applies to the population, and not to the individuals who belong to that population. Conversely, "the non-true value score" is regarded as "an error" – thus designating persons within the population (of not close to average scores) as such.

Clearly human beings should not be considered "an error." Single cases that contradict group data should not be thrown away but be described and understood. It is the "true value mythology" that should be given up in psychology as a science of human being's life experience.

2. On the neo-Galtonian research paradigm and the inference revolution

One of the defining features of North American psychological methodology is to depict a person as a mixture of many relatively independent "variables" (Danziger, 1997), and then try to study a number of such variables. For example the MMPI has over 500 items – clustered together into more than 200 different "scores on variables." These hypothetical entities have been extracted from the over 500-item responses by using factor analysis. Ironically speaking, human being is viewed as if they were determined by precisely those many variables in which psychologists have

61

Part 2   EMERGENCE OF TEM

interest. Other aspects of subjects' lives are never focused on. Such other features are considered as residuals or errors to be controlled by random-sampling. This is clearly opposed to the holism of German – Austrian methodology.

The methods of the North American schools of psychology before World War II were already largely influenced by the English neo-Galtonian research paradigm and the statistical methods that were the product of that paradigm. We know that this direction was opposed to Wundtian paradigm of Germany (Popple & Levi, 2000). In addition, it is very important that North American psychology owes its philosophical basis to British empiricism. Thus, the origins of two directions were already formulated in the Old World.

Francis Galton respected the importance of heredity so that he regarded the notion of regression as important. The notion of heredity tends to be stable one, even though Galton himself emphasized and demonstrated the notion of regression by collecting the data of parent – child pair-wise data. Actually, regression means the process of going back to an earlier or less advanced form or state. Of course that original meaning of the term has vanished from our contemporary uses in psychology. The North American thought cannot prefer the notion of "going back" (regression) – nor are there methods of "going forward" (progression) developed by contemporary statistics. Instead, the notion of being quasi-related somehow – correlation rather than regression – is currently preferred. The notion of correlation tends to emphasize the stable and/or progressive process. Last but not least, the notion of regression include time and change. But the notion of correlation is timeless and the score of correlation coefficient seems to be regarded as an index of stability. As Molenaar (2007) pointed out that each subject in the population should obey exactly the same dynamical law governing the psychological process under investigation (homogeneity), and that the dynamical laws should have time-invariant statistical characteristics (stationarity).

The "inference revolution" (dated approximately to 1940-1955 – Gigerenzer & Murray, 1987) created a mono-vocal orthodoxy of the inferential techniques and introduced it as standard scientific practice in psychology. Within that orthodoxy, the

Chapter 4   Beyond Dichotomy

notion of random sampling occupied a central place. According to Gigerenzer (1993),
in psychology and in other social sciences, probability and statistics were typically
not used to revise the understanding of our subject matter from a deterministic to
some probabilistic view (as in physics, genetics, or evolutionary biology), but rather
to mechanize the experimenters' inferences – in particular, their inferences from
data to hypothesis. Gigerenzer (1993) emphasized that this use of statistical theory
contrasts sharply with physics, where statistics and probability are indispensable
in theories about nature, whereas mechanized statistical inference such as null hypothesis testing is almost unknown. Inferential statistics should not be abused in the
researches of psychology.

The neo-Galtonian research paradigm and the inference revolution are not
originated in the same thought. But they allied and promote directly the North
American psychology tide both Watson (1934) and Toomela (2007) pointed out.

3. On the situation of psychology in Japan

Psychology in Japan before the Meiji Restoration (feudal era) should be separated from what we now call psychology (Sato, 2002, pp. 33-35) and Takasuna (2007)
agree this view. But the story was not about a single trajectory of "importing psychology from the Western." As Sato (2003) pointed out there were at least six trajectories
that led to the acceptance of modern psychology in Japan. And the "new psychology
as experimental psychology" was introduced by a young man named Yuzero Motora
via the United States (Sato & Sato, 2005). He studied psychology at Johns Hopkins
University supervised by G. Stanley Hall and after returning to Japan, he founded
the first department of psychology in Tokyo Imperial University (Now University of
Tokyo). Though Motora studied and taught psychophysics and experimental psychology mainly, he also had interest in Hall's genetic psychology and methodology of
the questionnaire-style research.

Although the starting point of psychology in Japan was an amalgam of German

Part 2 EMERGENCE OF TEM

– Austrian thought and North American thought, the younger generation of psychology went Germany to study psychology. Toomela (2007) insists that the German – Austrian way of thinking disappeared from the forefront of research in psychology, especially at Germany under Nazi Regime. But one of the representative thought systems of Germany psychology, Gestalt psychology was influential and popular pre-World War II period in Japan.

In pre-World War II period in Japan, there were a number of young lecturers and associate professors who went to the United States, Germany, and other European countries to study psychology. At that time, studying abroad was one of the prerequisites for becoming a full professor at a national Japanese university (Takasuna & Sato, 2004). Usao Onoshima (1894-1941) and Kanae Sakuma (1888-1970) were among them, and they studied Gestalt psychology in Berlin from 1923 to 1925 under the supervision of Kurt Lewin. The young Lewin was then the lecturer in the Institute of Psychology in Berlin (with Max Wertheimer, Wolfgang Köhler and Kurt Kofka as his colleagues). Gestalt psychology was widely accepted by Japanese psychologists – from acoustic perception to children's personality structure.

Later Lewin visited Japan in 1933 on the way of a round-the-world trip. First, Lewin came to the United States as a visiting professor at Stanford University (1932). From there he traveled to Japan and was warmly welcomed. But just then Hitler established political power. So, on the way to home at Moscow, he gave up the idea to go back "Gerty land" (Gertrud was his wife's name) and went to the United States instead. Tokyo, Seoul, Moscow and Berlin were connected continued railway at that time – in 1935 it took about 40 days from Tokyo to Paris in the sea route, but it was possible to cover that distance in 15 days by using Trans-Siberian Railway. This was the fastest route at that time.

4. Japanese psychology after World War II

After World War II, Japan was occupied by the allied military power. After

Chapter 4   Beyond Dichotomy

Japan's defeat in the Second World War in 1945, and during the period of the occupation, many aspects of Japanese government were reformed under recommen-
dations of the General Headquarters of the Allied Power. Reforming the Japanese
education system was one of its most important agendas (Sato, Namiki et al., 2004).
All education based on Shintoism, as it had been before the war, was abolished, and
a new scientific and democratic educational system was built. Psychology was given
a prominent place in the new system as a fundamental part of scientific education.
Counseling, guidance, group dynamics, and educational measurement among other
disciplines, were introduced from the United States. New psychological technologies
and multidimensional personality tests such as the MMPI, as well as new types of
mental tests such as the WAIS, were also introduced (Sato, 2005).

This is the situation that old Japanese saying says that "Bon festivals for the de-
ceased and New Year's ceremony have come together!" In our contemporary sense,
this means "The Olympic Games and FIFA World Cup are held on the same date."
Japanese psychologists experienced a big shock by its differences from what they had
known (Oyama et al., 2002). Whether fortunately or not, they have the basic knowledge to digest American new trends.

5. Beyond dichotomy and toward a creative synthesis

It is extremely important work that psychologists criticize carefully and multi-
laterally the problem included in methodology of present psychology. The authors
have accumulated discussion for about 20 years (Sato et al., 2000). Toomela's discussion fundamentally sympathizes with ours. We are glad that the way of discussion
is similar to ours. Geological and/or intellectual marginality might be shared both
Toomela and authors. Toomela's discussion seems to involve a harmony target
though we agree with German – Austrian psychological thinking. For example,

1. Mere statistical analyses based on accumulated data should not be considered
   as definitive – but exceptional cases should be also analyzed (Omi, 2006 –

Part 2   EMERGENCE OF TEM

corresponding to Watson's feature 6).

2. The biggest evil associated with ever more complicated nature – and increasing frequency of application – of statistical methods in psychology is that psychologists stop thinking (Omi, 1997 – corresponding to Watson's feature 8).

3. One and the same sentence in a questionnaire can convey different meanings among the individuals (Omi, 1998, – corresponding to Watson's feature 1).

We agree with Toomela's (2007) warning that reliance on linear statistical data analysis procedures in too many cases rule out the possibility for discovering person types and other more complex aspects of mind. Psychological experiments and investigation cannot succeed by using fragmented variables, so psychologists are caught in their own trap of oversimplification of human mind and its circumstances.

First of all, we need to expand the objects of investigation in psychology. Sensation and perception, cognition, personality and intelligence, these of course hold their proud position in the objects of psychology. But now we can declare that life experience is the major alternative important object of psychology. This leads psychologists to think about human as a whole. And subjects should be not remaining anonymous. They are as real – or more so – as characters from novels or theatre plays human beings all over the world know and resonate with. Consider a description of the psychological state of Hamlet as "Participant 007 who was observed in interaction with a part of the skeleton of *Homo sapiens*" – the real experience of contemplation of being and non-being becomes eliminated from the depiction.

"Anonymous" is rather a new word. In the German – Austrian or Wundtian paradigm, subjects were not anonymous. And subjects were interchangeable with experimenter. Academic psychologists are at first the most important group of subjects for psychological research in the 1890s and then show a progressive decline in the next decade. This ideological stance was passed on to younger and/or American generations of psychology (Danziger, 1990, p. 74).

As a result of Galtonian turn, especially North American thought, subjects should be regarded as just object and also regarded as members of supposed population. Subjects (= objects of investigation) might be appreciated because they could have measurable characters or variables – but not be respected as subjects (= active makers of their lives) themselves. Looking back into the early period of psychology psychologists focused on the mental states such as consciousness – or on behavior In either the psychological traditions of Wundt, Oswald Külpe, Lev S. Vygotsky on the one hand, or Ivan P. Pavlov, Vladimir M. Bekhterev, John B. Watson and Burrhus F. Skinner on the other, sampling was an unnecessary operation to be performed by a researcher (Sato, Yasuda et al., 2007).

After throwing away the notion of sampling and a deterministic view, we propose here "systemic view" and "relationalistic view." So, now, new type of subjects is needed – and has already appeared – in psychology's investigations. Hermans & Kempen (1993) proposed to regard subjects as active participants in psychological research, especially in interview research. Interviewing is an appropriate method to research individual life experiences in the first place. But after World War II, with the emergence of the standardized survey interview, individuals became accustomed to offering information and opinions that had no immediate bearing on their lives and social relations (Gubrium & Holstein, 2001). So individuals are obliged to play a role of passive respondents.

Life experience of each individual must be respected. In this context, Molenaar (2007) proposes to focus on the intra-individual variation. He emphasizes that psychologists have to start with analysis of intra-individual variation based on replicated time series designs. We agree this is one of the ways to arrive at general laws about idiographic regularities. But here we introduced the alternative way to achieve Molenaar's (2007) manifesto.

We claim that sampling free methodology and quantity-free methodology is needed. One of our ideas is HSS and TEM (Valsiner & Sato, 2006). Historically Structured Sampling (HSS) is a method of sampling individual cases based on their previous (up-to-now) knowable life course histories analyzed as a series of bifurcation points (Sato, Yasuda et al., 2007).

The notion of HSS relies heavily upon the notion of equifinality. Human life ex-

Part 2   EMERGENCE OF TEM

perience functions as an open system, not as closed system. And open system has an Equifinality Point (EFP). Equifinality means that the same and/or similar state which may be reached from different initial conditions and in different ways in the course of time. The notion of trajectory is very important to study life experience as EFP. Trajectory Equifinality Model (TEM) is a new proposal to describe human development from the perspective of cultural historical approach. TEM depict the variety of trajectory itself. Never need to calculate the mean score and standard deviation. And open-systemic view doesn't need the concept of population.

Socio-cultural psychology deals with higher psychological functions that are mediated by signs (Rosa, 2007). Life experience as an object of psychology may be thought that is mediated by signs. Every circumstance around human has sign, so we should try to depict the life experience as sign-mediated processes. Molenaar (2007) is concerned with the possibility that idiographic (individual-focused) approach results create the great number of possible models describing an individual. He emphasized that every individual is in some sense unique; unique models may also be necessary for every different situation, setting, developmental phase, historical period, even a mood swing. However, each psychological research should have one's own focus. In HSS and TEM, by focusing the EFPs as research questions, could propose a limited number of models.

6. Concluding remarks

Toomela's discussion (2007) successfully demonstrated that the history of psychological method is not a simple progress from the old and inferior methodology to new and superior one, and that predominant methodologies in current psychology are not necessarily superior to minor or old ones. It is expected that one could explore what has been inhibiting German – Austrian psychological thinking and whether North American thinking and German – Austrian thinking could aufheben in the near future or not. In Japan, the expectation to German – Austrian style psy-

Chapter 4　Beyond Dichotomy

chology has appeared in this decade. The journal *Qualitative Research in Psychology* (in Japanese) started in 2002. Qualitative psychology in Japan has become accepted and the Japanese Association of Qualitative Psychology launched at 2005.

Part 3
Development of TEM

Chapter 5

Sampling Reconsidered

Idiographic Science and the Analyses of Personal Life Trajectories

Keywords

Sampling, Idiographic Science (IS), Classifying Science (CS), Population, Historically Structured Sampling (HSS)

Our knowledge, our attitudes, and our actions are based to a very large extent on samples. This is equally true in everyday life and in scientific research ... In science and human affairs alike we lack the resources to study more than a fragment of the phenomena that might advance our knowledge. (Cochran, 1963, p. 1)

What is sampling? And why do we need to pay attention to it? Sampling is an inevitable operation in any research project – involving selection of some specimens of a class from the whole class. Yet there is more than mere decision of "whom to select" at stake here – sampling is predicated upon the realities of accessibility of the phenomena for investigation. After deciding what to investigate, researchers plan to how to access the phenomena what they want to know. Social scientists may focus on states, biologists may focus on bushes or animals, and psychologists most likely focus on human beings or their nearest phylogenetic relatives.

Furthermore – psychologists' real interest may be in some special aspect of those human beings – their mental properties for instance. Here is the access lim-

73

Part 3 DEVELOPMENT OF TEM

itation involved in sampling – these properties cannot be selected independently of the cooperation by the whole – the real persons who decide to participate in a study (or decline to do so), who cooperate with the procedures (or – undermine those by lukewarm or disruptive participation strategies). Thus, the researcher faces a difficult task – for knowing the selected properties, psychologists should select a particular human being as a whole (because mental properties never appear by themselves) – yet the interests of research are a part of the whole.

1. Two ways to generalized knowledge

1.1. The trajectories of Idiographic Science (IS) and Classifying Science (CS)

In any research project we have a problem – we can only study some of the members of the set of all of the phenomena – yet we want to arrive at conclusions that cover the whole set. Hence, the issue of how we select what we study is crucial for our knowledge. This issue is subsumed under the general question of sampling. We locate and select a specimen – *a* sample (a singular example) – from the whole multitude of the phenomenological field we want to study. Yet the reasons for selection of any specimens are not in the nature of such individual case. Instead, we use the individual case – or a selected group of individual cases – for creating generalized knowledge (Molenaar, 2004; Molenaar & Valsiner, 2005). Cultural psychology uses ways of generalization that are based on systemic analyses of singular phenomena (Valsiner, 2003a). It therefore leaves aside the set of methodological axioms of classificatory, inductively accumulative ways of arriving at generalization. That latter logic of generalization is inductive in its nature, and requires the creation of collection of specimens ("a sample" – a sub-set of N specimens of all N + N' cases that make up the class X). On the basis of such collections, formal rules of generalization are set to make claims that are considered to apply to the full class X ("the population"). Hence, we have two lines of thought involved in the process of generalization (Figure

Chapter 5 Sampling Reconsidered

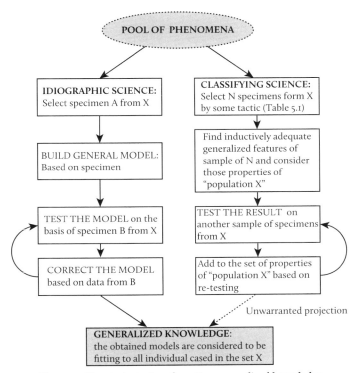

Figure 5.1. Two trajectories of creating generalized knowledge

5.1).

The two trajectories make different use of the selections from their common phenomenological field. The trajectory of Idiographic Science (IS) is based on the selection of single cases – together with their structural and/or temporal context – developing a general model that fits the systemic nature of a single case, testing that model on other single cases, and arriving at a generalized model that fits the generic organization of the selected aspect of phenomena. Many sciences are by default limited to this trajectory of knowledge construction – the object of investigation may be present in a singular form (e.g., the Moon that circles the Earth), yet their goal is to generate knowledge about processes that fits phenomena beyond the single case

Part 3   DEVELOPMENT OF TEM

(e.g., empirical "Moon science" is expected to provide generalized knowledge about processes of the formation of the universe, or general geological processes on the Earth).

The second trajectory – we call it that of "Classifying Science (CS)" – is built on the assumption that multiple specimens of the same class (category) are needed to arrive at trustable knowledge (and, conversely, a single case does not allow generalization). CS creates collections of specimens – selecting cases from the phenomenological field and treating such sub-set as "a sample."

This tactic of CS leads to the de-focusing of the systemic connections of each of the sampled specimens from the original phenomenological field (Valsiner, 2005). If such connection is irrelevant for the kind of research tasks of a study, this tactic may afford new generalized knowledge about the full set ("population") of the specimens. Yet the critical issue is if the knowledge about the full set is applicable to each and every individual member of that set. This is possible only if the full set is a crisp set (i.e., all its members are of the same quality). If, however, the full set is a fuzzy set – a set where its members belong to it by varying degrees of membership – then the transfer of generalization from population to a generic individual case (see Figure 5.1) constitutes an unwarranted projection.

The trajectory of IS follows the line of classical tactics of generalization in psychology. Wilhelm Wundt is usually credited with being the principal representative of experimental psychology in Germany. As the successor to Johann F. Herbart and Gustav T. Fechner, and the first to bring the new scientific psychology to real fruition (Wozniak, 1998), Wundt's voice has been historically prominent in the shaping of the discipline. Researchers' aims are to clarify the nature of mental phenomena and they turned adults into objects of psychological analysis quite naturally. The problem of specimen selection would never be focused under such intellectual situation. Phenomena and specimens are inseparable at the start point of scientific psychology – in the course of the whole sequence of study.

Wundt stressed the distinction between psychology and natural science. He pointed out that "two directions for the treatment of experience," should be divided.

Chapter 5   Sampling Reconsidered

And he continued:

> ... one is that of the natural sciences, which concern themselves with the objects of experience, thought of as independent of the subject. The other is that of psychology, which investigates the whole content of experience in its relations to the subject and in its attributes derived directly from the subject. (Wundt, 1896/1897, p. 3)

According to Wundt, the discrepancy between investigation theme and subject was completely alien to psychology such a science. But on the other hand, Wundt's plan of mental phenomena supposed the two levels – the lower and higher mental functions. Wundt claimed that the higher mental processes, involving the truly human, symbolic aspects of experience, can only be understood within a social context, using a non-experimental methodology (Leary, 1982). For the latter, Wundt emphasized a non-experimental methodology and wrote the ten-volume work of *Völkerpsychologie*. However, to say the least, this program was not followed by psychologists including his students. Experimental methodology won psychologists' affections.

However, a parallel epistemological framework arose from experimental psychology – by taking experimentation out of the laboratory and transforming it into large-scale questionnaire studies. In the U.S. context of late 19th century, it was called "child study movement." It found an enthusiastic audience among scientists and professionals as well as the lay public (van Drunen & Jansz, 2004). Taine (1875) and Darwin (1877) were pioneers who described the development of their own children using observation methods. But the most influential work was done by the German developmentalist William Preyer (1882).

The usage of the biographical method allowed for the analysis of the development of the individual as well as the institutional and social conditions that influenced the developments (Bergold, 2000). Pioneers tried to describe and understand the developmental phenomena of children. Because they observed only a few children, they were still working within the IS trajectory. Yet the social demands upon psychology led to the proliferation of the second – CS – trajectory. The applied

Part 3   DEVELOPMENT OF TEM

practice of mental testing in France in the 1890s (Alfred Binet) and its parallel focus on "child study" in the United States were building their generalizations upon the CS trajectory. This was put into practice by G. Stanley Hall. Hall learned experimental psychology in Germany and was one of the founders of American psychology. Much of his professional life was dedicated to the area of child study. Within the "child study movement," studies were performed in which parents and teachers acted as researchers' allies.

1.2. Creating norms: The child becomes a classificatory object

Developmental psychology has developed in parallel with child psychology – yet the two areas differ substantively (Valsiner & Connolly, 2003b). Child psychology is non-developmental in its nature – it compares children of different ages as homogeneous groups. Educational psychology and experimental pedagogy might also tend to treat children as specimens who form similarity groups (e.g., age sets, school grade grouping: "first-graders," "fifth-graders," etc.). By creating such similarity categories, psychologists moved away from careful look at phenomena and replaced it by comparison of outcomes of psychological functions as those appear in comparison of similarity groups. Thus, the focus on phenomena disappeared. Child psychology started to treat children as a social classificatory object – whose "fit into a category" explained the particular phenomena that were the basis for such fit.[1] History of psychology tells us child psychology established the normative data of development of childhood. Yet the processes of development were no longer in focus of child psychology – a characteristic of the area that remains this way to our present day (Cairns, 1998; Valsiner, 2006).

In contrast, developmental psychology has concentrated on processes. For example, Arnold Gesell – one of the students of G. S. Hall, was eminently involved in describing ontogenetic progression in children. In his introduction chapter of *The first five years of life*, Gesell (1940) emphasized that concepts such as habit, intelligence, and mental abilities can never explain the ever-changing organization of child. He suggested that the notion of growth be made into the key concept for the interpretation of development. He didn't intend to regard inter-individual differences as static state.

> There are laws of sequence and of maturation which account for the general similarities and basic trends of child development. But no two children (with the partial exception of identical twins) grow up in exactly the same way. Each child has a tempo and a style of growth which are as characteristic of individuality as the lineaments of his countenance. (Gesell, 1940, p. 7)

Thus, Gesell himself tried to depict the normative process of behaviors changes for understanding the determinants of growth. Though Gesell recognized the trajectories of infant development, he proceeded to depict the normative development pattern. His interest of infant hygiene made him consider the normative data rather than difference of trajectories.

Danziger (1990, p. 65) undertook an analysis of major American and German psychological journals to show the percentage of empirical studies in which "an exchange of experimenter and subjects roles" occurred. More than 30% of psychological research (1894-1896) in *American Journal of Psychology*, *Philosophische Studien and Psychological Review*, the roles of experimenter and subjects were exchange-possible. Though the percentage declined from 31 to 8 over a 40-year period, it still remained in 1930s. One the other hand, in late-coming journals such as *Journal of Educational Psychology* (founded in 1910) and *Journal of Applied psychology* (founded in 1917), there were few (almost no) studies in which an exchange of experimenter and subject roles appeared. Danziger (1990) pointed out that individuals were treated as an object of invention rather than as the subjects of experience. His point of view resonates with our view of dissociation of specimens and phenomena. Our look at sampling emphasizes the organism-centered experiences of growth.

Part 3   DEVELOPMENT OF TEM

2. What is a sample?

The reason researchers want to know about the properties of samples – is for the sake of generalizing to another abstract unit – population. Sampling means a procedure choosing sub-groups or elements from a population according to some criteria. Once the criteria are set, the sampling procedure treats all the sampled specimens as members of a qualitatively homogeneous class.

However, the nature of autopoietic systems – their self-regulation that leads to reproduction – acts in ways contrary to the simple image of taking a number of similar objects out of an urn. At the first glance, a selection of biological materials from biological world seems to be a kind of sampling as well. The selection of materials leads to critical impact to the progress of biological investigation of the transformation of the materials. The typical case of this situation has been shown in the field of genetics at its very beginning. The pioneer of genetics, Gregor Mendel, chose seven characters of garden peas as biological materials during the late 1850s and early 1860s. Yet these were sampled not for the sake of identifying some "essential cause" that remains behind the varieties of peas. He needed to demonstrate the specific ratio of segregation by hybridization – and revealed the duality of genetic encoding through crossing different kinds of peas with one another. He did not find out what the "prototypic" or "true" pea is like – as is the case of much of psychology's sample-to-population generalization effort (see also Valsiner & Rosa (2007b) – on the semiotic experiment). The search for a "true pea" – or for "the true score" in psychological testing – presumes that such "true" and static abstract entity exists. That assumption itself is untenable in the case of all living systems that exist only through their exchange relations with the environment.

The research directions in genetics since Mendel have concentrated on the sampling of theoretically relevant structured varieties of the biological materials that were selected for investigation. Following along the same lines of thought, the discovery of the structure of DNA by James Watson and Francis Crick in 1953 became

Chapter 5   Sampling Reconsidered

possible. It would have been a very different matter if these two youngsters had tried out to randomly sample the different base pairs for their model. The structure of the DNA may be a long chain of base pairs the location and function of many of the sub-sequences may be obscure – but by no means is that structure random. Nor is it possible to study the human genome through assuming that all base pairs make up the "population."

2.1. The meaning of "population"

Population is a *collection* of specimens of a particular category – be these *people*, or organisms of a particular *species* – that are located within some universe. Usually it is defined as a crisp set (where each member of the set belongs to it with full extent of membership). Given the inter-specimen variation[2] within each grouping of biological, sociological, anthropological, or psychological specimens it would be more adequate to define a population in terms of a fuzzy set – where each member of the set belongs to it by some measure of extent of membership (membership function). Populations are heterogeneous classes.

The concept of population eliminates the systemic qualities of the whole. As any collection it is devoid of structure – the specimens belong to a population if the inherent systemic connections between them are eliminated, or de-emphasized. Thus, all the leaves of a given tree form a "population" (of leaves of that tree) only if they are taken separately from their location on the tree. In other terms – a full tree is a tree (= a system uniting all leaves), not a "population of leaves of the tree." The quintessential example of a population of the leaves of the given tree is the collection of fallen leaves in the autumn – leaves can be collected (as a sample that approaches the full population) independently of their history (of locations on the tree). Such leaves become statistical population – an abstraction that approximates the "real" population, but is not the same (nor is it representing the original system). In an example from the human level – a military unit in a war situation (consisting of soldiers of various ranks and roles, all operating as one unit) becomes a "population" after all of its members end up buried in separate graves in a cemetery. All the graves

Part 3   DEVELOPMENT OF TEM

in the cemetery are the "population of the cemetery" – that can be studied in full (i.e., listing each and every member of the population) or by generalizing from a "random sample" of graves to the whole of the cemetery. One can see that the history of the whole – the actions of the military unit – cannot be restored from any version of sampling of the outcomes of their action (i.e., their distribution in the cemetery).

2.2. Logic of generalization based on the homogeneity assumption

The basis for using the sample-to-population generalization is the assumption of "homogeneity" of the phenomena under study in their basic essences. If one can believe in the homogeneity of a class, the arbitrary sampling is enough to do any research. But, in fact, unignorable variation within the sample (inter-individual or intra-individual) needs to be recognized. For integrating two contradicting concepts – homogeneity and variation – another intervening concept is needed. Usually the variation becomes regarded as "noise" that obscures the "pure essences" of the properties. This look at the reality of phenomena is built on static, a-historical, and essentialist philosophical grounds that are challenged in contemporary psychology (Hermans, 2001, 2002; Valsiner, 1986c). Here the "noise" becomes the "essence" of the phenomena – and instead of static ontology researchers begin to look at dynamic equilibria and disequilibria.

The focus on interdependency of persons and environments does not fit well with the notion of random sample. Looking back to the history of science, random sampling is discussed on the context of logical inference. The American semiotician Charles Sanders Peirce insisted that:

> The truth is that induction is reasoning from a sample taken at random to the whole lot sampled. A sample is a random one, provided it is drawn by such machinery, artificial or physiological, that in the long run any one individual of the whole lot would get taken as often as any other. (Peirce, 1896/1957, p. 217)

Yet it is precisely Peirce who repeatedly demonstrated how science cannot be

Chapter 5   Sampling Reconsidered

built solely through the inductive techniques (see Rosa, 2007), and actually operates through the unity of induction and deduction in the form of abductive inference (Wirth, 1997). It involves the selection of phenomena, formation of hypotheses, and creation of new knowledge at the intersection of deduction and induction through a "leap" of inference.

Randomization is thus a product of an atomistic axiom as applied to complex world. It presumes the independence of each randomized object from one another. If that assumption is applicable, randomization is necessary because the quality of inference should be guaranteed through minimizing imbalances of selection of the specimens. Such inference has aim to understand not sample itself but population. Applicability of this axiomatic may depend upon approximation. For instance, its applicability to the grain growing on various agricultural plots (i.e., the basis of R. A. Fisher's development of variance-oriented statistics) may possibly be claimed. Yet it is an unfeasible assumption when human beings, social groups, or societies are concerned.

2.3. The notion of sampling in the natural sciences

In various biological fields, ecological research has been using sampling frequently. Recently, its importance is noticed in relation to with views of nature preservation, biological resources, and biomass energy. Sampling as well as experimental design has been based on Fisher's "three principles" – local controls, randomization, and replication. A major problem of data sampling in biological field can be explained by how to apply the Fisher's principles.

Selecting a number of individuals of organisms in some areas is an essence of ecological research. Then, the mass of organisms, their growth rate and death rates are needed. However, biological population produces descendants – who are needed for maintenance of the species. Hence, stable living environment causes population to reproduce the stable number of descendants. What matters for our knowledge of the ecological system is the relative balance of individuals who exit the system (hence the need to know the death rate, or emigration rate) with those who enter (by

Part 3   DEVELOPMENT OF TEM

birth, or by immigration). The most popular method of understanding death rate is "mark release." That is, marked individuals are "released" to living environment. Afterwards, they are "recaught." The death rates are estimated from these individuals. This method is applied to marine and freshwater animals and birds and other animal species.

The practices of the fishing industry can be seen as depending upon the practice of sampling. As it is a productive industry, its wellbeing is dependent upon controlled catching of fish as well as the affording of the remainder of the fish populations to reproduce themselves. Knowledge of the nature of the fish populations – through sampling – makes it possible to decide upon quotas on catching the fish so that the population would not become extinct – nor grow beyond the conditions afforded by the environment. Yet it is very difficult to estimate the death rate. It is done on the basis of measuring the samples of living organisms over time – as in case of observations of the whale population. Yet the sociopolitical decisions – establishing hunting quota on one or another species by representatives of *Homo sapiens* – depend on the values give to one or another population size estimate in relation to its decline (= death of numbers of specimens).

2.4. Sampling in the behavioral sciences

Looking at history of psychology at its independent starting point of scientific study of psychology, random sampling was never taken into account. For example, in Fechnerian psychophysics it wasn't necessary to consider a human being as a sampling unit. Fechner only needed to define the concept of sensation and stimulus. Likewise, Wundt's psychology succeeded with this basic attitude. The focus on the phenomena of the psyche in general did not need the notion of sampling at all.

In the early period of psychology, psychologists focused on the mental states such as consciousness – or on behavior. In either the psychological traditions of Wundt, Oswald Külpe, Lev S. Vygotsky on the one hand, or Ivan P. Pavlov, Vladimir M. Bekhterev, John B. Watson, and Burrhus F. Skinner on the other, sampling was an unnecessary operation to be performed by a researcher. However, as the subject

Chapter 5   Sampling Reconsidered

matter of psychology gradually became to have interests in groups of people – such as school classrooms filled with pupils or army recruits in military training – sampling came into focus (Danziger, 1990). Danziger outlines how temporal trends exist in the use of different categories of research subjects. Academic psychologists are at first the most important group of subjects for psychological research in the 1890s and then show a progressive decline in the next decade (Danziger, 1990). Human beings were replaced by rats and army men – all treated as homogeneous classes rather than individualities. A military unit is a "sample" from the population of the given army as a whole – representing the latter precisely because of its homogeneity. In contrast – a writer, poet, or a painter do not represent any population – their creativity stems from their immediate personal experiences.

Expansion of the areas of research for psychologists into the public domains changed the sampling method of psychology and led to random sampling. The idea of random sampling seems to be imported from social survey. At the U.S. presidential election in 1936, a then-unknown pollster named George Gallup predicted that Roosevelt would win the election, based on a random sample of 50,000 people. On the other hand, the *Literary Digest* poll, which was based on 10 million questionnaires mailed to readers and potential readers (over 2 million were returned) failed to predict the winner. The success of Gallup and the failure of *Literary Digest* highlight random sampling as a proper method for prediction of pubic opinions.

3. Sampling and statistical theories

Sampling theory can be traced to the late nineteenth century. Basic statistical techniques for probability sampling were first proposed by Jerzy Neyman (D'Onofrio & Gendron, 2001). Neyman's seminal work "On the two different aspects of representative method: The method of stratified sampling and the method of purposive selection" was such landmark work (Neyman, 1934). Nevertheless, the importance of representativeness of data wasn't considered before World War II. Although there

Part 3   DEVELOPMENT OF TEM

were some statisticians such as Yule (1929) and Neyman (1934) discussing the random sampling, McNemar (1940, p. 331) lamented that "the sampling inadequacy of so many researches" was "a reflection of the scanty treatment of sampling" in the textbooks on statistical method in United States. He insisted that "a large amount of psychological research must depend upon sampling for the simple reason that human variation exists."

Here we can note that sampling is the method for dissipating the idea of the existence of variation within a population. McNemar (1940) pointed out that at least 90% of the researches in psychology are interested in making an inference about the similarity or difference of two groups. Sampling theory has been valued because the biased interpretation easily occurred in research using hypothetical tests (Marks, 1947). Therefore, McNemar (1940) insisted that the validity of a scientific inference must depend upon the precision of data on which it is based. Interestingly, he used the word "the universe" in spite of "population" so that psychologists' concerns might focus on understanding the universal mental state (not human being or organisms). Securing a representative sample was easily attached to systematic sampling procedures, including random sampling.

In his 1934 paper, Neyman claimed that the method of stratified sampling was preferable to the method of purposive selection. As Smith (1976) notes the importance of the paper to statistical sampling is enormous especially in the area of social survey within a period of 10 years. These 10 years approximately match the age of "inference revolution." The "inference revolution" (dated approximately to 1940-1955; Gigerenzer & Murray, 1987) created a monovocal orthodoxy of the inferential techniques and introduced it as standard scientific practice in psychology. Within that orthodoxy, the notion of random sampling occupied a central place.

It is interesting to have a look at how methodology of sampling had attracted psychologists' interest over time. Figure 5.2 shows the number of journal papers include "sampling" in the title before World War II.[3]

Interestingly, journals on educational psychology were the places where sampling issues were discussed very often during this period. Spearman published his

Chapter 5   Sampling Reconsidered

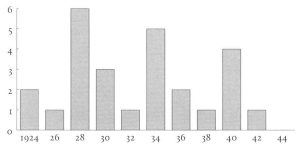

Figure 5.2. Referencing the topic "sampling" in 1924-1944

"The sampling error in the theory of two factors" on the *British Journal of Psychology* in 1924. This paper was one of the earliest papers that use the term of sampling in the title. The period of the 1920s was precisely the time when psychology moved from being a primarily laboratory science to becoming a discipline that tries to be relevant in the public and applied areas of society. As a result, the questions of selection of persons by some criteria became emphasized.

3.1. Steps in sampling

Usually, the word "sampling" means "sampling the specimen as a unit." Sampling always implies "to sample" – that is, to take – the specimen (a person, an organism, a marble out of an urn) to investigate it for the sake of a general goal. Although we insist that phenomena-oriented sampling is better than specimen-oriented sampling, this distinction is vague and many researchers seem to be familiar with the specimen-oriented sampling, it may be useful to consider the sampling from the prevailing view. Under such assumption, we know there are three steps in the psychological sampling and investigation:

Step 1. Focus on selected properties (basis for sampling)

Step 2. Sampling of the human participants

Step 3. Measuring the selected properties through the cooperation of the participants

Step 2 is critical for sampling – it is here that the focus changes from psycholog-

Part 3   DEVELOPMENT OF TEM

ical phenomena of individuals to that of the amorphous character of "the sample."
At Step 2, the size and the representativeness of the sample of research participants
in relation to "population" – rather than their representativeness as to *how well the
targeted phenomena are present in each individual* – becomes an issue. It is here where
the quality of the target phenomena easily gets lost in the discourse of samples –>
population generalization narrative. Comparison of samples leads to comparative
statements about populations – which cannot easily be translated back to each and
every individual case in each of the compared populations (Valsiner, 1986c). The notion of samples – and of sampling – is an example of the utilization of elementaristic
linear causality schemes (Valsiner, 2000, p. 73). As we will show in this chapter, in the
case of socio-cultural psychology that scheme of causality is not applicable. Corre-
spondingly, the notion of sampling needs to be transformed.

3.2. Changing the axiomatic base: Historicity of life courses

If psychology tries to understand the individual in her/his generic form(s), we
should apart from the philosophy of randomization. If there is anything random in
human conduct it is not the position of a particular person within a social structure,
but specific features of conduct in the person's movement from the present setting to
the next anticipated future state. Even there the randomness is bounded by limits of
past history (Valsiner, 1997) and future anticipation (Valsiner, 2003b). At most, we act
in quasirandom ways in our search for non-random forms of conduct that grant our
adaptation to the not-yet-known future.

We can find it there was a bifurcation point of our concerns on the sampling
methodology. Researchers in psychology (especially social psychology) have taken
a course to random sampling in the past 50 years. Other scientists moved along on
a different trajectory. According to Egon Brunswik, proper sampling of situations
is more important than that of persons (Brunswik, 1947). Brunswik was a fighter
against statisticians in those days (see Hammond, 1948). His Viennese background
(see Benetka, 1995) made him competently skeptical of the "dust-bowl" statistical
empiricism that began to dominate the United States after World War II. Brunswik

Chapter 5   Sampling Reconsidered

is one of the eminent pioneers of ecological validity. Recognizing the unity of per-son-environment relations leads to the understanding of inevitability of sampling of actor <> environment units.

Hence we can see that sampling is a topic with venerable – yet ideologically situated – history in the social sciences. What contemporary science of psychology needs is clarity about how to construct adequate methods for specific research pur-poses – and not a discussion about whether one or another category of methods is better (or worse) by virtue of their ontology (Valsiner & Diriwächter, 2005).

3.3. Types of sampling

Although the methodology of psychology has been dominated by the principle of random sampling, other sampling methods are being designed. We once consid-ered the different notions of sampling in the social sciences (Table 5.1).

In general, random sampling is regarded as one of the probabilistic sampling techniques. But we want to emphasize here that "random" and "representative" are not same concepts. In purposive sampling, subjects are selected because of some pre-set characteristics. In other words, the selection of participants is made by human choice rather than at random. Purposive sampling is popular in qualitative research. Patton (2002) has proposed the following cases of purposive sampling (Table 5.2).

Here we add the explanations of some of Patton's sampling methods. "Inten-sity" is a method of picking information-rich cases that manifest the phenomenon intensely, but not extremely. "Politically important cases" is a method of picking cases that are important for political reasons. Of course, the scientific and political aspects of researches (especially ones of cultural psychology) are interdependent but are hoped to be reciprocally reinforcing. "Confirming or disconfirming" is a method of picking cases to seek out confirming or disconfirming evidence. So this may be used second stage of researches. Both taxonomies are organized from the perspec-tive of sampling – it is assumed that the researchers are "drawing a sample" from "a population." So these taxonomies lack a consideration of the nature of human lives – including those of researchers.

Part 3   DEVELOPMENT OF TEM

Table 5.1. Different notions of sampling in the social sciences

Random	A sample of objects is selected for study from a larger group (called population). Each object is chosen by procedures that are designated to be random – it is "by chance" that the objects are selected. Each object in the population has an equal chance of being selected into the sample. Within that sampling mode sub-types exist: cluster sampling (population is divided into clusters, followed by random selection of the clusters), or independent sampling (samples selected from population are mutually free of affecting one another).
Representative	The act of selection is based on the proportional representativeness of the objects in the population. The sample includes a comparable cross-section of varied backgrounds that are present in the population. Sub-types are stratified sampling (first divide the population into sub-groups, then select from these groups) and matched sampling (each object in one group is matched with a counterpart in another).
Theoretical	The underlying theory if the researcher determines whom to select for the study. Our new introduction (HSS) belongs here.
Practice based	A practitioner – a clinical psychologist, teacher, nurse – who wants to do research on their field and experience treats his or her clients as research subjects. Ethical protections of subjects' rights are in place, but the agreement by persons to participate is set up within the field of their indebtedness to the researcher as the provider of some other practically needed services.
One-point break-through	Even if researchers hope to access the ideal kinds of subjects, exceptional circumstances and/or special conditions may prohibit that. In such case, the researchers struggle to access anyone who accepts the research proposal-literally fighting against tight access barriers. Undoubtedly such sampling is far from being "non-biased" or "random" yet there is no need to criticize such a sampling as "biased." Depending on the research theme, it's preferable to do something rather than nothing. And it may develop into a version of relational network based sampling as below.
Relational network based (i.e., the "Snowball Method")	The researcher engages the members of the first selected (and agreeing) participants to bring to the sample the members of their relationships networks. A crude sub-type is quote sampling (researcher may be given a "quota" of how many and what kinds of objects he/she needs to bring into the study.
Convenient	Researchers in university ask students to participate into their research. Cognitive psychologists like to regard them as adults and developmental psychologists like to regard them as adolescent. And comparative psychologists like to regard them human being. So university students are convenient samples of psychology studies.
Capricious	The researcher takes whoever happens to agree to participate.

Chapter 5   Sampling Reconsidered

Table 5.2. Purposive sampling (from Patton, 2002)

Extreme or deviant case
Intensity
Maximum variation
Homogeneous
Typical case
Stratified purposeful
Critical case
Snowball or chain
Criterion
Theory-based or operational construct
Confirming or disconfirming
Opportunistic random purposeful
Politically important cases
Convenience
Combination or mixed purposeful

The sampling rhetoric implies that the researcher is an omnipotent "boss" of the population – like a Napoleon as general of large armies – who can by select a sample from the whole set of available and equally willing subjects. We know that this is almost never the case – the researcher is not "in control" (but needs to go through complex persuasion techniques to secure subjects' cooperation; Günther, 1998), and the selection process is sequential so that the previously selected subjects may be known to the latter ones. Last but not least – different subjects have their own active reasons for (or against) participation. Sampling is thus a cultural negotiation process. Here, we see culture as the key to any research encounter, and consider human beings as open systems.

3.4. Sampling in socio-cultural psychology

Adoption of culture as a central concept in psychology leads to the necessity of taking a new looks at some of the key methodological problems in the discipline (Valsiner, 2001b, 2003a). Among those is the systemic nature of human psychological processes that becomes highlighted by the reinsertion of cultural or higher psychological processes into our models of the mind (Sato & Valsiner, 2006).

Part 3   DEVELOPMENT OF TEM

Cultural psychology is the new synthetic direction in contemporary psychology that emerges from the developmental traditions of Lev Vygotsky, Karl Bühler, and Heinz Werner. It brings back to psychology the crucial role of history. Vygotsky similarly maintained that psychological functions are internalized relations of a social order and are structured by this order. Vygotsky explained that in modern society:

> ... the influence of the [technological and social] basis on the psychological superstructure of man turns out to be not direct, but mediated by a large number of very complex material and spiritual factors. But even here, the basic law of historical human development, which proclaims that human beings are created by the society in which they live and that it represents the determining factor in the formation of their personalities, remains in force. (Vygotsky, 1930, cited in van der Veer & Valsiner, 1994, p. 176)

Cultural psychology requires a theoretical perspective and a rigorous methodology. Focusing on the sampling method, sampling the specimens together with their contextual and historical surroundings is needed. This indicates a return to the practice of sampling of the phenomena – and a move away from the tradition of sampling of specimens. Cultural psychology uses the individual-socioecological reference frame (Valsiner, 2000, p. 73 – see Valsiner & Rosa, 2007b) where the idea of separating the object of investigation from its contextual surroundings equals elimination of the phenomena one wants to study.

This is the good starting point to innovate new methodology in psychology. To begin with, if not the individual but the process is understood, a new methodology concerning a new sampling is needed. It presumes that the definitive database for any scientific generalization in developmental and cultural psychology is a single case (rather than a sample. Molenaar, 2004; Molenaar & Valsiner, 2005). This is in contrast to the usual sample-to-population generalization in which the systemic nature of the single case is irreversibly lost in the process of generalization. What contemporary science of psychology needs is clarity about how to construct adequate methods for specific research purposes rather than a discussion about whether

Chapter 5   Sampling Reconsidered

one or another category of methods is better (or worse) by virtue of their ontology (Valsiner & Diriwächter, 2005).

To summarize, sampling is an inevitable operation in any research project. Any research effort, unless it analyzes the whole realm of the given phenomena, requires some way of sampling. Some specimens of the existing (known) pool of all specimens are selected, which means others are left out. That selection is best accomplished on the basis of the history of the objects of investigation (Valsiner & Sato, 2006). It is the processes of development that result in a variety of histories of the same class of phenomena.

3.5. Generalization – Knowing about what? Population or generic models?

The issue of generalization is another side of the coin when we consider sampling. Sampling is a tool for generalization – and not a goal in itself. As has been pointed out elsewhere (Valsiner, 2003a, 2007), there are two trajectories for generalization – from samples to populations, and from a single case to a generic model (which is further tested on other selected single cases).

Size and representativeness of sample are taken into account for good generalization. Usually one might consider that small size of sample inevitably mean non-representative. But Yin (2003) insists that small sample size doesn't lead to biased sampling.

> A common complaint about case studies is that it is difficult to generalize from one case to another. Thus, analysts fall into the trap of trying to select a "representative" case or set of cases. Yet no set of cases, no matter how large, is likely to deal with the complaint.
>
> The problem lies in the very notion of generalizing to other case studies. Instead, an analyst should try to generalize findings to "theory", analogous to the way a scientist generalizes form experimental results to theory. (Note that the scientist does not attempt to select "representative" experiments.) (Yin, 2003, p. 38)

Part 3   DEVELOPMENT OF TEM

Yin (2003) proposes to distinguish between "statistical generalization" and "analytical generalization." Statistical generalization refers to the ability to make statistical inferences about a population based on research on a small sample of that population.

Socio-cultural-historical phenomena in cultural psychology are studied with a different type of universality in focus that is available to researchers through analytic generalization. In this sense, our contemporary socio-cultural psychology continues the general traditions of Fechner, Wundt, Külpe, Skinner, and modern cognitive science based on the early mental experimentation (Simon, 1999). The generalization from population to sample trajectory is limited in its knowledge construction power because of its hidden assumption of the average (or prototypic) phenotype allowing us to infer the causality for its generation. This assumption is untenable (Valsiner, 1984, 1986c).

Socio-cultural psychology deals with higher psychological functions that are mediated by signs (see Rosa, 2007). Hence the elementaristic forms of causality are not applicable in this area – and we need to return to the historical traditions in the discipline to find alternatives (Valsiner, 2000). As was mentioned above, Wundt accepted the distinction between cultural studies and natural science (Nerlich, 2004). As Diriwächter (2004) suggested, in order to understand higher psychological processes, only historical comparisons, the observation of our "mind's" creations (*Beobachtung der Geiste-serzeugnisse*), could be looked at. So, a trajectory of non-experimental and non-statistical psychology is needed. Assumptions of the statistical paradigm do not afford this kind of approach, and need to be abandoned (Baldwin, 1930). In the first place, the aim of statistical work is to assume *a priori* separate status for objects that are actually held together by systemic links, thus replacing the real systemic order by a statistically reconstructed artifact (Valsiner, 1986). The statistical route of inductive generalization constructs a reality and consistency in the form of larger, more abstracted and homogeneous objects (Desrosières, 1993, p. 236). The "population" becomes a new created object – to which generalizations are legitimately made. Yet it is impossible to take such constructed sign. "population" – as

Chapter 5　Sampling Reconsidered

an equivalent to a structured order of a society. A step further-back projection of generalizations about "population" as if those were generic models that work within each and every individual case within the population is a theoretically unwarranted move (Valsiner, 1986). So it isn't necessary for us to critically examine the premises of statistical methodology in socio-cultural psychology.[4]

Changing the axiomatic is needed and is in the process of happening these days. Cultural psychology might be a promising program because cultural psychology, especially socio-cultural approach, regards persons as systems rather than units. And cultural psychology is one of orthodox (legitimate) heritages of Wundt's *Völkerpsychologie* which study (the products of) the higher processes.

3.6. Development as a process: Constructing histories

There has been much inconsistency in maintaining a developmental focus in psychology (Cairns, 1998; Valsiner & Connolly, 2003b). However, that focus is inevitable if one deals with socio-cultural phenomena in their basic form – that of open systems. In the most general sense, the developmental perspective is based on the axiom of becoming which takes two forms:

X – [becomes]　–> Y
X – [remains]　　–> X

The axiom X – [remains] –> X is not the same as the identity axiom of non-developmental perspectives – X = [is] = X. Being is conceptualized as an ontological entity, while remaining is a process of maintaining an emerged state of a system is implied. Both becoming and remaining are processes that guarantee both relative stability and change in the case of development. Epistemology of psychology tends to overemphasize the stability of human nature. Here we'd like to appreciate the possibility of change and regard the stability as the result of remaining. If one can find the stability, we ought to seek the conditions that interfere with the process of becoming.

Part 3   DEVELOPMENT OF TEM

All human development is contingent on the encounters with the world –
events influence persons' life. We mean "contingent" as unexpected and/or uncon-
trollable. It doesn't necessarily mean that contingent life is uncertain life – yet it is
life filled with phenomena of ambivalence (Abbey, 2007). For example, the meaning
of events related to reproduction is by no means warrantable. The notions of "love,"
"justice," and so on are culture-bound, as well as systems of marriage (and notions
of concubinage, levirate, etc.), family, and economics (Escobar, 1995; Radaev, 2005).
At different age periods the particular features of the relations with the environment
differ. The more one ages, the more he/she comes to meet various experiences. Personal life history is constructed through semiotic means and leads to the wisdom of
human living.

Furthermore, no one experienced same events similarly to one another. Many
dramatic events (viral infections, etc.) may selectively capture one person, but not
others. And even if such events occur in some persons, the influences of such events
are different for each person. A boy/girl who has to be taken to a hospital may begin
to aim in life to become a medical professional, while another might try to avoid any
encounter with medical settings. A psychologist who experiences a similar situation
reminded him/her of the fact that one lives only once. Someone (e.g., a successful
pickpocket) may encounter a happy event (of success in his activity), and the other
(the "donor" of the stolen purse) would not consider the same event happy. Clearly
there are many life events – each of which may, or need not, happen. Life is contingent on the conditions of living. Medical sociologist Arthur Frank claims that the
patients' onset of illness is somewhat contingent but experience of illness influenced
the patients life course (Frank, 1995).

4. Socio-cultural experiences on the trajectories of living

Contingent experiences such as illness inevitably play some role in the person's
life. It's not a developmental task and of course it's not pure biological necessity.

Chapter 5   Sampling Reconsidered

Rather, it is socio-cultural experience within which all persons are guided by the internalized cultural meaning systems. Here, we can regard the socio-cultural events as contingent ones. Even illness isn't eternal. Some contagions are completely eradicated, and new contagion such as AIDS appears. And HIV infection rates are varying in time and place. So being affected by a contagion is principally a socio-cultural experience. Another example is an Amyotrophic Lateral Sclerosis (ALS). ALS, also known as Lou Gehrig's Disease, is a progressive and ultimately fatal neuromuscular disease. So if one would suffer from the ALS, the ALS would severely influence one's life. The person suffering from ALS needs to live in the different way.

Besides medical events like illness, our life events are contingent and no one is in control. For example we cannot control our parents' lives. One child's parents might die when he/she was one year old. The other child's parents would move to a foreign country. Alternatively, we cannot control a relative position of an academic achievement. Suffering from AIDS or ALS influenced one's life. Parents' deaths influence one's life too. However, the developmental theory tends to disregard such contingent events. So we need the new methodology to understand human life from the perspective of contingent events as socio-cultural experiences.

It is important that the event has the historicity in the double meaning that the individual experiences the contingent event. Such events are embedded in historical context and individuals have their own historicity. Socio-cultural psychology is therefore necessarily historical. A sampling method such as random sampling doesn't treat these contingent events. Thus there is a need to create a new way to consider the act of sampling.

It's difficult to sample randomly contingent events because they are just "contingent." We should devise the new sampling methodology so that we might treat the contingent experience as a socio-cultural experience. Suppose one person happened to know he/she was stricken with mortal illness and researchers should know his/her experience. Handing a questionnaire to fill in is one of the representative methods. We can get the scores on scales such as fear of death. We even compare the scores of the mortal illness and the healthy, if possible. Yet such comparisons tell us nothing

Part 3   DEVELOPMENT OF TEM

about the real transformation of persons over their particular life course trajectories. Contingent events such as suffering deadly disease influence one's total life and transform the structures of human existence. The basic notion of psychological science needs to be built upon idiographic assumptions (Molenaar, 2004; Molenaar & Valsiner, 2005). Sampling should be dependent of the theory and the methodology derived from the method, rather than a direct import from manuals on methodology. The theory we use here is that of development – looking at human lives not as "variables" but as transforming structures (Valsiner & Connolly, 2003b).

5. A new philosophy of method: HSS (Historically Structured Sampling)

Historically Structured Sampling (HSS) is a method of sampling individual cases based on their previous (up-to-now) knowable life course histories analyzed as a series of bifurcation points. It makes it possible to contrast individuals who have arrived at the present state (equifinality point) through vastly different life course trajectories. The notion of HSS relies heavily upon the notion of equifinality that originated in the General Systems Theory (GST) of von Bertalanffy (1968) and is rooted in the early work of Hans Driesch (1908).

Human psychological structure functions as an open system, not as closed system. A central place in it is given to the notion of equifinality. The notion of equifinality originates in Driesch's biological work. Driesch performed a series of experiments agitating sea urchin cells during division and causing them to fragment. Instead of forming a partial embryo, Driesch found that the cells formed an entire one. Here, the same final state may be reached from the different initial conditions and from different ways. This is what von Bertalanffy (1968) called equifinality. Despite Driesch's vitalist general philosophy, von Bertalanffy built his organismic perspective on the basis of multilinear developmental model along similar directions. Equifinality is the basic characteristic of open systems, and unilinearity is merely a special case

Chapter 5   Sampling Reconsidered

of multilinearity (within which equifinality dominates).

Von Bertalanffy pioneered the organismic conception of biology from which the GST developed. He regarded living organisms including human beings as not closed systems but open systems (Valsiner & Sato, 2006). Von Bertalanffy (1968) outlined the principle of the equifinality as crucial for the open systems:

> In any closed system, the final state is unequivocally determined by the initial condition: e.g., the motion in a planetary system where the positions of the planets at a time t are unequivocally determined by their positions at a time to ... If either the initial conditions and or the process are altered, the final state will also be changed. This is not so in open systems. Here same final state may be reached from initial conditions and in different ways. This is what is called equifinality, and it has a significant meaning for the phenomena of biological regulation. (von Bertalanffy, 1968, p. 40)

HSS intends to select individual cases for the study through consideration of their historical trajectories moving through a common temporary state (equifinality point). In other words, HSS focus on the individual events and/or states considered as Equfinality Points (EFP). Equifinality means that the same state may be reached from different initial conditions and in different ways in the course of time. Then researches try to depict multilinearity, that is, trajectories to such EFP. It plays the central role in the selection of cases of developing systems in case of HSS. Any psychological states and/or life events in what researchers have interest are structured historically. The researcher decides which aspects of the historically organized system are the objects of investigation – the EFP becomes a part of the conceptual scheme in the researchers' own interest.

5.1. Trajectory Equifinality Model (TEM)-based on HSS

Trajectory Equifinality Model (TEM) is a new proposal to describe human development from the perspective of cultural historical approach. It is important to emphasize that equifinality does not imply sameness – which is an impossible condi-

Part 3   DEVELOPMENT OF TEM

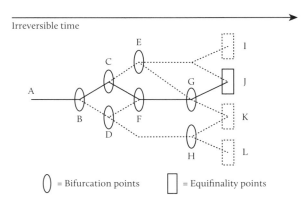

Figure 5.3. Actual life course trajectory and its crucial change possibilities

tion in any historical system. Rather, it entails a region of similarity in the temporal courses of different trajectories. After establishing the equifinality point, trajectories should be traced. Depicting the TEM makes it possible to grasp the trajectory with irreversible time (Figure 5.3).

In Figure 5.3, the rectangle J is the supposed Equifinality Point (EFP) on what researchers focus in their researches. For this EFP, there are many pathways to pass. Seven ellipses "B thorough H" are Bifurcation Points (BFPs) in this TEM. We can call them *passage points*. Of course, many passage points are both EFP and BFP, but main EFP should be focused along researches' interests. Researchers may find many passage points. But no matter how many points we can find, the natures of all points are not equal. Some points are trivial, and the others are crucial. Some are inevitable, others suggested these points were inevitable.

TEM is the method to describe persons' life courses within irreversible time after researchers' focusing important events as EFPs. We propose some notions for practicing TEM to construct models. The first one is notion of irreversible time and this notion originates in Henri Bergson. Next, Bifurcation Point (BFP) is a point that has alternative options to go. Last but not least, *Obligatory Passage Point* (OPP) originated in the context of the sociology of science (Latour, 1987). OPP is a phase and/or event persons inevitably experience. There are two types of OPP, indigenous and

Chapter 5   Sampling Reconsidered

exogenous. The former includes species-specific biological transition points – such as cutting of teeth in infancy, menarche, or menopause. The exogenous OPP is set up by the environment and/or custom.

The act of using the HSS and TEM involves the following steps (Valsiner & Sato 2006):

A) locating the relevant Equifinality Point (EFP) – as well as all relevant OPPs – in the generic map of trajectories necessarily present for the generic system of the processes under investigation (theoretically based activity),

B) empirical mapping out all particular cases – systems open to study that move through these points, and

C) comparison of different actual trajectories as these approach to the equifinality point by superimposing onto each trajectory a pattern of theoretically meaningful "range measure" – derived from (A) – that specifies whether the given trajectory fits into the realm of selectable cases.

Since EFP depends on the researcher's focus and/or research questions, we set up *Polarized Equifinality Points* (P-EFP) for neutralizing implicit value system of researchers. P-EFP makes researchers notice the possibility of invisible trajectories.

5.2. Examples of HSS: Three studies that explicate the TEM

We introduce here three studies using the TEM model that is the basis for the HSS method of sampling. In the case of each of the three – on adolescents' abortion experience, girls' decisions to start making cosmetics, and infertile wives to abandon to continue receiving reproductive treatments – we outline the structures of personal life-decision histories through an analysis of various bifurcation points.

[1] Infertility in Japan

Infertility is a phenomenon that is strongly influenced by the cultural and social context. All over the world, as well as historically, societies have oriented young generations, i.e., married couples, towards childbearing. The inability to bear children has always been marked with negative connotations. This situation is the same in Japan. Couples suffering from infertility have diverse experiences. They select a be-

Part 3   DEVELOPMENT OF TEM

havior based on these experiences, which is linked to their goal – such as undergoing fertility treatment. It is important to understand the trajectory of infertile experiences from the viewpoint of persons who have chosen fertility treatment and have also considered adoption. Both, being "conscious of infertility" and "considering adoption" are not merely personal experiences and/or life course options, but they are historically structured experiences.

Yasuda (2005) interviewed nine couples that had continued to be unable to have children after fertility treatment and who had been considering adoption, in order to evaluate their experiences with infertility. She described the diversity of infertility experiences after fertility treatment along the passage of time, using the descriptive TEM developed in the process of her research. From the interviews, she was able to extract the participants' views on how to deal with the social systems of fertility treatment and adoption.

In this research, trajectories start from the point of beginning fertility treatment. People continue to have fertility treatment so long as infertility does not end. Some may be aware of adoption. Some others continue to have fertility treatment, whereas others may end treatment and try adoption. In the latter case, Turning Point 1 is observed (Some women end fertility treatment without being conscious of the possibility of adoption. Most may consider adopting children, but some do not select this option because they do not recognize it as a social system for having children). Type 1 individuals become aware of adoption before they end fertility treatment and as a result, they change over from fertility treatment and try this option. This suggests that it is important to let people suffering from infertility know that adoption is one social system for having children. It is also essential to inform the options that are available to them. In fact, most couples said that they wanted help in getting to know methods of adoption that were available to them, because they could not have children, in spite of continuing fertility treatment. They realized that adoption was an option and have persevered with it. Type 2 people were conscious of adoption while undergoing fertility treatment but did not try it. These couples could not agree regarding adoption between the couple, though they continued to live together after

102

Chapter 5   Sampling Reconsidered

Table 5.3. Couples categorized by the transition processes of conduct selection

Type 1	Had become conscious of adoption before ending fertility treatment (Turning Point 1), and had changed over to the adoption option from fertility treatment.
Type 2	Had become conscious of adoption after fertility treatment, but had not attempted adoption because of disagreement between the couple. They had ended fertility treatment (Turning Point 1) and had decided to live without children.
Type 3	Had ended fertility treatment deciding to live without children (Turning Point 1), but later, they had become aware of the possibility of adoption (Turning Point 2), and had tried it.
Type 4	Had ended fertility treatment (Turning Point 1) and later they had become aware of adoption (Turning Point 2). However, they had not been able to realize it. So they had given up trying adoption (Turning Point 3), and had decided to live without children.

ending fertility treatment. Few Type 2 couples considered adoption after they ended fertility treatment. That is to say, the appearance of Turning Point 2 happens within a wide range of time. Type 3 people had ended fertility treatment, and afterwards they became aware of adoption and have persevered with adoption. Adoption cannot necessarily possible just because the couple wish to do it. Type 4 people did not realize the possibility of adoption and have given up. Giving up adoption is regarded as Turning Point 3 in Yasuda's study.

Three basic experiences were revealed in the interview: "stopping fertility treatment," "considering the possibility of adoption" and "deciding not to adopt." In this study, the nine couples were classified into four types (see Table 5.3).

Obviously, the four categories described above are not static, *a priori* ones. They are the results of dynamic trajectories of nine couples. Therefore, the trajectories could be defined using the TEM. With the intent of understanding the experiences of the couples, including those after stopping fertility treatment, Yasuda focused on the experience of stopping fertility treatments as an EFP, and decided the experiences of considering the possibility of adoption as an OPP and those of deciding not to adopt as a BFP. Yasuda depicted the diversities of their experiences that converged into and diverged from EFP (Figure 5.4, which refines TEM by Sato, Yasuda et al. (2004) and TEM by Yasuda (2005), which are derived from the same data. By depicting the data

Part 3 DEVELOPMENT OF TEM

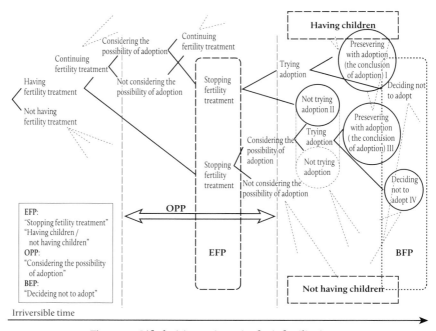

Figure 5.4. Life decision trajectories for infertility issues

with TEM, they set the EFP as the condition of couples that either became parents or not. In other words, they consider a "couple with children" and a "couple without children" as polarized EFPs. Either one of these conditions is neither superior nor inferior to the other, but is considered equal.

Naturally, the decision not to have children should be considered equal to the decision to have children. Namely, the decision not to have fertility treatment and adoption should be equal to the decision to have fertility treatment and adoption. It is important not only to present choices, but also to guarantee the choice of trying nothing.

Figure 5.4 shows the life histories that were told by the couples or the wives. The four heavy circles represent the four categories. However, logically there should be more categories. In this study, Yasuda could identify only four categories partly because of restrictions in participant recruitment method that resulted in a small

Chapter 5　Sampling Reconsidered

sample. However, this small sample size did not cause a sampling error. From a different perspective, we can say that we have envisioned the diversity of infertility experiences without participants. There could be many infertility experiences that cannot be understood by certain research techniques. TEM is a method of describing experiences that facilitates understanding of the diversity of experiences that cannot be perfectly grasped, but must exist.

In her study, Yasuda (2005) was able to explain the diversity of infertility experiences along the flow of time with TEM that was developed in the process of this study. It sets the stage for potential use of HSS – for further investigation of the infertility-related decisions. By using TEM, she will be able to select participants and adjust the focus of analyses according to the research question: "How do people select fertility treatment?" and "How do people select the social system of adoption as a way of having children?" among others. In fact, the couples could change their mind at any time, and she explained the importance of the sincerity in making these selections. At no time, was it necessary to make a choice, and all possible choices were to be equally respected.

Later she asserts that making choices is not necessarily perfect. For example, adoption cannot be considered as merely a way to have children. To begin with, adoption is basically a social system to ensure children's happiness. Therefore, people trying adoption need to consider not only themselves, but also the children. Further this presents the important consideration even with regard to fertility treatments. While having treatment, people tend to pay attention only to giving birth to children, but they have to think of the children's happiness after they have them. Various factors regarding the selection of adoption must be taken into account.

Regarding fertility treatment, people who start it have a chance to select one treatment over the other. Fertility treatments have progressed as the biological technologies have improved. So, selections also can only be secured under those, and have kept up with the times. Therapeutic procedures such as "host mother," "surrogate mother," and other fertilization techniques have not yet been approved in Japan. Incidentally, it is necessary to examine the ethical meaning of selecting

Part 3   DEVELOPMENT OF TEM

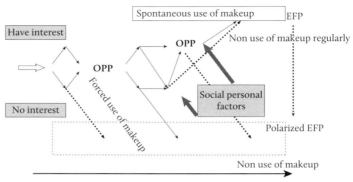

Figure 5.5. Personal histories of makeup use in Japan

these treatments. Available choices and wishes that can be realized are restricted by social, cultural, and ethical conditions. Therefore, it is important to grasp and depict the diversity of people's experiences within the limits of possibilities. Actually, the social systems that are involved in "fertility treatments" and "adoption" are different. So considering each case with the social systems deliberately is important. TEM is a good scheme for depicting the diversity of infertility experiences, because infertility experiences themselves are embedded in other social subsystem such as "fertility treatments" and "adoption operation." Needless to say, each society and/or culture has a unique way to prohibit or allow such reproductive techniques.

[2] Use of cosmetics by Japanese women in the united states

In Japan, most women wear facial makeup, and some Japanese women feel that this is a duty. Most studies concerning women's makeup have focused on women who use cosmetics, and not on those women who do not. Kido's study focused on both groups of women (Sato, Yasuda et al., 2004). The purpose of this study was to clarify the psychological and behavioral process by which Japanese women begin to use cosmetics (or not) and the transition in their use of makeup. Five Japanese women were interviewed and were depicted in the TEM in Figure 5.5. Being forced to use makeup is an OPP. Society facilitates women's spontaneous use of makeup.

Next, to clarify this transition, Kido (2006) examined women who had experienced acculturation. Five Japanese women who had studied at a college in the United

Chapter 5 Sampling Reconsidered

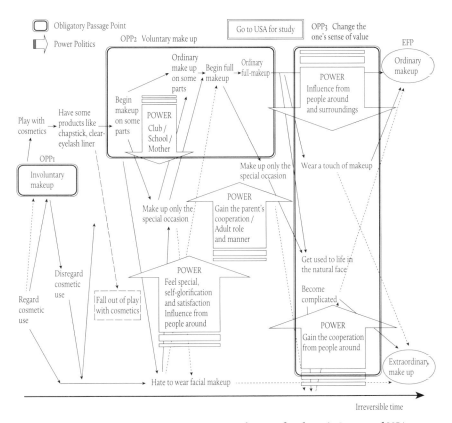

Figure 5.6. Five Japanese women's TEM on the use of makeup in Japan and USA

States were interviewed. All the interviews were taped with permission. The content of each interview was clustered into four groups (e.g., "adaptation," "a choice made to express one's qualities") using the KJ method. The KJ method is one of famous idea and/or category generation method in Japan. KJ method is one of famous idea generation methods in Japan. KJ Method is a technique for summarizing information. The original KJ method was developed by Jiro Kawakita in the 1960s (See Kawakita, 1986). In Kido (2006)'s case, all relevant events and facts of cosmetic experiences are written on individual cards and collated. Cards that look as though they belong

Part 3   DEVELOPMENT OF TEM

together should be grouped. This grouping procedure should be repeated and lastly aggregated and abstract categories are expected to be emerged. After using the KJ method, Kido (2006) depicted their life courses using the TEM (Figure 5.6).

In this model, Kido (2006) found three Obligatory Passage Points (OPPs). When all the interviewees lived in Japan, they felt that they had to use makeup, but could choose not to do so in the United States. Therefore, it seems that in Japan, strong social forces (a form of power politics) almost forced one to wear makeup. In addition, once a pattern of makeup use was established, it seems to have become a habit.

[3] Psychological process of abortion

Arakawa & Takada (2006) applied the Trajectory Equifinality Model (TEM) to investigate the psychological process of abortion experience because pregnancy and abortion are constrained by time, permitted only up to the 22nd week by "mother's body protection law" in Japan. Therefore, abortion choice is strongly affected by society and culture. Arakawa & Takada (2006) interviewed three young women (21-27 years old) who had terminated their pregnancies.

The results of the interviews are depicted in Figure 5.7.

As illustrated in this figure, the time between "taking notice of unusual physical condition" and "abortion surgery" is strictly limited, and pregnant women had to do and decide several things (discussing with the partner, doing tests by using pregnancy check kits, going to a clinic, deciding if they should give birth or not, signing up, and worrying about their obscure future) before the time limit.

Based on the TEM, Arakawa & Takada (2006) divided such events into two types. The first type is the events in which variety is not tolerated. To terminate their abortion, doctor's diagnosis and signing the certificate of consent are necessary. Besides such institutional constraints (OPP), there are certain other trajectories all of which have to be passed. The first is "using a pregnancy check kit." Arakawa & Takada (2006) pointed out that the reason women hesitate to go to a clinic is because there is no turning back. The second one is "not thinking of giving birth." The reason for this is assumed to be due their age. Although there were alternatives, they did not select them. This shows that non-institutional constraints also affect the women's choice.

Chapter 5　Sampling Reconsidered

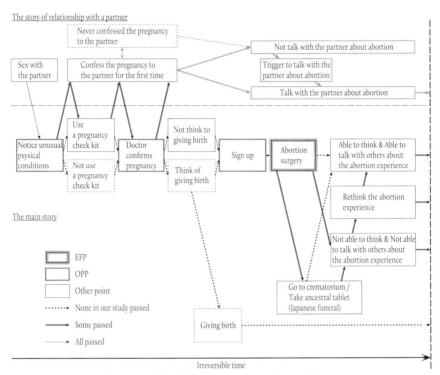

Figure 5.7. The TEM of abortion experience in Japan

The second type is those events in which variety is tolerated. For example, as far as "talking with the partner about abortion or not" is concerned, some women could talk about their abortion, but other women could not. "The timing that women confess pregnancy to the partner" and "Meaning of abortion experience" also varied. Many responded that "It depends on the relationship with the partner." "Meaning of abortion experience" also depends on creating a positive meaning.

Arakawa & Takada's (2006) study illustrates how TEM reveals the points a woman has to pass, and where she may not have pass. And TEM is suitable for visualizing the social direction, that is, what kind of power in the culture and the society affects women's choices at the decision making process of abortion. The psychological theories of choices and/or options like TEM should connect theories of social sciences.

109

Part 3   DEVELOPMENT OF TEM

Amartya Sen, the winner of the Nobel Prize for Economics in 1998, emphasizes the importance of choice.

> Choosing may itself be a valuable part of living and, a life of genuine choice with serious options may be seen to be – for that reason – richer. (Sen, 1992, p. 41)

Cognitive science tends to treat decision making as a cognitive process and individual situation might be abstracted. But cultural psychology tries to treat one's living with choosing. Our analytic efforts (depicted in Figures 5.3-5.7) show five TEMs. Yet the appearances of these TEMs are not same. Of course, these are TEMs because they are based on the new sampling practice (HSS). And TEM is versatile so that we can depict the various trajectories.

6. Conclusion: Re-thinking sampling and re-building theories

Sampling is a process of selecting something for inclusion in a research project. Sampling should be done to increase information richness. So we should plan to make a good sampling design. Sample design refers to the means by which one selects the primary units for data collection and analysis appropriate for a specific research question (Handwerker, 2004).

TEM is a strategy for qualitative research similar to the grounded theory (Glaser & Strauss, 1967). But we proposed HSS and TEM as a set of methodologies. HSS and TEM depend on each other. HSS is a sampling method based on the systemic view, while TEM is a way of describing the full life history of the cases that includes both the actualized moves of the past and possible (considered) actions which – for one or another reason – were left within the realm of possibilities. Sampling in this respect equals that of the systems' life histories within the "landscape" of life events. In the latter, both actualized and non-actualized trajectory options can have an impact to the present decisions undertaken to face the future. Our suggested HSS method thus

110

Chapter 5   Sampling Reconsidered

allows for a developmental perspective of the socio-cultural phenomena.

Last but not least, theories are tools that help us look at phenomena (see Valsiner & Rosa, 2007b) – and are not orthodoxies to follow. Our outlining of TEM is to find out how participants make sense of their experiences in order to come to a decision by evaluating the different bifurcation points. This conforms to an explanatory model of conduct. This view is not one of prediction and control, but of bounded indeterminacy.

Notes

1) The best example of such categorical reasoning is in the failure to define intelligence – other than by the method that is classified "intelligence test." The phenomena of intelligence – problem-solving in any everyday context – are lost in the "measurement of intelligence" by way of tests.

2) This is axiomatically granted by the nature of these groupings not as collections of specimens but as open systems where inter-specimen variability is constantly amplified.

3) Journals were *British Journal of Educational Psychology, Child Development, Journal of Abnormal and Social Psychology, Journal of Applied Psychology, Journal of Comparative and Physiological Psychology, Journal of Consulting Psychology, Journal of Educational Psychology, Journal of Social Psychology; Political, Racial and Differential Psychology, Psychological Bulletin.*

4) And not only in that area – the inferential problem of confusing individual generic levels of knowledge with that gained on "populations" is present everywhere in psychology, with possible exceptions of experimental psychology and (some examples of) neuropsychology.

Chapter 6

Depicting the Dynamics of Living the Life
The Trajectory Equifinality Model

Keywords

Life ccurce, Life trajectory, Trajectory Equifinality Model (TEM), Three Layers Model of Genesis (TLMG)

The history of the organism is the organism. (Murray, 1938, p. 39)
The flow of the river never stops and yet the water never stays the same.
From *Hojoki: Written from a small square hut* (KAMO-no-Chomei, 1212)

Hojoki is a famous essay in Japanese literature as an expression of mujō (無常), the transience of the world. The author – KAMO-no-Chomei (1155-1216) – was a monk who renounced the ordinary life in the then-capital Kyoto and lived his last years in simple huts in the countryside. He was one of the great critics and poets at that era. The notion of the flow of river that he evoked is suitable for considering the dynamic aspect of life. A river is a natural stream of water. Even though a river consists of water; the water within a river is never a river itself. And if the time were to stop – we would not be able to distinguish the water and the river.

The notion of the river is not at all simple. The boundary of river and land is vague and changeable. The status of river is vague – nothing would ever be forever. Nevertheless, this complication is a comfortable as a metaphor of life. If we take the systemic view in psychology and we regard human being as the open system, the

Part 3   DEVELOPMENT OF TEM

subject of study is not a discrete individual, but a relationship with the environment. And the boundary of the subject and environment is not so clear. The time flow never goes back with in life – yet the representation of time has many variations (see Yamada & Kato, 2006). In this chapter, we try to show the new notion and methodology for depicting the dynamics of the living and to detect obstacles of depicting the dynamics. We re-consider the life stage theory, the life course paradigm, and the methodology of rating scale, because these seems to be the obstacles to pursue understanding the dynamics of the living.

The study of a life course cannot exist without the notion of time. But psychologists and sociologists don't take the notion of time seriously. One of the reasons why they tend to disregard time is that their desire is to seek a depiction that focuses on stability. Actually many of them might "find" the stable structure of personality and stable trail of life course as they construct it through data analyses that are blind to variability and dynamicity. This aspiration leads to the correlational studies. For example, psychologists often like to do research to find the correlation between some biological factors and personality – while ignoring the factors of culture. This is a very attractive seduction for personality psychologists because they have an inferiority complex in their relation with what they construe as "the truly natural" sciences. In fact to do appropriate science, both stability and/or structure are very important for psychologists and sociologists.

Changes are not too complicated. If psychologists abandoned their dreams of revealing a time-free "true state" of affairs and started considering time seriously, we would easily find another possibility. The Trajectory Equifinality Model (TEM) which we describe in this chapter is a new methodological device for psychology. It is based on the systemic view and takes the notion of irreversible time seriously.

114

Chapter 6   Depicting the Dynamics of Living the Life

1. Obstacles in treating the dynamics of the living in psychology and sociology

Differently from Kamo's Heraclitan idea as expressed in the beginning of this chapter, the historiography in the European tradition – especially the usual focus on Ancient Greece – seems to adjust its mode of thinking to the stable ways where thoughts treated as analogs to the classical Greek architecture. Such stability leads psychologists to build stage models of life development. In contrast, historiography in Japan seems to assimilate the notion of the flow of the river – nothing would ever be forever.

Stage theories entail the idea that when we develop, we go through a number of states that can be described as temporarily homogeneous. This is similar to constructing the building in the main view of history in Western culture. There are many eminent stage theories in psychology. Among them, Freud's psychosexual stage theory, Piaget's stage theory of a child's thinking, Kohlberg's stage theory of moral values, Winnicott's development stages, Erikson's developmental stage theory of learning self-esteem and trust. For example, Freud took seriously the psychosexual energy and hypothesized psychosexual stage theory (Table 6.1).

After observation of children in many times and places, Piaget posited that 4 stages of cognitive development. Sensorimotor Period (birth to 2 years); Pre-operational Thought (2 to 6 or 7 years); Concrete Operations (6/7 to 11/12) and Formal Operations (11/12 to adult). In a similar vein, Erikson posited his stage account (Table 6.2).

Kohlberg developed a three-level six-stage model of moral development, where each level is broken down into with two stages (Table 6.3).

Even though stage models theorists might insist that they treat the time with in their models, the time within the stage model seems to be discrete. Stage models depend on chronological age – which means the superiority of biological factors is implied.

115

Part 3   DEVELOPMENT OF TEM

Table 6.1. Freud's psychosexual stage theory

Oral stage	from birth to 18 months
Anal stage	from about 18 months to 3 years
Phallic stage	from 3 to 6 years
A period of latency	from 6 to 12 years
Genital phase	from 12 years onwards

Table 6.2. Erikson's eight stages and its tasks

Infancy	Trust vs. Mistrust
Toddler	Autonomy vs. Shame and doubt
Preschool	Initiative vs. Guilt
School age	Industry vs. Inferiority
Adolescence	Identity vs. Role confusion
Young adult	Intimacy vs. Isolation
Midlife	Generativity vs. Stagnation
Old age	Ego integrity vs. Despair

Table 6.3. Kohlberg's six-stage model of moral development

Level 1: Pre-conventional		
	Stage 1	PUNISHMENT AND OBEDIENCE Heteronomous morality
	Stage 2	INSTRUMENTAL EXCHANGE Individualism/instrumentalism
Level 2: Conventional		
	Stage 3	INTERPERSONAL CONFORMITY Mutual interpersonal
	Stage 4	Social system and conscience
Level 3: Post-conventional		
	Stage 5	PRIOR RIGHTS AND SOCIAL CONTRACT
	Stage 6	UNIVERSAL ETHICAL PRINCIPLES

Maslow's (1943) "hierarchy of needs" model seems to avoid such tendency. Differently from the usual way of psychologists to study mentally ill or neurotic people, Maslow looked at exceptional people such as Albert Einstein and Eleanor Roosevelt. But, Maslow's model carries with it an ideal value system and retains in a linear pro-

Chapter 6   Depicting the Dynamics of Living the Life

gressive model. Both stage model and hierarchy model do not regard the flow and continuity of life as important.

1.1. Life course studies and the notion of life trajectory

In life course studies we can find a contextual view of trajectories:

> The life course is age-graded through institutions and social structures, and it is embedded in relationships that constrain and support behavior – Both the individual life course and a person's developmental trajectory are interconnected with the lives and development of others. (Elder, 1998, pp. 951-952)

All of the core principles of life course theory have special application to this transition to lifelong development and aging, the role of human agency in making life choices, the constraints and opportunities of the historical time and place, the timing of events and transitions, and the forming and dissolution of linked lives (Elder, 1985; Daaleman & Elder, 2007). Five core principles define the life course as a paradigmatic framework:

1. human development and aging as lifelong processes,
2. human agency,
3. historical time and place,
4. the timing of events in a life, and
5. linked lives.

However, when we look at the empirical uses of the "trajectory" in life course studies we discover that it means just a "pathway." It describes a path of the life lived – but not the dynamics of moving towards the future. Macmillan & Eliason (2003) pointed out that trajectories often referred to long-term involvement in or connection to social institutions and corresponding role. For example, McQuellon et al. (1998) tried to "measure" the trajectory of psychosocial recovery over the first year after Bone Marrow Transplantation (BMT). BMT patients were assessed by many scales – including physical functioning, mood etc. – at four times, namely, base-

117

Part 3   DEVELOPMENT OF TEM

line (n = 86), hospital discharge (n = 74), 100 days (n = 64) and at 1-year (n = 45). And authors found that the recovery trajectory in this patient population showed three distinct trends. These were, (1) linear and improved over time, (2) the trend for overall quality of life was parabolic (worsening at discharge, then improving), (3) the trend for patient concerns over time was linear and worsening.

A trajectory is considered to be the stable component of a direction toward a life destination and is characterized by a given probability of occurrence. A trajectory refers to the tendency to persist in life course patterns (Wheaton & Gotlib, 1997, p. 2). The notion of a life trajectory might be likened to that of a canal. And though the notion of life trajectory allow to change or shift from the established trajectory, it might lead to the feeling of "life on concrete (non-fragile) track." Even though Lerner & Busch-Rossnagel (1981) emphasized the individuals' subjective aspect – in their words, individuals are producers of their development, the researches in sociology of life course tends to prefer to the statistics-based longitudinal analyses in which the dynamism of life course is only assessed the point researchers set, so dynamics of living tends to be easily eliminated.

1.2. Can Structural Equation Models (SEM) reflect the dynamism of development?

The life course studies tend to use the correlational efficient. Even they use more complicated technique like the Structural Equation Models (SEM), the basic nature of such models has not changed. Because SEM fully depends on the correlation coefficients as input data – and such dependence conceals both the dynamic and qualitative aspects of the phenomena. Historically speaking, the notion of the correlation was invented to measure the *degree* to which the two variables are *linearly* related. Sir Francis Galton developed the idea that Karl Pearson further elaborated mathematically and invented the formula on the calculation of the correlation efficient now named after him. Because these two eminent statisticians intended to verify the power of heredity, that coefficient was designed to grasp only the stability, not variability, of the relationship between two variables. Even as the result of cal-

Chapter 6   Depicting the Dynamics of Living the Life

culation of correlation coefficient is based on each variable's variability, the result is interpreted as if it pertains to the essential relations between the qualities implicated by the "variables."

1.3. Assigning numbers – creating static properties – and scale types

The problems begin even earlier than the calculations of correlational relations. Already at the moment of psychologists' quantification of qualitative phenomena – an act of signification in semiotic terms – the question of what kind of scales are implied is crucial. Scale properties are important. In his seminal paper, Stevens (1946) proposed four levels – scale types – of measurement: nominal (or categorical); ordinal; interval; and ratio. The latter two are combined as continuous variables. He proposed the hierarchy of measurement scales for psychophysics. Although this idea has been criticized by statisticians, it still remains a core organizational framework for quantification in today's psychology. Importantly, the four levels measurement are not convertible in a symmetric way. A number created at the ratio scale level can be converted "down" to interval level and to the ordinal level. But the reverse is not possible – an ordinal level number cannot be converted "up" to the ratio scale level. Five years later, Stevens (1951) proposed the "permissible" mathematical operations for each type of scale – nominal, ordinal, interval and ratio. However, Stevens's proposal has been watered down – the scale types are regularly treated as if they were upwardly convertible – ordinal scale data are analyzed like ratio scale data.

Once a number becomes assigned to a phenomenon, psychologists move to operate with numbers as if these were meaningful. All numbers in psychology calculated in any imaginable way – usually on the basis of convenience of statistical analyses packages rather than honoring their representative meanings. This fits the master narrative of measurement in psychology – psychology tends to use statistics to disguise its discipline as scientific. To continue this disguise, substantiation of "mind" is inevitably needed. And the construct of psychology such as self, personality and many other characteristics are *a priori* regarded as substantive and stable. As Peter Callero has pointed out:

Part 3   DEVELOPMENT OF TEM

... There is a tendency [in mainstream psychology] to focus on stability, unity, and confor-
mity and de-emphasize the sociological principles of social construction. The self that is
socially constructed may congeal around a relatively stable set of cultural meanings, but
these meanings can never be permanent or unchanging. (Callero, 2003, p. 127)

The easy way of number assignment in empirical studies of psychology and sociology entails the politics of rating scale. It profoundly dominates the act of creating
stable constructs through methods created to "measure" them. While focusing on
such static constructs, efforts to reconstruct underlying processes which are involved
in the rating scale has fragile foundations.

Even research on life trajectory study addicting the correlational coefficient
might be unknowingly embedded in creating unrealistic knowledge. On one hand
there is a pre-set theory-driven explanation (e.g., a stage theory) that is treated as a
given. On the other hand there is the empirical correlational paradigm which turns
variability into stability displays. Both theory-driven nature and using the rating
scale strategy lead it to a scientific-like but fragmented view of human beings. It is
a reductionist view. It's high time to overcome reductionist perspectives – hence a
new vision of trajectory is needed. We need another way to access the dynamism of
life trajectory and such new methodology needs to grasp the change (not stability)
and emphasize the cultural meanings as Callero (2003) insisted.

We propose the new notion of trajectory as a combination of vectors that represent co-existing directions of psychological orientations. A vector is described
both by size and direction – so that vectors might express different tendencies and
their relationship, and the combination of vectors might be suitable to depict the
movements along the life trajectory. But before we step forward, let's look back one
of major dispute on the credibility of quantitative studies.

1.4. The person-situation debate, and beyond

Personality psychology is inherently embedded in the closed systemic view.

Chapter 6   Depicting the Dynamics of Living the Life

And the personality theory is the fuel tank of non-dynamic view using correlational coefficient method. Once personality psychology had a chance to transform, but it didn't. Here we take a brief look at the debate in personality psychology. A diagnostic measurement system is a lens that actually obscures the dynamics of living one's life.

Personality psychology, developmental psychology and clinical psychology have failed to develop in the direction of the dynamic and idiographic psychology. In psychology, both time-conscious and dynamic (not psychodynamic) view of life are rare. Personality psychology, developmental psychology and clinical psychology would be in a position to treat human life as a whole and depict dynamic transformation within time. But all projects have been

> ... as soon as a psychologist reject the idea of closed-systems of psychological phenomena and accepts an open-systems viewpoint, his treatment of the time dimension in psychological research would change. (Valsiner, 1986a, p. 352)

Walter Mischel (1968)'s *Personality and assessment* changed the quality of discussion on personality studies. As Hermans & Bonarius (1991) pointed out, this publication is of particular historical significance in personality psychology. Mischel (1968) transformed discussion on the personality and the debate between personality psychologists and Mischel has been called "person-situation debate." Mischel's perspective was influenced by social behaviorism of his time – as he insisted on the role of situation, claiming that situational determinants accounted for more of the behavioral variance than individual differences did. So "situationism" is the best label of his position. The illusion of cross-situational consistency might be revealed as myth. Over-time stability is supported by the similarity of situation. Person tends to select the preferable situations. During the debate, typology, trait theory and psychodynamism found the situationism as their common enemy. Not surprisingly many objections to Mischel's claim emerged from various points of view. Idiographic approaches and the focus on the life story analyses were among them. Yet these were not direct objection to Mischel's claim – in their core they actually accepted the central core of

121

Part 3   DEVELOPMENT OF TEM

it.

After the debate, a new frame of personality theory has emerged. Ironically speaking, situationism fosters the integration of psychodynamic theory, trait theory and typology which were all attacked by Mischel (1968). New type of personality theories have eclectically created in the personality related area. New theoretical frame fully depends on a multivariate statistical methodology. One of such a new trend is called the "Big Five" (Goldberg, 1990). One of the representative models of "Big Five" is the OCEAN Model (McCrae & Costa, 1996) which propose five factors including O: Openness to experience, C: Conscientiousness, E: Extraversion, A: Agreeableness and N: Neuroticism. Another theoretical frame is a personality disorder diagnostic system included within the DSM-system. Many personality disorders appear and vanish with hundreds of multidimensional studies.

Even Mischel's claim might directly attack the cross situational consistency and over time stability of personality studies, his claims were supposed to doubt the way of method which are based on correlational coefficients. So relying on the new statistical technique also based on the correlational coefficient (that means SEM) in personality study is no other than the return which longs for cross situational consistency. On the other hand, trajectory focused study in life course study is also based on the correlational coefficient so this is no other than the reversion which blindly take seriously the over time stability.

Recently, McAdams & Pals (2006) tried to release the definition of personality from the old-fashioned "personality as an entity." They defined personality as an individual's unique variation on

1. the general evolutionary design for human nature, expressed as a developing pattern of
2. dispositional traits (the person as actor),
3. characteristic adaptations (the person as agent), and
4. integrative life stories (the person as author) complexly and differentially situated in
5. culture.

Chapter 6　　Depicting the Dynamics of Living the Life

From the perspective of cultural psychology, the latter three are enough.

The new look at personality gets rid of the trait concept. Traits – as well as linear and bipolar dimensions – never grasp the transformation of personality. In the "new Big Five" of McAdams & Pals (2006), they didn't refer to the over time stability of personality based on the rating scale. If so, they were obliged to treat the life course study and it became ruined. Here we find it's time to seek the new type of both theoretical and practical scheme for "dynamics of the living."

2. Rethinking the rating scale: Toward the new views of trajectory

Common language terms are usually represented as point-like. A word – "a bird" – despite its various nuances of sense, ranging from anatomical referencing to poetic overgeneralization – is still represented in our speaking or writing by the same form "bird" in a point-like fashion (Abbey & Valsiner, 2005). In case of a point, there is no direction. Vectors have direction and size. But vectors do not cross each other. Vectors are just orientations in some direction. They are not depicting the actual course of development of trajectories, which are essentially combinations of vectors. They depict the development. Vectors are time-free (Table 6.4).

Psychologists who want to measure mental state use the point-scale measurement. It, point-scale, is located within the realm of point. In personality tests, intelligence tests, all questionnaires where you quantify some of the data, time-less and direction-less score is produced. Calculated number has serial order. Increasing and decreasing on the uni-dimensional static scale can be expressed. So point-scale orientated research couldn't express the transformation.

Vector models are hybrids of point models and trajectory models. Point models are quantifiable. Vector models can use quantification in estimating vector size. But at the same time they are richer because they use direction which is not quantifiable. You can say how big or how long this vector is but you cannot quantify which way it is oriented. Kurt Lewin wanted to construe field psychology which included vector

Part 3   DEVELOPMENT OF TEM

Table 6.4. Point, vector and trajectory on psychological depiction

	Size	Direction	Time
Point	No	No	No
Vector	Yes	Yes	No
Trajectory	Yes	Yes	Yes

psychology. But the title of Lewin (1943) paper 'Defining the "field at a given time"' well reflects his interest is mainly in the field – and not time. It was after the publication of Frank's (1939) cultural-philosophical article on "time perspectives," Lewin adopted the term (Nuttin & Lens, 1985). He defined it as "the totality of the individual's views of his psychological future and his psychological past existing at a given time" (Lewin, 1952, p. 75). He pointed out the children's narrowness of time-perspective in here and now life space. We can learn from Lewin that vector is suitable for applying the study of space and/or field not for time. So we adopt the different concept of *trajectory* to go step further. The notion of trajectory has been used in life course research – based on correlational relations across time.

Here we change the meaning of it by comparing with the notion of point and vector. How can one reach the trajectory model from the point model? Imagine someone is asked to rate the life satisfaction on the 7-point rating scale.

Good   1   2   3   4   5   6   7   Bad
                         ○

The circle on 4 reflects "so-so satisfaction" of the rater. If we are allowed to superimpose (add) the arrow of vector around the score, that makes us understand a little clear.

Someone might depict a trajectory including circle and vectors like this.

Chapter 6 Depicting the Dynamics of Living the Life

The number rated "4" is reached through different directions. This is the simplest trajectory model. Another might depict a trajectory including circle and vectors like this.

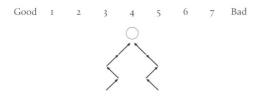

This is just the model of trajectory and we can find an equifinality point; to which real and possible trajectory would reach.

Returning to the problem of longitudinal life course studies using psychological scales, the repeated administration of scales only interpret the number on the unidimensional scale. The score might be compared on the dimension of number. But comparison such as this ignores the uniqueness of each person's trajectory (history). Not a score but a trajectory should be recognized if a person is considered as an active, goals-oriented agent. The number observed in a scale is depiction of outcome – while the trajectory is depiction of the process.

Knowing the process make you see what outcome is/can be generated – and not the other way round – from the outcome you cannot reconstruct the process. The point model asks direct questions about phenomena that underlie the "measures" – such as – "what is the *true state* of life satisfaction?" This question is impossible in case the vector model is assumed – it would create a method where you are put into some ambivalent situation about being satisfied and observe the *direction of further movement* from that situation. However, the vector model does not provide a developmental and/or historical look on the life satisfaction – since the vector consists of time-based unfolding of sequence of outcomes. A vector is detected by at least two points in some sequence in a space of coordinates.

Developmental and/or historical look need the trajectory model. And trajectory model gives us an enhanced opportunity to explore the complex life history. Surely we agree that trajectories are considered in life-course sociology – yet there they are

Part 3   DEVELOPMENT OF TEM

treated as vectors discovered after the fact, in a retrospect on the life course past. Yet human lives are lived from the known onwards to the not yet known. The methodology of TEM allows us to look at potential and/or unrealized trajectories of both the past and of the possible future. Furthermore, it allows a conceptualization of how the trajectories are in the process of construction.

3. Considering trajectories-in-the-making

3.1. TEM: Making the past, creating the future

The Trajectory Equifinality Model (TEM) grows out of the theoretical need of contemporary science to maintain two central features in its analytic scheme – time, and (linked with it) – the transformation of potentialities into actualities (realization). We should start from deductive viewpoint. Of course each person's life trajectory is idiosyncratic. Here is the place where the notion of "abduction" is truly needed. Charles S. Peirce (1908) advocated the importance of abduction as a method of inference in addition to the traditional ones, i.e., deduction and induction. He emphasized that neither deduction nor induction contribute the smallest positive item to the final conclusion of the inquiry – all that is done by abduction. TEM depends on systemic view and the view has a greater affinity for the Oriental "inclusive separation" – it is an example of anti-dichotomy logic. It's not a uni-linear process but multi-linear process. TEM can easily depict the variation of trajectories.

Dynamism is expressed by the depicting the social power. Even if there were many alternative options, person wouldn't choose some options. TEM is the hypothetical model of trajectories to a similar experience of equifinality which researchers focused on. TEM depicted from the empirical data might reflect a real abductive inference. TEM is neither the result of inference and nor the result of empirical testing. Such attitude may resonate with the efficiency of model notion by Bruner (1986). He stressed that schema and mental models provide meaning and organization to experiences and allows the individual to "go beyond the information given."

Chapter 6   Depicting the Dynamics of Living the Life

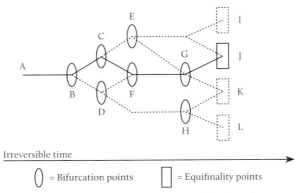

Figure 6.1. **Multilinearity of trajectories** (modified after Valsiner, 2001b)

The term *equifinality* is widely known due to Ludwig von Bertalanffy who is the founder of General Systems Theory (von Bertalanffy, 1968). We have created a new method on the basis of this notion (Sato, Yasuda et al., 2004; Valsiner & Sato, 2006; Sato, 2007; Sato, Yasuda et al., 2007; Sato, 2009). Sato, Yasuda et al. (2007) emphasized that equifinality does not imply sameness – which is an impossible condition in any historical system. Rather, it entails a region of similarity in the temporal courses of *different trajectories*. The notions of equifinality and trajectory are highly trans-related. Simply speaking, TEM is the method to describe persons' life courses within irreversible time after researchers' focusing important events as EFPs. After establishing the equifinality point, trajectories should be traced. Depicting the TEM makes it possible to grasp the trajectory with irreversible time (Figure 6.1).

The rectangle J is the supposed Equifinality Point (EFP) on what researchers focus on in their researches. For this EFP, there are many pathways to pass. Seven ellipses, indicated alphabetically as "B thorough H," are passage points and many of them have options to go. We call the passage point which has an option as "Bifurcation Point (BFP)" in this TEM, and have proposed some notions for practicing TEM to construct model (Valsiner, 2001b; Valsiner & Sato, 2006; Sato, Yasuda et al., 2007).

Part 3   DEVELOPMENT OF TEM

3.2. Basic notions of TEM

[1] TEM and HSS

The history of TEM is interdependent on the sampling methodology named the *Historically Structured Sampling* (HSS). It is developed in contrast to random sampling – which is highly recommended in psychology because of its apparent "fairness" (randomness). There is a paradox in the use of "random sampling" – it is needed because individual human beings are not homogeneous. As a famous statistician of his day, McNemar (1940, p. 331) insisted that "a large amount of psychological research must depend upon sampling for the simple reason that human variation exists." McNemar regarded the human variation as an "error" – a deviance from the "true value." His view had a lack of historical thinking. He really ignored the historicity of human lives. Human variation is the result of life course of each person and it is not timeless phenomena but time-dependent phenomena.

How should we consider the problem of sampling? If the theoretical implications of TEM are taken as the starting point, then HSS is the necessary sampling tactic to use for the study (Valsiner, 2009). We introduced that concept as a counterpoint to the non-systemic practice of "random sampling" and its less random analogs (Valsiner & Sato, 2006; Sato, Yasuda et al., 2007). This methodology of "random sampling" focuses on persons just because they are assumed to consist of a selected variety of features labeled "variables" (Sato, Watanabe et al., 2007). HSS focuses on the lived experience of any person within the irreversible time. Here, the lived experience should be regarded as true open-systemic phenomena. And all lived experience is embedded in specific time and place, namely culture. Personality is not a "dependent variable" for the lived experience, but an open-systemic phenomenon.

Thus, the new sampling method should reflect both real life courses and researchers' research questions. We call this new methodology as Historically Structured Sampling (HSS). The notion of HSS entails a radical move from other accepted methods of sampling – random sampling being the most glorified – to a version of non-random sampling of individual cases (Sato, 2007). From the viewpoint of sampling philosophy and technique, the procedure of HSS consists of "equifinality sam-

Chapter 6   Depicting the Dynamics of Living the Life

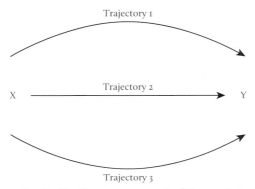

Figure 6.2. Equifinality point as a result of three trajectories

pling" i.e., the equifinality point which researchers have an interest is the experience to focus on.

[2] Equifinality and trajectories

Equifinality is the principle that in open systems a given end state can be reached by many potential means. It emphasizes that the same end state may be achieved through many different means, paths and trajectories. Variability of trajectories means richness of life. So the very first place of the conceptual adventure, equifinality and trajectories are highly intertwined with each other.

Von Bertalanffy preferred *equifinality* better than "goal," equifinality isn't the deadend like goal point. When the EFP has reached, EFP transforms to a new point to newly emerged finality. Actually, from the view point of research methodology, EFP is the focus point of focus (Y) that allows the different trajectories (1, 2, 3) to be charted out (Figure 6.2).

[3] Polarized EFP

Since EFP depends on the researchers focus and/or research questions, EFP only shows one aspect of phenomena. We need to show some kind of complement set of EFP. So we set up Polarized EFP (P-EFP) for neutralizing implicit value system of researchers. Excerpt from Yasuda (2005)'s study, she approached the infertile experiences of married women in Japan looking at their reconstructed histories of moving

Part 3   DEVELOPMENT OF TEM

between the PFEPs containing "having children" and "not having children" as the two opposites within the same whole. Both having children and having no children should be considered as equivalent equifinality points.

[4] Irreversible time

Under the influence of Bergson's philosophy, Valsiner (2000) insisted that the irreversibility of time is an absolute given for the study of all living phenomena. Irreversible time is the characteristic of real time never to repeat any happening of the previous time period. Time flows from an infinite past towards an infinite future. We don't intend to refer the representation of time. We try to put the basic feature of time into our model. Even if we felt we do same things, time might pass. There is no timeless repetition, we pose.

[5] BFP and OPP

Bifurcation Point (BFP) is a point which has alternative options to go. Obligatory Passage Point (OPP) is a concept originally emerged in the context of the geopolitical term (Latour, 1987). For example, the Strait of Gibraltar is the strait that connects the Atlantic Ocean to the Mediterranean Sea. So we can say that the Strait of Gibraltar is the OPP from the Atlantic Ocean to the Mediterranean Sea, and vice versa. Converting it in the context of TEM, OPP means a phase and/or event persons inevitably experience through initial condition to EFP.

[6] Multifinality and ZoF

Multifinality simply implies the multiple-ness of finality. But in the meaning sphere of TEM. It is used for finality after EFP. This means that multifinality refers to various pathways and finality from the same beginning point. In the context of TEM, multifinality implies the diversity after the points of EFP or Polarized EFP (P-EFP). And the different view point, EFP is set by researchers. Even researchers might focus on the EFP from their own research interest, each participant has their own life and finality (aim and/or goal). In their paper on the prevention of HIV/AIDS, Mitchell et al. (2004) showed the utility of focusing the variation, they examined multifinality (looking prospectively) and equifinality (looking retrospectively) to identify both normative and less common combinations of risk/protective configurations. We

Chapter 6　Depicting the Dynamics of Living the Life

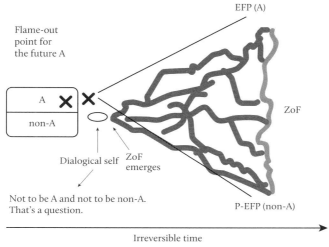

Figure 6.3. Zone of Finality (ZoF)

use the multifinality point when the finality after EFP is clear. But if not, we use the term *Zone of Finality* (ZoF – Figure 6.3). Zone of Finality (ZoF) is the finality of participants after the EFP. EFP derives from the researchers' insight rather than participants' landscape of the aim and/or goal. ZoF might compensate the complacency of researchers. The reason we use the ZoF in place of multifinality is that the future perspective might be ambiguous itself.

[7] Social direction and social guidance

The focus on social direction derives the notion of directed social cultural power. It might be said that the "common sense" provides tradition, social norm and social pressure. On the other hand Social Guidance (SG) is the power of defense against the Social Direction (SD). SG is the power supplied from the intimate persons such as a family, friends, teacher and others. Simply speaking, SD is defined as the power of inhibition to go to EFP, and SG is defined as the power of promotion to go to EFP.

[8] Transformation of an open system

TEM is a tool for depict both real and imaginary trajectories to equifinality points and it doesn't include the tool of depicting the state of each person as an open

Part 3   DEVELOPMENT OF TEM

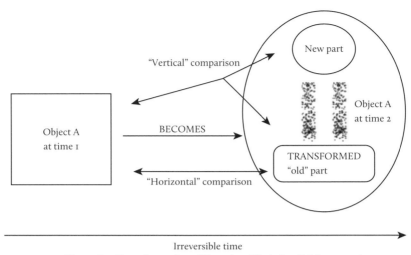

Figure 6.4. **Transformation of form** (modified after Valsiner, 2001)

system on a trajectory. An open system sometimes transforms and almost maintains it. We consider that maintaining is the form of transforming. To trans-form implies changing of form, i.e., some form of the previous kind turns into a new form (Figure 6.4). So the number generated by quantitative measures cannot depict the whole process of transformation.

Transformation involves something becoming something else. That is one aspect of development. Whatever is there before becomes transformed into something else. Secondly, whatever is there before maintains itself. So also that maintenance, the steady state of developing organism is also developmental phenomenon. This will be particularly crucial in autism. Autism is a domain of very slow development. You have to wait for a long time and for very good circumstances when the autistic child would break out of the cycle of autism.

3.3. Empirical studies for depicting dynamics with TEM

Because the methodology of TEM has only a brief history, there are not so many studies using TEM till today. But we can show a list of leading TEM studies.

Chapter 6   Depicting the Dynamics of Living the Life

Table 6.5. Studies using TEM

Reference	Topic
Yasuda (2005)	Giving up the infertility treatment
Kullasepp (2006)	Becoming psychologists
Kido (2006, 2011)	Wearing makeup habitually
Cortés (2008)	Dropping out from higher education
Yasuda et al. (2008)	Adolescent abortion
Tanimura et al. (2008)	Japanese women aiming to get married before 26-year-old

Life events studied with using TEM are neither abstract experience nor abstract psychological process (Table 6.5). These are the lived experience embedded in culture within irreversible time. For example, abortion is a highly cultural-historically val-ues-laden event. Some cultures never allow the abortion today. In Japan the abortion operation is restricted before 22-week gestation today but was allowed 8-month before. Similarly, becoming psychologists in Estonia in 2000s (Kullasepp, 2006) may be different from becoming one in other country. And again, aiming to get married in Japan in 1980s (Tanimura et al., 2008) are desperately different experiences of Japanese women in 21st century. All these are dramatic real life experiences. Yet nothing can be more misleading in science than abandoning the general view on the quality of the whole as it relates with its parts (Valsiner, 2009).

Here we show an example of the TEM study on the dropping out from the higher education.

Following Sato, Yasuda et al. (2007), Cortés (2008) review the steps in using TEM (Figure 6.5). These are: (1) defining relevant Equifinality Regions (EFR) and Obligatory Passage Points (OPP) in the map of trajectories of the process, (2) empirical mapping out all cases moving through these points, and (3) comparison of actual trajectories as these approaches to the equifinality region. Extending the original focus, Cortés (2008) proposed the equifinality "regions" instead of equifinality "point" because the notion of regions hints the geography and/or place. So a region goes together I-"positions" of Dialogical Self (DS; Hermans, 2001). Cortés tried to integrate

133

Part 3   DEVELOPMENT OF TEM

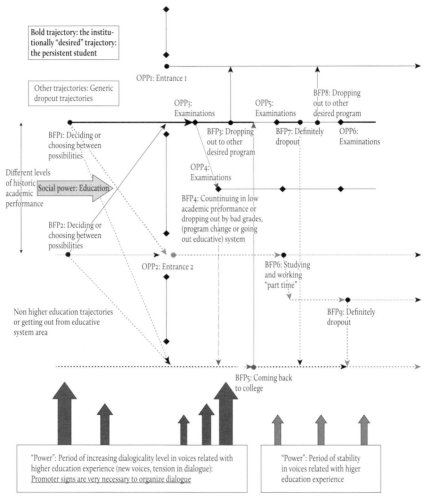

Figure 6.5. Cortés (2008)'s TEM

TEM and Dialogical Self. He defined two polarized equifinality regions – "I as an educated (higher education) person in X field" and its opposite polarized I-position, "I as a non-educated (higher education) person."

The strategy for construction of the TEM presents two related levels of organi-

Chapter 6　Depicting the Dynamics of Living the Life

zation of the dropout phenomena: an ontogenetic level to depict different possible trajectories with dropout events in the aim to construct the web of historical trajectories of individuals and a "quasi-microgenetic" inquiring level by focusing the previous moments of dropout events that lead the dropout decision and the consequent decisions and what happened after the decision.

The act of using the HSS and TEM involves the following steps (Valsiner & Sato, 2006; Sato, Yasuda et al., 2007):

(A) locating the relevant Equifinality Point (EFP) – as well as all relevant OPPs – in the generic map of trajectories necessarily present for the generic system of the processes under investigation (theoretically based activity),

(B) empirical mapping out all particular cases – systems open to study that move through these points, and

(C) comparison of different actual trajectories as these approach to the equifinality point by superimposing onto each trajectory a pattern of theoretically meaningful "range measure" – derived from (A) – that specifies whether the given trajectory fits into the realm of selectable cases.

Since EFP depends on the researchers focus and/or research questions, we have proposed to set up Polarized Equifinality Points (P-EFP) for neutralizing implicit value system of researchers. P-EFP makes researchers notice the possibility of invisible trajectories. Preparing the questions is an important procedure to do qualitative study including TEM. For example, Ayae Kido focused the experience of "Wearing makeup habitually" and interviewed 5 females. Questions made are 7 items in three categories (Kido, 2006).

The participant's immediately close female person such as mother, sister and the others were asked about the way of makeup style that they use them, the attitude for makeup they take, and whether the participant long for a way of makeup of them or not.

The participants were asked about when and how were they passively worn makeup first time, hen did they wear makeup spontaneously first time, and when her did they were makeup habitually in life? General questions includes items like what

Part 3   DEVELOPMENT OF TEM

does the makeup mean for them at that time?

All contents of the interviews were recorded with permission. The records of all interviews were divided meaningful sentences units for further analysis. One unit might consist of a sentence or sentences. Japanese scholars sometime use the KJ method. KJ method developed by a Japanese ethnologist, Jiro Kawakita in the 1960s (Kawakita, 1986). The KJ method was developed as a result of having difficulties in interpreting ethnographic data in Nepal. The KJ method builds upon Charles S. Peirce's notions of abduction and relies upon intuitive non-logical thinking processes (Scupin, 1997). Each unit (sentence) written on card is to be categorized step by step. First, exact same expressions in units are compiled. Almost other units are left. Second, similar expressions in units are compiled and are given some abstract label that characterizes gathered units (i.e., new unit emerges). Some units originally and new units emerged in second step are now materials for next step of compiling. Compiling and labeling procedure is conducted repeatedly (usually 4 or 5 times) so that abstract and/or aggregated categories might appear. These repeated compiling procedure results in getting different level of abstract labels. In Kido's case, all relevant events and facts of cosmetic experiences are written on individual cards and collated. Kido ended up with four categories from her interview data. For TEM, the highest level of categories is not needed. Moderate level of labels is needed to depict trajectories (Kido, 2006; See also Sato, Yasuda et al., 2007).

3.4. Focusing on the dynamics in the personal decision making

We need a further step to describe the dynamics in human development. The theoretical issue to consider is like this. Mori (2009) expresses the concern that TEM expresses just the superficial sequence of events, not the dynamics of human experience. What happens at the specific decision making point to determine which way he/she take? To explain the mechanism around the BFP (Bifurcation Point) appears to be necessary for understanding the dynamics of the livings within irreversible time. After reaching BFP, for example, circle c in this Figure 6.6, if there are two or more concrete finalities, these are called as multifinality. And if not so concrete and

Chapter 6   Depicting the Dynamics of Living the Life

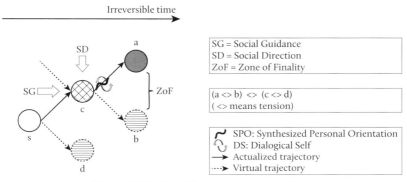

Figure 6.6. Social guidance and social direction

only the ambiguous image is seen, such a situation may be better to be called as the Zone of Finality (ZoF). Each person on the own trajectory has his/her orientation which has developed through the life course. We call this orientation as "Synthesized Personal Orientation (SPO)." SPO takes forms of goal, adoration and dream.

As usual, SPO automatically leads to next finality. But sometimes, objections and/or barriers might happen. This is the point of severe decision making. We can assume here two powers are simultaneously at work at the point. These are Social Direction (SD) and Social Guidance (SG). Both SD and SG are conveyed through everyday social exchanges at home, school and other social situations. And relative gravity (direction and power) of SD and SG determine the selection.

Significant others may play different roles in this scheme. They sometimes stand with a person as an agency of SD (for example, a social norm) and sometimes guide a person from the power of SD to reach solution (making decision). Because, there are many significant others around one person – like a convoy attempting to persuade him/her in one or another direction. From the theoretical view point, there are many bifurcation points to make decisions about moving along one or another of the trajectories. Seeking the decision making points doesn't inevitably need the EFP Instead, analyzing powers around the decision making points allows TEM research broader perspective than before.

Part 3 DEVELOPMENT OF TEM

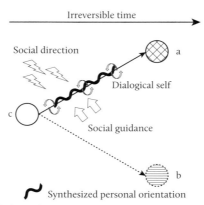

Figure 6.7. **How dialogical processes construct trajectories** (Sato & Valsiner, 2010)

Then we look closely the transition process between c and a in Figure 6.6. As we say later, we can conceive this transition process by using Three Layers Model of Genesis (TLMG).

What would happen at the one trajectory from a point (see in Figure 6.7) to another point a? In the figure before (i.e., not this one), the lines between points are straight and direct but if looking at closely, we can see the two opposite powers which conflicts between social direction and social guidance. So the Synthesized Personal Orientation (SPO) reflects the fluctuated orientation and open-systemic nature of human being within irreversible time. A person proceeds with one's orientation as an open system (which means orientation is not internal derived) and struggle to realize own orientation against the Social Directions (SD) with support of Social Guidance (SG) supplied by the intimate social relationships.

For example, before World War II, Japanese university did not open their doors to women. So if some women hoped to go study at university, social direction strongly suggested not to study. But of course, universities of other countries such as in the U.S. opened the door to women around that time without restrictions. Ms. Tsuruko Arai (1886-1915) entered graduate school of Columbia University and was supervised by Edward L. Thorndike. She could earn Ph.D. Degree in 1912 (Sato, 2007). In her life situation her family and teachers encouraged her much to go study

Chapter 6   Depicting the Dynamics of Living the Life

abroad. Thorndike in graduate school of Columbia University also encouraged and supervised her.

Traditional psychology has easily attributed outcomes of positive development to single causal factors, such as motivation, while the term "social support" tends to be used to explain the social relationships needed to overcome the bad condition. But such explanation by motivation is not appropriate for open-systemic view − by which the achieving person is constantly relating with the environment. Dialogical self emerges when synthesized personal orientation fluctuates. Inspired by both William James' American pragmatism and s Russian dialogical orientation, Hubert Hermans created a theory of self on a new basis − the unity of opposites involved in a dialogue. The Dialogical Self Theory presupposes a multivoiced person with not just one dominant I-position, but several I-positions, which are temporally and spatially structured (Hermans & Kempen, 1993). The self is defined as a "dynamic multiplicity of relatively autonomous I-positions in an imaginary landscape" (Hermans, 1999).

Temporally and spatially structured "I-positions" have different voices and "I-positions" are relatively independent each other. But in some points, they cause conflicts. Thus, "I as a" and "I as b" appears by turns and conflict occurs. Back to the Ms. Tsuruko Arai of about 70 years before in Japan, Tsuruko as a non-educated and Tsuruko as an educated girl might cause conflict. This scheme can really represent the superficial calm but deeply dynamic process on the way from one BFP to another point (before making decision).

The Three Layers Model of Genesis (TLMG − Figure 6.8) is useful for understanding ontogenesis through the prisms of two other time frames (Valsiner, 2007). At the lowest level, micro-genetic level, the process of *Aktualgenese* (this German word was translated into English "microgenesis" by Heinz Werner) is constantly at work. But in macro-genetic − that of ontogenetic − level nothing needs to change. It is in between the two levels − the meso-genetic level where changes are consolidated to be either taken as novelties to the macro-genetic level, or become regulators ("promoter signs") of the micro-genetic processes. Ontogenetic maintenance can happen through SDs (Social Directions), the promoter sign can be derived from a

Part 3 DEVELOPMENT OF TEM

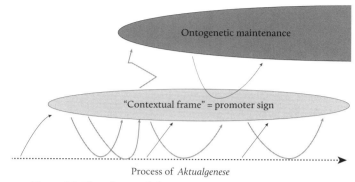

Figure 6.8. The scheme of Three Layers Model of Genesis (TLMG)

social norm, habit or any conservative tendency.

Setting Equifinality Points (EFPs) lead to put both potential trajectories to EFP and Polarized EFP (P-EFP) on the trajectory. But of course this is the demand for researchers not for participants. Sometimes people cannot do anything because selection is difficult (Hamlet or Buridan's ass phenomena). But the other time, even after selecting one option, people bother. Here we can see that the dialogical self is useful again. That is, bothering persons have dialogue with themselves. What if I had selected another option? How I would be now? This form is easily converted into another form with dialogical self. Which is better for me now, I as one or I as another? For example, two choices of university A and B for a person, he/she self-dialogue is I as a student of A university better than I as a student of B university? There are many more severe choice situations. We move to the situation of intractable disease patient to think about more severe decision making process.

4. General conclusions

A person is not the pile of traits and a life trajectory is not a single line connecting the discrete time points which researchers arbitrary set. If we take time seriously,

Chapter 6   Depicting the Dynamics of Living the Life

we should not say such things. There exist many obstacles to our efforts to take time seriously in studies of psychology and sociology. Uses of stage theories and reliance on correlation coefficients, as well as an implication that trajectory is merely a unitary path (rather than a range of options) within the life course paradigm that we outlined in the beginning of this chapter are some examples. Taking the equifinality principle into account is one of the breakthrough in describing the dynamics. Accepting the premise that different initial conditions produce different trajectories to arrive at a similar final state is the reality of open systems.

The Trajectory Equifinality Model (TEM) hopefully overcomes such obstacles The dynamics of living in real context should be understood by using the notion of signs as organizers of the future – hence assuming a constructionist stance. Vygotsky (1978) pointed out that the developmental process is mediated by cultural tools. Human development is mediated by signs – and because of such mediation the potential for a person's moving in various directions in one's life course exists. Life stage models of development cannot conceptualize this dynamism. Of course, existing life course studies struggle to understand the continuity of life as well. But they can never depict the dynamics of the flow of the lived experience within in the irreversible time. They might cover outcomes of processed that are charted over time – creating a trajectory *post factum* – but never accessing the real processes embedded in time. Actually, the practice of life course research sets up longitudinal "contact points" at fixed intervals – yet relevant transitions can happen at any moment in between these points. To use an analogy – model of life course studies look like fixed net fishing. In contrast, TEM is one of the ways to understand the flow and the continuity of life from the view point of the agent whose life course is under study.

Last but not least, we consider the notion of transform within our discussion. We need the transforming mechanism model which leads to depict the dynamic process of life trajectories. Depicting the maintenance of a similar state is also dynamic. Superficial maintenance never implies static state of covert system. Sometimes covert dynamism might result in the overt static state. Looking at the trajectories as they are being constructed can be used for creating the new way to depict the coher-

Part 3   DEVELOPMENT OF TEM

ence, dynamism and variation of idiosyncratic life within irreversible time.

Chapter 7

The Authentic Culture of Living Well

Pathways to Psychological Well-Being

Abstract

This chapter deals with cultural construction of life courses – in illness and in health. Patients – or people who have fallen ill, in general – are usually treated by the health-care institutions as "vehicles of disease" as they are assigned new social roles in the medical setting. The inner world of patients has been respectfully disregarded as residual features of no central importance. Even as two disciplines – medical sociology and qualitative nursing research – have recently tried to transform the situation, their way of understanding patients' narratives and meaning making processes should be of enlightening value for the medical profession. Assuming a process-oriented research standpoint that takes the notion of time seriously is imperative for such efforts. Since the social power of the medical profession intrinsically controls the patients' lives – in or out of medical settings – a new type of qualitative research on illness and wellness as built from the viewpoint of patients is needed. Both micro-ethnography and a qualitative approach in cultural psychology are promising and useful approaches for applying to this new mission. Thick description of one's daily life is needed and it might be called "life ethnography." Theoretically the notions derived from Trajectory Equifinality Model (TEM) such as zone of finality and multifinality are useful to understand the personal-cultural construction of the feeling of being (and staying) alive – and well.

Keywords

Trajectory Equifinality Model (TEM), Promoter sign, Future perspective, Life with Illness (LWI), Multifinality

Part 3   DEVELOPMENT OF TEM

A key axiom in medical anthropology is the dichotomy between two aspects of sickness: disease and illness. Disease refers to a malfunctioning of biological and/or psychological processes, while the term illness refers to the psychosocial experience and meaning of perceived disease. (Kleinman, 1980, p. 72)

Open-ended plasticity occurs when organisms respond to new stimuli by constructing new adaptive developmental paths or trajectories. (Ginsburg & Jablonka, 2007, p. 221)

For a long time, it has been thought that the idea of culture is the one that relates a person with a specific location – country, community, or the like. The uses of the term in history of anthropology reinforced that idea. However, cultural psychology – building on the centrality of the notion of signs as emphasized by Charles S. Peirce, which is also traceable in the work of Lev Vygotsky – has the possibility of offering a theoretical base that allows us to think about culture without being "caught" in any particular place. Valsiner (2001c, p. 32) insisted that "culture belongs to person," since culture is functioning within the intra-psychological systems of each person. And it is through signs that culture acts as the mediator within a person.

In this chapter we look at sickness experience as cultural organizers of human lives. As the quotation indicates at the top of this chapter, Kleinman (1980) insisted that two aspects of sickness should be differentiated: disease and illness. Then we take the notion of illness more seriously than one of disease. Earlier Eisenberg (1977) pointed out this discrepancy between illness and disease. He said that patients suffer illnesses; doctors diagnose and treat diseases. And also he said that illnesses are experiences of discontinuities in states of being and perceived role performances. Diseases, in the scientific paradigm of modern medicine, are abnormalities in the function and/or structure of body organs and systems. And the patient represents and implies a person being patient from the medical doctor's viewpoint.

We aim to invalidate the notion of the patient as "person who must be patient" – and follow all the orders of the medical system. Instead, we focus on the person's "Life with Illness (LWI)" – it is a life with extra difficulties (introduced by the disease)

Chapter 7   The Authentic Culture of Living Well

– yet it is a person's life filled with all the ordinary pleasures and disappointments. We all know illnesses are experiences of discontinuities in states of being and perceived role performances (Eisenberg, 1977). Even so, a person should not be called as "patient = suffering person." He/she lives with illness. Life with illness is one of the forms of human life. And it leads to the construction of its own peculiar kind of culture.

1. How Trajectory Equifinality Model (TEM) deals with Life with Illness (LWI)

The Trajectory Equifinality Model (TEM; Valsiner & Sato, 2006; Sato, Yasuda et al., 2007; Sato et al., 2009) provides a good frame for understanding ruptures and reconstructions in personal culture under the conditions of sudden pathogenesis. TEM is the method to describe persons' life courses within irreversible time. The term equifinality is widely known because of Ludwig von Bertalanffy, who is the founder of General Systems Theory (von Bertalanffy, 1968).

Equifinality is the principle that in open systems a given end state can be reached by many potential means. It emphasizes that the same end state may be achieved through many different means, paths, and trajectories. Variability of trajectories means richness of life. So the very first place of the conceptual adventure, equifinality and the trajectories that converge upon it are highly intertwined with each other. Von Bertalanffy preferred equifinality better than "goal," equifinality isn't the dead-end-like goal point.

The reason why TEM is suitable for describing LWI is because TEM has incorporated the notion of a polarized equifinality point – an imaginary complementary class of usual and/or singular events that might exist – in contrast to the equifinality point that represents healthy life. Both the equifinality point and the polarized equifinality point are devices for relativizing the value system in existence. The polarized equifinality point is the place in irreversible time at which the personal culture of the

Part 3   DEVELOPMENT OF TEM

person with illness becomes transformed into a new form. Here one can observe a new value system in its cultural emergence. That can happen in many ways – multi-finality is useful for describing the person whose experience leads to new culture and new aims in life.

In medical sociology there exist investigations of patients' lives from the perspective against an official medical system. The study of chronic illness trajectory model by Corbin & Strauss (1991) is one of such studies. However studies from medical settings easily confound the patients' perspectives and the perspective of the medical system that is controlling patients' lives. The orientation of illness trajectory then should be criticized from the describing of the lives of people with illness. TEM is recognized as a promising method for the illness trajectory framework.

We propose the importance of the micro-genetic approach especially in describing the life of patients or persons who are ill; in general, psychological research on human beings as medical patients has been rising since the latter half of twentieth century. At first, medical sociology and the studies of nursing became focused on research of social "deficits" of the patients (Parsons, 1951a). Then, patients from non-middle-class backgrounds did not fit well into the social regime of medical settings, and that misfit needed to be studied. Ethnography emerges as a useful resource because the mission of ethnography is to depict culture.

2. Illness trajectory framework from nursing rsearch and medical sociology

2.1. Historical context of ethnography: The archeology of anthropologies

Ethnography is defined as the art and science of describing a group or culture (Fetterman, 2008). This term also refers to qualitative methodology or reports to describe a behavior pattern of the people through fieldwork (LeCompte & Preissle, 1993). Ethnography originated from early (cultural) anthropology and spread to other social sciences. Each discipline has its own way of studying diverse customs, so the

Chapter 7 The Authentic Culture of Living Well

deliverables are widely variable in the same "ethnography." For example, micro-ethnography is commonly-used type of ethnography in psychology. Micro-ethnography is the study of narrowly defined cultural groupings such as a school classroom. Micro-ethnography is suitable for the study of "Life with illness," especially the refractory and/or progressing disease.

To understand the features of micro-ethnography, let us start with looking back at the history of the anthropologies. This chapter gives weight to ethnography as methodology and explains how it is used in psychology today. Ethnography originated from early (cultural) anthropology, more properly from Bronislaw Malinowski's work in the 1920s (e.g., Malinowski, 1922). He was also the pioneer of "empirical" fieldwork – and he also worked in the field – where he developed currently accepted anthropological research methods (such as participant observation). The term "empirical" implies another kind of anthropological research. Though now the anthropologist seems to be a fieldworker, as a person who actually goes to his research field, the typical anthropologist before Malinowski was not. This old type of anthropology could be called "armchair anthropology." Armchair anthropologists depended on speculative discussion and got the data for their research from others who actually visited a field – usually places far away from their academic homes. The problem is, of course, all of their discoveries could easily become products of fantasy. Fieldwork, and ethnography as its product, got a foothold because they were expected to be a method to describe human life and behavior more directly.

The political aspect of anthropology cannot be ignored when we look back at its history. A number of anthropologists in the past worked as a part of a national strategy because ethnography was useful for understanding the culture of the people in their colony. This colonial anthropology aimed to make their colonial occupation easier and firmer by collecting the information about the different cultures through the European ways of seeing. Actually, the early "positive" anthropology transformed from armchair anthropology with using the real observation of the field, however the aim of anthropology could not be transformed. This academic program should obey the interest of government and follow the mission to know the "native" of

147

Part 3   DEVELOPMENT OF TEM

conquests/colonial lands (see Kuklick, 1991). The cooperation among government and anthropologists became pronounced in war time, especially during World War II (WWII). The study by Ruth Benedict is one of the notable examples. In her book, *The Chrysanthemum and the sword*, as a cultural anthropological study, she showed indigenous features of Japan (Benedict, 1946). Although the book was published after WWII, the content was based on her war-time research. To understand the culture of Japan was considered to attribute to a strong position of control after the war.

New uses of ethnography are being adapted in urban sociology (see Kharlamov, 2012). Fieldwork and ethnography already attracted another discipline of social science in the 1920s. Sociologists in the United States applied those methods for exploring their interests. The so-called "Chicago school" tried to study a different culture within their own country. For example, Cressey (1932) described the social world of dancers and guests in the ballroom, and Whyte (1943) proposed the collision of local and total society as a cause of delinquency through observing various groups and communities in a slum district of Boston that was mostly inhabited by immigrants from Italy. Urban sociologists transformed the meanings of the term "ethno" from ethnic group in another country into some group who have different cultures in the same area (country). Subjects of research also could be varied.

"Anthropology of science" provides a unique example. Bruno Latour took a laboratory as his research field. A laboratory is not only the place of production of scientific knowledge but also the community in which scientists practice their daily works in a unique manner. In *Laboratory life* (Latour & Woolgar, 1979) and *Science in action* (Latour, 1987), he studied how the scientific truth was made, focusing on the process and network. One of the most important keys to this process is to grasp the local practice as it proceeds with time and build upon social relationships. Today, it is not enough to know about an unprecedented field. We may apply these perspectives to another more significant issue.

2.2. Life ethnography
Recently, the subfield of life ethnography has emerged as a type of ethnographic

Chapter 7   The Authentic Culture of Living Well

research to describe the lives of people. People, especially those who have incurable and progressive diseases, face continuous transformation of their symptoms and body. Life ethnography should not eliminate time, because the disease process is an ongoing and never-stopping experience.

The key points of life ethnography can be summarized into following points:

1. Description of the system of "life with illness"; patients live with various factors affecting their lives including caregivers, technology, institutions and so on. They also each have a historical and cultural background. Each researcher may take different methods to write a life ethnography, but it is important to understand the life of a patient within their network.

2. Understanding each case through exhaustive fieldwork.

3. Notion of time and the emergence of signs of guidance – e.g., "the aim of life." Ethnography is to discover how people create signs that make them behave in various ways.

Mundane (daily) diaries and medical documentation are useful for understanding "time-full" process. The new possibility of bridging between medicine and psychology has just emerged. Life ethnography of refractory and/or progressive disease brings us the new exciting challenge. That is the dynamism under the maintenance process with the immobile body.

Although each discipline, including psychology, has different rules for describing a phenomenon with ethnography, the following points are shared in common:

1. Understanding human behavior including the context of his/her living through fieldwork.

2. Multi-method: participant observation, interview (both dialogue and group), document study and so on.

3. Generating hypothesis that is suited for explaining the phenomenon systematically through gradual focusing.

The unit of description – how and what should be described – differs between disciplines. There are a few exceptions to these methodological trends, but to summarize: anthropologists focus the structure of relative, ritual, customs, and so on;

Part 3   DEVELOPMENT OF TEM

sociologists place more importance on institution; psychologists place a special emphasis on behavior, speech, and interaction of the people. This type of ethnography is called "micro-ethnography" because it is a method for disclosing micro-genetic behaviors and psychological processes.

The term "micro-genetic" – originating in Heinz Werner's version of rendering the notion of *Aktualgenese* – is important for describing human behavior within a specific time and space, or chronotope. According to Bakhtin's conception, the chronotope refers to the interconnectedness of time and space in literature. The word "chronotope" literally means "time space" and is defined by Bakhtin (1984) as the intrinsic connectedness of temporal and spatial relationships that are artistically expressed in literature. Today, this notion is applied to narrative analysis. Life ethnography and narrative analysis of the life with illness become important promising areas in cultural psychology. Because we can understand that a disease experience is not only a biological/physiological event but is a socio-culturally constructed event.

Life ethnography fits well with medical anthropology. Medical anthropology focused on the social processes and cultural representations of health, illness, and the nursing or care practices. Alan Young showed how the concept of post-traumatic stress disorder (PTSD) was made into a disorder (Young, 1995). Disorder tends to be attributed to personal problems, but it cannot be constructed without medical and political background. Arthur Kleinman showed how the experience of chronic patients could be transformed, focusing on their narrative (Kleinman, 1988). Symptoms of chronic disease are not experienced as pure medical meaning, but experienced as a bio-psycho-social meaning. And illness is not simply a personal experience; it is transactional, communicative, and profoundly social. But again, we use "life ethnography" for emphasizing "life of person with illnesss" not of a patient in a medical setting.

2.3. Illness trajectory model

Life of patients and/or developmental process of patients rarely gain a primary focus in psychology. Mental illness is an exception, because this is the main target of

Chapter 7   The Authentic Culture of Living Well

clinical and/or abnormal psychology. This is a clear gap in our knowledge – lives of patients should be treated from a psychological perspective. We have developed the new framework for it – the look at persons' construction of their future life pathways based on reconstructing the past. Anselm Strauss and his colleagues started studying chronic illness in patients as early as 1960. Following intensive work, they focused on the conceptualization of managing and shaping the course of an illness (Phipps et al., 2003). Furthermore, Corbin & Strauss (1991) developed a chronic disease trajectory framework following over 30 years of research on a variety of chronic illnesses. Because their model/framework is grounded on the research and practice of nursing, this is welcomed by nursing care models of different chronic diseases such as cancer, trauma, diabetes, mellitus, and stroke, among others (Kabinga & Banda, 2008). Corbin and Strauss's chronic illness trajectory model prescribes that the life course of chronic patients should be divided eight phases (they later added one more phase). Specific nursing management steps are invented for each phase. Illness, instead of disease, implies that lives of patients are embedded in social, cultural, and family context.

Although the phases from the chronic illness trajectory model are static and useful for nursing management, they are not useful for the lives of patients. Burton (2000) summarized the eight phases (instead of nine) of the illness trajectory framework:

> The first stage in a trajectory (pre-trajectory) occurs before the onset of symptoms, and consequently before a formal diagnosis is made. This emphasizes the importance of illness prevention within a framework for managing chronic health problems. When signs and symptoms appear (trajectory onset), these can pose a significant threat to the physical, social or psychological integrity of an individual (crisis phase). The onset of symptoms may precipitate a period of illness that requires active intervention, usually in an in-patient setting, to prevent the worsening of symptoms, or the prevention of complications associated with the effects of the illness (acute phase). Where intervention is effective, a period of stability may be reached which will require varying degrees of intervention to maintain individual health (stable phase). An individual will, however, experience challenges

Part 3   DEVELOPMENT OF TEM

to their recovery either directly or indirectly associated with their illness which require a reappraisal and adaptation of interventions, usually without admission to a hospital setting, to promote coping and stability (unstable phase). Responses to these challenges to recovery will at some point, however, be unsuccessful, and the patient's recovery may deteriorate (downward phase) to such a point that the patient may be terminally ill (dying phase). (Burton, 2000)

Corbin and Strauss's trajectory framework sets the illness trajectory up as a series of phases. Trajectory phasing represents the many different changes in status a chronic condition can undergo during that course (Corbin & Strauss, 1988, p. 16). Phases are not simple time durations. They depend mainly on physical symptoms. A bio-psycho-social model of disease is not disregarded, but symptom-oriented phasing is necessary for the medical setting. Their framework as a grounded theory was developed from an extensive research program on dying, and was refined in studies that included a range of settings and patient groups (Corbin & Strauss, 1992).

The aim of medicine is to save lives – which really means overcoming disease until the moment of death. So the value systems of patients' lives are embedded in a simple and/or uni-dimensional medical meaning system. This is inevitable. So if we want to think of the "life itself" of a patient, we need to think about the life trajectories that are far from the medical setting. The word "life" is not an antonym of the word "death." It implies daily activity (everyday life) and course of individual (life course, lifelong development).

When a patient goes to the doctor, he/she is seen not as a person who needs help with his or her health, but as a person who has an affected area to be treated. Even worse, he/she is seen as a potential component for the medical factory! Here Bakhtin's notion of addressivity (Moro, 1999) provides us the analyzing viewpoint in the micro-genetic level. Sometimes modern professionals, including medicine, lose the addressivity of his/her profession. Medical professionals tend to deal with a patient as a part of an ill body rather than as a human being.

A patient is treated as an anonimous body by medical professions, i.e., medical

Chapter 7   The Authentic Culture of Living Well

techniques direct to an faceless body. These states may be the lack of addressivity (Bakhtin, 1986). It is also a trait of the outlook of modern human beings. If the (dialogical) act doesn't conclude without the addressee, the act of the medical-care personnel doesn't conclude. Moreover, the problems are acute – the patient cannot reply to the medical discourse. The lack of dialogue will bring patients the feeling of imperfection and the duty of "concentrating on treatment." However, the person tends to live with the expected prospects, and the person cannot help thinking about the thing after treatment. If the present medical-care personnel are busy, it seems possible to adopt a system including a support person such as a Child Life Specialist (CLS). A CLS is a pediatric health-care professional who works with patients, their families and others involved in the child's care in order to help them manage stress and understand medical and various procedures (Armstrong-Dailey & Zarbock, 2001). CLSs are trained professionals with expertise in helping children and their families overcome life's most challenging events. They focus on the psycho-social development of children, and encourage effective coping strategies for children and their families under stress (Swanson, 2005). For a productive research orientation, different perspective is needed. For a productive research orientation, we need to focus on the living process of patients rather than the dying process of patients. Here, we rename the living process "life trajectory."

2.4. Life trajectories for the person with illness

Life trajectory approach, not illness trajectory approach, focuses on each illness person's life – not the process for dying. It's a thick description for the lived life of a person with an illness. Depicting dynamics of living may lead to understanding the thickness of life. Pursuing life trajectories depends on the new methodology of Trajectory Equifinality Model (TEM; Valsiner & Sato, 2006; Sato, Yasuda et al., 2007; Sato et al., 2009). In the case of uses of TEM, researchers focus on subjectively important events of the person and treat those as the Equifinality Points (EFPs). The history of TEM is interdependent on the development of the notion of Historically Structured Sampling (HSS; Valsiner & Sato, 2006) the function of which is to replace

Part 3   DEVELOPMENT OF TEM

the standard random sampling techniques for systems that do not satisfy the axiom of independence of its elements. All human systems consist of non-independent parts and cannot be "randomly" sampled. From the viewpoint of sampling philosophy and technique, the procedure of HSS consists of "equifinality sampling" i.e., the equifinality point in which researchers have an interest is the experience to focus on.

Sato, Yasuda et al. (2007) emphasized that equifinality does not imply sameness – which is an impossible condition in any historical system. And the more important thing is setting the polarized equifinality point in TEM. Since equifinality point depends on the researcher's focus and/or research questions, EFP only shows one aspect of phenomena. We need to show some kind of complement set of EFPs. So we set up Polarized EFP (P-EFP) for neutralizing the implicit value system of researchers. P-EFP makes researchers notice the possibility of invisible trajectories. Since the setting of P-EFP might be regarded as the pluralizing of the finality points, it implies the multifinality of the life. TEM has focused the trajectory in the past for equifinality point, but now, the description of future perspectives of each person is regarded as a new practical issue of TEM.

TEM has been developing for a few years quickly and the notion of multifinality is the promising brand new idea to depict the uncertainty of ongoing life within time.

Bifurcation point is the location on a trajectory when and where new direction emerges. Bifurcation Point (BFP) is a point that has alternative options of where to go. What would happen at the BFP?

According to Sato & Valsiner (2010), we can see in Figure 7.1 the two opposite powers that conflict between social direction and social guidance. Each person is supposed to have his/her original orientation to EFP. It is called "Synthesized Personal Orientation (SPO)" and SPO reflects the fluctuated orientation and open-systemic nature of a human being within irreversible time (Sato et al., 2009). A person proceeds with one's orientation as an open system (which means orientation is not internally derived) and struggles to realize his/her own orientation against the Social Directions (SDs) with support of Social Guidance (SG) supplied by the intimate social

Chapter 7   The Authentic Culture of Living Well

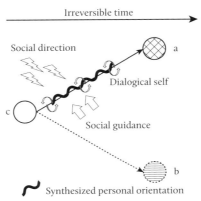

Figure 7.1. **The making of the future: BFP as the point of transformation and blooming time** (Sato & Valsiner, 2010)

relationships. The focus on social direction derives from Valsiner's (2001b) idea and it should be defined as some kinds of sociological cultural power. It might be said to include "common sense," tradition, social norm, and social pressure. On the other hand SG is the power of defense against the social direction. SG is the power supplied from the intimate persons such as a family, friends, teachers, and others. Simply speaking, SD is defined as the power of inhibition to go to EFP, and SG is defined as the power of promotion to go to EFP.

3. Lessons from life of intractable and/or chronic disease and notion of finality: Uncertainty and genesis of multifinality

3.1. The patients' life of intractable and/or chronic disease

Akasaka (2009) examined how people with chronic Inflammatory Bowel Disease (IBD) live with their illness and describe their experience of pain. IBD is a group of inflammatory conditions of the colon and small intestine. And it is an illness of uncertain etiology. Six patients with IBD were interviewed regarding their medical history and experience of illness. From their descriptions, four steps in the process of

Part 3   DEVELOPMENT OF TEM

coming to terms with their illness were identified: "confusion; fear of change," "seeking an explanation and encountering a diagnosis," "uncertainty; seeking future," and "reconstructing meaning." Because the IBD is an illness of uncertain etiology, the third phase of "uncertainty" has a double meaning. These are uncertainty of cause and uncertainty of prognosis. And patients tend to illusorily correlate the hypothesized cause and their worsening symptoms.

Nishida (2010) examined communication deficiencies and misunderstandings between care receivers and caregivers through one in-depth case study. In this case, the care receiver suffered from a severe progressive disease (Amyotrophic Lateral Sclerosis, ALS) and lived in a single household. The study finds the following problems in the patient's situation:

1. caregiving services were subdivided among a number of separate subgroups by provider and this grouping seems to be lack of organization from the receiver's position;

2. though the patient had difficulty in self-determination as his disease progressed, nobody played a coordinating role in providing care. Both patients and caregivers struggle with oppression, but avoid straightforward communication – because patients need the care to live and caregivers need to keep their jobs.

Hidaka (2010) has engaged in life ethnography work with the ALS patients. He says that it's important for patients not only to respond to a life-threatening condition, but also to express their experiences and get involved in patients' advocacy activity. Some patients have used them to write a book or report for telling their experience to the society. Capacity of patients' communication has been developed based on new computer technologies.

However, there are problems for continuous use of assistive technology. A research showed one-third of assistive technology is abandoned within 3 months because of the lack of effective supporter(s). On the other hand, in a few exceptional cases, a few patients have been using assistive technology continuously with a supporter. Hidaka (2010) reported one person with ALS using his cheek for communication at home with 24-hour-a-day care. This person should stay in bed during the whole day with a respirator, but he can enjoy using a computer for writing and communicating others. His activity is supported by many people around him. These include family members, medical and co-medical staff, and the peer supporter. The peer supporter is a person with the same disease (in this case, ALS) and has a specialized skill (in this case, computer technology). The peer supporter knows both disease and technology, so he can deliver necessary and sufficient support for the person with the illness in bed during the whole day. In this case, the person with severe ALS got ALS a long time ago and now he has finality that was never construed before his pathogenesis.

3.2. Frame of transition process of pathogenesis of intractable and/or chronic disease

These are three examples of uncertainty in the life with illness. And uncertainty is the important feature of the transition process of becoming patients. We can identify the frames of transition as follows. Frame is the key concept, which is derived from Fogel's (2006) work on dynamical system approach. Salgado & Goncalves (2010) insist that frame is not a static concept but runs in sequence.

The frames from the perspective of life ethnography and life trajectory approach are below (Table 7.1). Here we use the term "frame" to focus on the meaning-making process of a person with illness.

Finality is the key concept of Trajectory Equifinality Model (Valsiner & Sato, 2006; Sato, Yasuda et al., 2007; Sato et al., 2009). Before getting an illness, a person has the singular finality of a healthy (and usually means normal) person, which is unique to each person. Each person could have their own finality respectively. But if person got an illness, the finality he/she has had is usually under crisis. The finality evaporates and uncertainty emerges.

From the theoretical demand of TEM, a singular finality should be relativized by another complementary finality, i.e., polarized EFP. For the TEM, the Polarized EFP (P-EFP) should be set so that the model might avoid evaluating the life course

Part 3   DEVELOPMENT OF TEM

Table 7.1. Frame of transition process of pathogenesis of intractable and/or chronic disease

Singular finality
Evaporation of finality = Uncertainty
Zone of finality
Multifinality

by a dominated single voice. Being affected by intractable and/or chronic disease is a moment when a previously formed finality (for healthy person) should evaporate. Then a P-EFP should replace the EFP, but it's difficult. Because not only EFP but also P-EFP has been set for the healthy person. P-EFP is not a second-best finality for new patients. So both EFP and P-EFP vanish simultaneously. Then uncertainty emerges.

Uncertainty is the period during which patients are in most unstable condition. For considering aspects of uncertainty, Hermans's theory of dialogical self in globalization era is useful. In the context of globalization, Hermans & Dimaggio (2007) referred to the notion of uncertainty. They define the experience of "uncertainty" as a condition where different authors ascribe alternative meanings. So a more detailed description is required. They see the experience of uncertainty as composed of four aspects: (a) complexity, referring to a great number of parts that have a large variety of relations; (b) ambiguity, referring to a suspension of clarity, as the meaning of one part is determined by the flux and variation of the other parts; (c) deficit knowledge, referring to the absence of a superordinate knowledge structure that can resolve the contradictions between the parts; and (d) unpredictability, implying a lack of control of future developments.

The experience of uncertainty characterizes a situation of multi-voicedness (complexity) that does not allow a fixation of meaning (ambiguity). Positioning as a healthy person is at stake and an "I-as-patient" position is not easily formed. Some kind of multi-voicedness emerges. Not a voiceless but a multi-voice situation creates uncertainty.

Some persons in uncertainty may hear no voice and need a voice from others.

Chapter 7 The Authentic Culture of Living Well

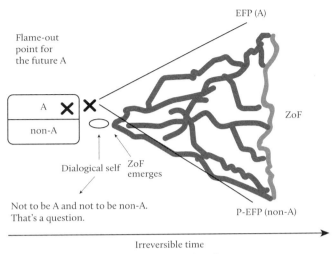

Figure 7.2. Zone of finality

Others may hear a lot of voices from others and be confused about which voice is adequate.

Struggling with such a vague situation, a "new" patient begins to accept the condition. And a position of "I-as-patient" is added to the repertory. After an uncertainty period, a new finality should be formed but it might be ambiguous. The Zone of Finality (ZoF) appears (see Figure 7.2).

Under a "usual" life, each individual has his/her own aim. It depends on the value system of healthy people. And equifinality point of an ex-healthy person should disappear when he/she gets severely sick. And a new equifinality point cannnot emerge soon after such a rupture. He/she tends to lose desire to achieve the original aim and sometimes a person loses the aim of life (some might choose to die). So when a flame-out or wreck experience evaporates the EFP, an alternative finality should emerge. But it's difficult to clarify this second-best finality, so the finality should be ambiguous and form the zone of finality. Here we use "zone" instead of "point."

Then the role of dialogical self is important. The person who is suffering should ask oneself (self-dialectically), "So what is the next aim? Which way should I take?"

Part 3   DEVELOPMENT OF TEM

Even though one cannot answer this question, one should begin to start new journeys. Even a next finality is neither clear nor discrete.

4. Quality of life and beyond

4.1. On measurement of "quality of life"

Quality of Life (QoL) is one of the well-known concepts in psychology and related areas. There are so many measurement scales of QoL now. We wonder whether quantitative measurement of quality of life is possible. It's an ironic contradiction. In the measurement of quality of life, the QoL of refractory and/or progressive diseases seems to be evaluated as low and valueless, because their sickness gets worse and – such development means an increase in hopelessness. For example, the patients with ALS disease gradually get worse – in the end they cannot move any muscle. Persons who gradually lose their muscular power should stay in bed all day and cannot move by themselves. Yet some patients can establish contact with friends and family by using Internet Technology (IT). They manage to control IT devices with the muscles they can use. One person uses cheek muscles for controlling a computer. Another uses left-foot muscles. Then can write books, paint, and so on. They are enjoying their lives in their own way.

Given this reality, any score of an Activities of Daily Living (ADL) questionnaire misleads us to estimate the quality of life to be low specifically when the score is regarded as the index of improvement. Barthel Index (BI) is a scale used to measure performance in basic activities of daily living. ADL scales focus upon a range of mobility, and self-care tasks, and ignore issues such as pain, emotions, and social functioning (Fayers & Machin, 2007). BI consists of many daily living activities. In one example of feeding, the standard is below. BI is evaluated by using in Japanese medical situations:

10 = independent,

5 = partial help with eating or needs help cutting,

Chapter 7   The Authentic Culture of Living Well

0 = unable.

So – if the person can't spread butter, the evaluator gives him 5 points to indicate the need for "help with eating." Spreading butter is the anchor to rate the level of feeding activity. Here we must note that even if spreading the butter might guarantee a good level of ADL, a person who cannot spread the butter should not be regarded as low ADL. But is this right? The item of ADL only reflects the viewpoint of medical professions.

Let us consider the Functional Independence Measure (FIM) (Keith et al., 1987). The FIM measures 18 items over six different domains by a 7-point scale: (a) self-care, (b) sphincter control, (c) mobility, (d) locomotion, (e) communication, and (f) social cognition. These items are construed from the viewpoint of medical professions, not from the patients' viewpoints. And more importantly (that means worse), scores on such items are difficult to change with the patients' situations.

4.2. Equifinality for the person with chronic disease and/or progressive disease

What's the equifinality for the person with chronic disease and/or progressive disease? Parsons (1951b) proposed the sick role concept. The sick role concept consisted of four main principles:

1. The sick person is not at fault for being sick;

2. The sick person is excused from usual (everyday) responsibilities;

3. The sick person must get well as soon as possible;

4. The sick person must seek professional help.

"Being sick" is not simply a "state of fact" or "condition" (Parsons, 1951b). The sick person is exempt from normal social roles. He/she should try to get well and also has to say "push myself to the max." Maxim one, first, is the institutionalized definition that the sick person cannot be expected, by "pulling himself together," to get well by an act of decision or will. In this sense also, he is exempted from responsibility, as he is in a condition that must be "taken care of." Maxim two, the second closely related aspect, is the exemption from normal social role responsibilities (Parsons,

Part 3   DEVELOPMENT OF TEM

1951b, p. 437). Maxim three is the definition of the state of being ill as itself unde-
sirable with its obligation to want to "get well." And Maxim four seems reasonable,
but let us not forget that any imbecilic act is prohibited and supervised by people
surrounding the patient.

One criticism of Parsons's sick role is that there are limits to its application. It is
good for a person with an acute disease but not for a person with a chronic disease
(such as diabetes mellitus, hypertension, and arthritis). How do we think about the
patients with refractory and/or progressive diseases? Is there no hope? Parson's sick
role is not cut out for the patients with refractory and/or progressive diseases. Patients really want to "get well" as Parson's maxim three says, but maxim four never
will be completed. On maxim two, they don't make themselves be exempt from
mundane social roles, instead, taking normal social roles such as being a father or
mother and using it as motivation for struggling with their difficulties. As Parsons's
four principles of sick roll indicate, the life should totally change compared with before being sick. Patients' aims and finality should be transformed. Usually, a healthy
person has his/her finality from the healthy person's viewpoint. Being healthy and
free of illness is one of the popular wishes for a "normal" person. Being healthy is
so ordinary to many people, it's difficult for healthy people that health status is not
permanent. And they often have anxiety, complaint, and other negative feelings to
pursue their wishes and dreams. Based on the health state, many people struggle to
live. And the premise (i.e., healthy state) is never doubted. Getting a disease is a very
big rupture and it deconstructs all aspects of life without disease. Singular finality
decays and uncertainty emerges.

Here let's consider disease as an adorable dimple. The noun patient is a denom-
inative noun. This noun comes from the adjective word, "patient." Disease could be
regarded as some positive feature like dimples on one's cheeks. Being sick is not a role
but an "individual characteristic" or "personal quality." Not "disease" itself, but "life"
with disease should be regarded as respectable. Even though the concept of QoL has
gradually been accepted as an important therapeutic goal for chronic diseases in the
most recent two decades, there is some confusion in the procedures to measure QoL

Chapter 7   The Authentic Culture of Living Well

and the aim to measure QoL.

Measurement of QoL has been developed by psychometrician, so quantification is regarded as an important principle. And quantification leads us to focus on the "objective" aspect of life experience of patients. If QoL of patients' life should be grasped from their subjective sphere, then we would need another kind of methodology.

4.3. The person as a co-investigator in research

George A. Kelly published *The psychology of personal construct* in 1955. He assumed the human is a scientist. That means people seek to make sense of the world as we experience it by building and testing hypotheses about "how the world works." Then each person creates and maintains an individual way of interpreting the world. He called this individual frame of interpretation a personal construct. The personal construct system made by this empirical process was called a personality (Kelly, 1955). Inspired by the scientific exploration of Kelly's work, Hermans & Bonarius (1991) regarded the participants in psychology studies as "co-investigators." This means that the subject/participant should also be allowed to take a much more active role in psychological research. Between investigator and participant of intersubjective communication constructs of interaction, such a process of interaction should not be understood as the communication of the professional and the layperson (i.e., patient). This intersubjective interaction should be regarded as the coalition of two different kinds of the professionals; the researcher has specific knowledge, and the researchee is also a specialist who knows the special condition of his/her own self (Hermans & Kempen, 1993).

The Schedule for the Evaluation Individual QoL (SEIQoL; McGee et al., 1991; O'Boyle et al., 1992) which is one of the methods of measuring QoL, might be also influenced by Kelly's position. The SEIQoL is designed to measure three elements of QoL: (1) those aspects of life a person considers crucial to his/her QoL, which are elicited by means of a structured interview, (2) current functioning satisfaction with each aspect, (3) the relative importance of each aspect of QoL, which is measured by

163

Part 3   DEVELOPMENT OF TEM

deriving the weight the person assigns to each in judging overall QoL (O'Boyle, 1994). Actually, the investigator asks the question of participants, "What are the important 5 domains for your QOL?" in the administration manual (O'Boyle et al., 1995). The especially important one is the process where five QoL domains are nominated. When this measurement is carried out as Hermans and his colleagues say, the intersubjective conversation is composed between the patient and the investigator of the patient's QoL domains. The patient can nominate any situation as the content of own QoL-related item. The situation inevitably includes his/her value system, beliefs. And the item is useful for the investigator to understand that patient. Because the nominated item reflects the aspects of the patient's self. If "Health," "Family," and "The relationship with medical staff" are called QoL items, they reflect the patient's value system. In other words, the patient conveys individual QoL to the investigator, from the specialist of his/her own life. Then, the investigator could learn about patient through using SEIQoL (i.e., patient's illness, ordinary experience, and individual situation) from their narratives and dialogical conversation are not only good for measuring individual QoL but also knowing the individual meaning system. In addition, when the patient can't list five domains, the investigator gives examples from his/her experience and an existing domain's list. Just then, the patient becomes an investigator who researches for the domain that relates to individual QoL within him- or herself. The investigator will help to expand choices of the patient's QoL domains as a co-investigator, not for study but for the patient.

5. Theoretical implications

5.1. Epigenesis is not necessary for multifinality

Waddington (1956) had an interest in explanation of the linking of genetic and environmental factors in development. In Waddington's own words:

One can make a mental picture ... of development of a particular part of an egg as a ball

Chapter 7   The Authentic Culture of Living Well

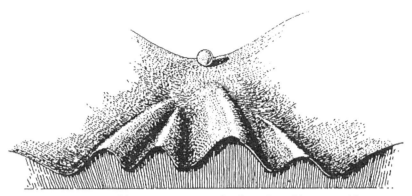

Figure 7.3. Waddington's "epigenetic landscape" (Waddington, 1966)

running down a valley. It will, of course, tend to run down to the bottom of the valley, and if something temporarily pushes it up to one side, it will again have a tendency to run down to the bottom and finally finish up in its normal place. If one thinks of all the different parts of the egg, developing into wings, eyes, legs, and so on, one would have to represent the whole system by a series of different valleys, all starting out from the fertilized egg but gradually diverging and finishing up at a number of different adult organs. (Waddington, 1966, p. 49)

Waddington's landscape (Figure 7.3) implicitly links to the increasing entropy. But in a human's life, some kinds of conversions appear. This is what we call equifinality points. Multifinality is not what Waddington suggested. His model's main character is a solid ball, which is a closed system. It never interacts with the surrounding field and never has the future perspective. The open-systemic nature of human is disregarded in Waddington's theories.

5.2. Multifinality from the perspective of life with illness

The notion of equifinality originates in Driesch's biological work. Driesch performed a series of experiments intervening with sea urchin cells during division and causing them to fragment. Instead of forming a partial embryo, Driesch found that the cells formed an entire one. Here the same final state may be reached from the dif-

Part 3   DEVELOPMENT OF TEM

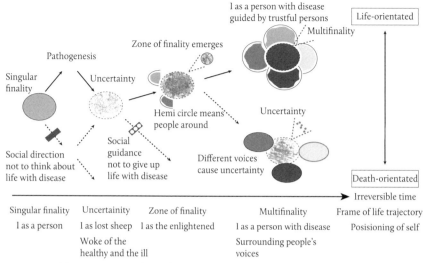

Figure 7.4. Hypothetical trajectories of intractable disease persons

ferent initial conditions and from different ways. This is what von Bertalanffy (1968) called equifinality. Despite Driesch's vitalist general philosophy, von Bertalanffy built his organismic perspective on the basis of the multi-linear developmental model along similar directions (Figure 7.4).

Life is ruptured when a person gets a disease. Singular finality is decayed and uncertainty emerges. Overcoming one's disease is the new aim and medical professions assist patients. It fits to treatable diseases. If patients recover fully, this story is not so bad. But, what if it is an intractable and/or chronic disease? From the viewpoint of patients, unclear prognosis image is formed (zone of finality), but this vague finality is repressed by clear finality derived from medical professions. Dominant messages from medical professions should be transformed into alternative massages from the perspective persons with disease. Some research on intractable disease patients has pointed out that uncertainty is the key notion of the state. In general, the well-planed equifinality point "A" disappears, then uncertainty emerges. The future is not clear. First, there is no voice to hear, then voices from medical professionals

Chapter 7   The Authentic Culture of Living Well

come next. Finally, many voices appear and make the person confused. Uncertainty reflects a complex process. However, the single finality from one voice is dangerous for the patients. Although multivoiced situations make patients confused, some other finalities should emerge. Multifinality is the notion for opposing the dominant story from the medical profession only. Multifinality ensures an atmosphere in which patients in the uncertain situation can select freely patients' own ways of living. Multifinality in one's own historical trajectory should not measure the variable in a person but should understand the whole person with illness.

The notion of multifinality in this chapter has two interwoven connotations. For understanding "QUALITY" of "LIFE" (Caution, it is not the abbreviation of QoL) with severe disease, we should distinguish different types of multifinality. Deconstructing the singular finality of the healthy person and reconstructing finality is a kind of multifinality. And constructing and differentiating the finality as a person with illness is another one. And an item-generating system for QoL such as SEIQoL is needed. In usual quantitative scales on QoL, items on the scales are provided from medical profession's perspective.

5.3. Multifinality as a spatial extension of finality

TEM is a new methodology derived from such a demand that is embedded in the context of ethnography. TEM has been developing for a few years quickly and the notion of multifinality is the brand new idea to depict the uncertainty of ongoing life. Social sciences, including psychology, benefit from utilizing the notion of multifinality because this can depict the emergence process of future perspective in the living. It's especially useful for treating the dynamic of living with disease. Parsons (1951b) proposed the sick role concept. "Being sick" is not simply a "state of fact" or "condition" (Parsons, 1951b). The sick person is exempt from normal social roles. Lacking a role means losing the guides from the world. An uncertain future emerges and then dialogical self occurs. Self struggles to encounter the promoter sign, which leads the sick person to certain future. Thick description of the lived life might be achieved by TEM with some notions such as Hermans's dialogical self and positioning. Dia-

Part 3　DEVELOPMENT OF TEM

logical self is the spatial extension of self. And Hermans clearly looked at the era of globalization. Researching the diversity of finality all over the world is a challenging task for cultural psychology. Hermans (2008) suggested that extension of the self in space leads to the study of the dialogical self as the interface of globalization and localization. TEM doesn't actually have the spatial viewpoint, but TEM can be applied to understand the different models of the sign in various cultures. The notion of multifinality brings us, especially people living and struggling with disease, such a new journey.

The restriction of activity resulting from illness causes the low QoL of patients and creation of alternatives leads to higher QoL of patients. The Schedule for the Evaluation Individual QoL (SEIQoL) stands on a constructive approach and is a tool for understanding the patient's QoL from the patient's perspective. Patients can decide their important domains for a custom-made QoL score. Constructing multiple QoL domains is really promising support for the patient. Family, medical professionals, and other people around the patient should bear such important task. TEM, from the perspective of time, and SEIQoL, from the perspective of place are both necessary for understanding the daily life of persons with disease. And the notion of multifinality bridges the time and place. The living experience of persons with illness should be understood from the perspective of chronotope and it means cultural psychology must open the door to new research and a new practice paradigm.

6. Concluding remarks

In cultural psychology, that general mechanism is found in the functioning of signs (semiotic mediation) (Valsiner & Rosa, 2007a, preface). Culture can be seen as a systemic organizer of the psychological systems of individual persons – culture "belongs to" the person. Again, culture "belongs to" each individual person. It is irrelevant that the persons "belong to" culture, ethnic group, or country, since culture is functioning within the intrapsychological systems of each person. Here culture is

Chapter 7   The Authentic Culture of Living Well

applied to an each subgroup of human being.

The person with a disease must be regarded as "having their own culture." Such a view brings the authenticity to the so-called "patients." In this chapter, we focused on the culture and/or meaning making of a person with illness. We proposed not to use the word "patient" because this is too often a medicalized word. This is because cultural psychology aims to describe the living person's life.

Social sciences, including psychology, benefit from utilizing the notion of multifinality, which makes it possible to depict the emergence process of future perspective in the living. TEM is the new methodology that is embedded in the context of ethnography. TEM has been developing for a few years quickly and the notion of dialogical self from Hermans makes it possible to understand the moment a healthy person confronts getting an illness. We should treat patients' lives within irreversible time from the ill perspective.

7. Future directions

In this chapter, we proposed to focus on life with illness (instead of patients' lives) as one of the forms of human life. And this leads to the construction of its own peculiar kind of culture. From the viewpoint of cultural psychology derived from the "sign" psychology of Vygotsky, culture is not necessary to hold the notion of actual time and actual place. The person is influenced by multiple signs of many "cultures." So we should focus the person to know culture within the person. Life with illness prepares to open the door to turn to a brand new form of cultural psychology. And its main premise is, "culture within person, not person within culture."

Appendix

Appendix 1

Historically Structured Sampling (HSS)

How can Psychology's Methodology Become Tuned in to the Reality of the Historical Nature of Cultural Psychology?

Abstract

Cultural psychology brings back to psychology the crucial role of history – which leads to the need for new methodology. Such methodology needs to fit the nature of phenomena – which in psychology are of open-systemic nature. Cultural phenomena are historical at all levels: personal (personal life histories), that of society (history of any given society) and at the level of the microgenesis of actions. Such historicity renders a number of habitual empirical practices – such as random sampling and generalization from samples to populations – inappropriate for science. Despite the tradition in psychology of that treats "random sampling" as normative for science, we show that it constitutes a conceptual dead-end street that moves psychology away from adequate strategies of generalization. Psychology at large can follow the lead of cultural psychology and look at individual cases as systemically organized within themselves, generalizing from such systemic organization of particulars to generic systemic models of the phenomena, with subsequent empirical testing of these models in selected new individual cases. We show the importance of the selection of individual cases for the study through consideration of their historical trajectories moving through a common temporary state (equifinality point). Some of these equifinality points are obligatory – set by the phylogeny of the species or by collective cultural construction.

Keywords

Historically Structured Sampling (HSS), Trajectory Equifinality Model (TEM), Ran-

Appendix

dom sampling, Equifinality Point (EFP), History

1. Historically Structured Sampling as a new innovation

In this appendix we propose the *Historically Structured Sampling* (HSS) – which is based on the acceptance of the *Trajectory Equifinality Model* (TEM) – as the core for the methodology of selection of the objects of investigation in psychology. This orientation grows out of our look at culture in psychology – especially as it brings to psychology the notion of history. The adoption of culture leads to the necessity to take a new look at some of the key methodological problems in the discipline (Valsiner, 2001a, 2003a, 2004). It is the systemic nature of human psychological processes that becomes highlighted by the re-insertion of cultural – higher psychological processes – into our models of the mind.

A major problem that blocks research in cultural psychology from developing new methodology is the issue of sampling. Sampling is an inevitable operation in any research project. Any research effort – unless it analyzes the whole realm of the given phenomenon – requires some way of sampling. Some specimens of the existing (known) pool of all specimens are selected – which means others are left out. The researcher generalizes from the studied specimens (sample) to all specimens (population) – and is likely to misjudge what is generalized as it is posited to be applicable to the non-studied cases. Yet, as we show, even moving the sample to cover the population is no automatic solution here.

1.1. The varieties of sampling

In existing methodological discourses, the notion of sampling takes a number of forms (see Table A.1.1).

As is obvious from Table A.1.1, different traditions in the social sciences have tried to modify the canonical version of sampling – that of random sampling – in ways that fit their epistemological goals (theoretical or representative sampling) or

Appendix 1   Historically Structured Sampling (HSS)

Table A.1.1. Different notions of sampling in the social sciences

Random	A sample of objects is selected for study from a larger group (called population). Each object is chosen by procedures that are designated to be random – it is "by chance" that the objects are selected. Each object in the population has an equal chance of being selected into the sample. Within that sampling mode sub-types exist: cluster sampling (population is divided into clusters, followed by random selection of the clusters), or independent sampling (samples selected from population are mutually free of affecting one another).
Representative	The act of selection is based on the proportional representativeness of the objects in the population. The sample includes a comparable cross-section of varied backgrounds that are present in the population. Sub-types are stratified sampling (first divide the population into sub-groups, then select from these groups) and matched sampling (each object in one group is matched with a counterpart in another).
Theoretical	The underlying theory if the researcher determines whom to select for the study. Our new introduction (HSS) belongs here.
Practice based	A practitioner – a clinical psychologist, teacher, nurse – who wants to do research on their field and experience treats his or her clients as research subjects. Ethical protections of subjects' rights are in place, but the agreement by persons to participate is set up within the field of their indebtedness to the researcher as the provider of some other practically needed services.
One-point break-through	Even if researchers hope to access the ideal kinds of subjects, exceptional circumstances and/or special conditions may prohibit that. In such case, the researchers struggle to access anyone who accepts the research proposal-literally fighting against tight access barriers. Undoubtedly such sampling is far from being "non-biased" or "random" yet there is no need to criticize such a sampling as "biased." Depending on the research theme, it's preferable to do something rather than nothing. And it may develop into a version of relational network based sampling as below.
Relational network based (i.e., the "Snowball Method")	The researcher engages the members of the first selected (and agreeing) participants to bring to the sample the members of their relationships networks. A crude sub-type is quote sampling (researcher may be given a "quota" of how many and what kinds of objects he/she needs to bring into the study.
Convenient	Researchers in university ask students to participate into their research. Cognitive psychologists like to regard them as adults and developmental psychologists like to regard them as adolescent. And comparative psychologists like to regard them human being. So university students are convenient samples of psychology studies.
Capricious	The researcher takes whoever happens to agree to participate.

175

Appendix

by giving particular practical means of finding research participants a fancy label (e.g., convenience, practice-based, etc.). That makes sense, since the belief in random sampling is nothing more than a belief – since in practice the randomness of any single choice (e.g., of a specimen from a population – to make a sample) is in principle impossible to ascertain.[1] Yet there is a bigger issue behind that practical impossibility of randomness of the "random sampling" – the role of the open-systemic phenomena in the selection schemes of sampling. The crucial issue for cultural psychology is whether any of the sampling schemes opens researchers' access to the phenomena of culture in psychological processes, or keeps these phenomena out of touch for the scientists. Psychology at large has been active in keeping researchers away from the crucial aspects of their phenomena (see demonstration in the case of personality inventories – Valsiner et al., 2004). But what is the situation in cultural psychology – the "up and coming" area in psychology (Cole, 1996)?

1.2. Culture as a problem for the social sciences

Culture is a historically emergent phenomenon. It emerged from the historical interchange of the species that was to become *Homo sapiens*, and the environment. In Max Weber's words,

> ... culture is a finite segment of the meaningless infinity of the world process, a segment *on which human beings confer meaning and significance*. (Weber, 1949, p. 81, added emphasis)

Weber's comment recognizes the unique, personal nature of experience that becomes organized by cultural tools – instruments and signs (semiotic mediators). It is the functional focus on cultural tools used within the psychological functioning of human beings that distinguishes cultural psychology from its cross-cultural cousin (see Valsiner (2003a) for elaboration of this distinction).

Our contemporary cultural psychology looks upon human psyche as social in its ontogeny and constructive in its microgenesis (Valsiner, 2000). Thus, cultural psychology is *necessarily a historical psychology* – and our current discourse about culture

Appendix 1   Historically Structured Sampling (HSS)

in psychology continues along the lines of *Völkerpsychologie* (Diriwächter, 2004), where the question of higher-level phenomena as those relate to the lower-level psychological functions was the central question. Relating of these levels when seen in time entails the synthesis of new (higher) levels, and de-differentiation (demolition) of previous higher structures. Emergence and dissipation go hand in hand in cultural organization of human psychological life.

The issue of how to make sense of part <> whole relationships that has haunted psychology all through its history re-surfaces in contemporary cultural psychology. In cultural psychology, it is that latter link – "vertical consistency" between general assumptions, theories, methods, and phenomena (Branco & Valsiner, 1997) that determines the adequacy of one or another look at sampling. We will first look at the traditional logic of "random sampling," and show that it misses precisely those aspects of systemic phenomena of cultural kind that cultural psychology studies. We then introduce another – theoretically based – notion of sampling – Historically Structured Sampling (HSS).

2. Design failures: "Blind spots" of "random" sampling

Despite use of the notion of population in our methodological discourse, there is a paradox – we talk about population as if it were fixed and finite (even if not possible to study, in full – for practical reasons), but in reality it is fluid, ever-changing, and infinite.[2] The population does not exist as a given – it develops as the specimens in it act, produce, reproduce, and change their own ways of being. Thus, in reality the conglomerate we call population is some collectivity of functioning systems that just "merely is" but exists in its own processes of movement – of the whole, and of its parts. The basic assumptions of systemic (in contrast with elementaristic) view on the phenomenon of "population" makes the difference in the ways the notion of sampling becomes crafted.

The traditional look at sampling is usually exemplified by the act of drawing

Appendix

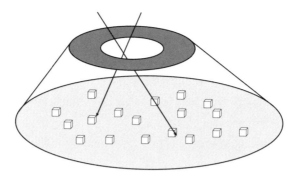

Figure A.1.1. A physical example of how sampling works in case of non-systemic phenomena

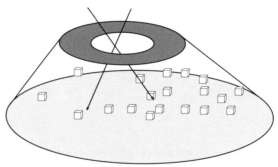

Figure A.1.2. A physical example of how sampling still works in case of non-systemic phenomena – unevenly distributed in the box

marbles from a box, at random (Figure A.1.1). It exemplifies the tradition of an atomistic world view where no systemic organization needs to be presumed. The objects to be sampled are assumed to be independent of one another, and of the context, and not possess any "counter-intentionality"[3] to the sampling efforts.

Given the surface of the box and the homogeneous nature of each of the marbles, each of them can be said to "have" equal probability of being drawn to the sample[4] – and hence any sub-group of the marbles drawn would provide evidence about the homogeneous category of these objects. This situation is still the same in case the marbles become unevenly distributed in the box (Figure A.1.2) – as long as they

Appendix 1 Historically Structured Sampling (HSS)

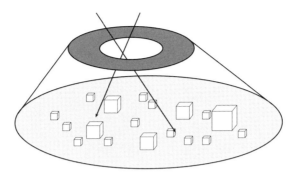

Figure A.1.3 A physical example of how sampling marginally works in case of non-systemic phenomena that form a quantitatively heterogeneous class

are homogeneous and the boundaries of the box ("search ground") are known, the sampling of the objects is sufficient for generalization from a homogeneous sample top homogeneous population.

The picture becomes complicated if the different specimens of the population vary quantitatively – while maintaining their homogeneous class nature in qualitative terms (Figure A.1.3). Some marbles are bigger; others smaller, the sample drawn from the box will be heterogeneous in quantity while still being homogeneous in quality.

Such separation of the qualitative and quantitative features of objects of investigation has been axiomatically accepted in psychology, and has made certain uses of statistical techniques (e.g., correlations – Valsiner, 1986b) possible. Yet this assumption is untenable – in any systemic phenomena, quality and quantity are directly mutually co-constructive – quantitative alterations lead to qualitative irreversible shifts (Prigogine, 1978, 1987).

Thus, traditional sampling as described in Figure A.1.3 misses the most crucial issue – that of systemic organization. Figure A.1.4 illustrates the case where different systemic linkages exist between the members of the population. Yet these links are not (yet) examples of systemic interdependencies. Rather, these are physical links. In the case depicted in Figure A.1.5, the traditional sampling that would create a

Appendix

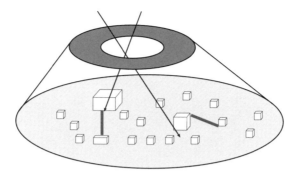

Figure A.1.4. An example of how sampling fails to work in case of non-systemic – yet linked – phenomena

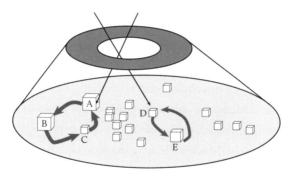

Figure A.1.5. An example of how sampling creates an error in case of treating systemic phenomena as if these were non-systemic objects

"sample" {A, D} is not representative of the systemic relations among the "members of the population" (systems A-B-C-A and D-E-D), but breaks down that functional systemic relation. Yet, without any doubt, all the "items" in the "box" can be viewed as detectable forms – like in Figure A.1.3. *The traditional sampling philosophy has the "blind spot" in axiomatically granted overlook of the interdependence of the elements in the field.* In other terms – sampling from an unknown "population" and hopes to generalize the results of the study to "the population" cannot answer any questions in cases where the phenomena need to be considered systemically organized.

Appendix 1   Historically Structured Sampling (HSS)

3. Why has the sample-to-population line of generalization survived?

Science is a social enterprise – and hence vulnerable to non-linear historical development. Technological progress does not automatically mean new breakthroughs in ideas, even if it may make such breakthroughs possible. The thinking in science is intellectually interdependent with the socio-historical context which the scientists inhabit (Valsiner, 2004; Valsiner & van der Veer, 2000). Even within the same historical period and within the same society, large differences exist between various disciplines in their way of generating knowledge.

The development of quantification of data in psychology is a good example of a search for precision that has ended in its opposite. In the name of consensually validated methods and data analysis techniques, the nature of phenomena has been lost from consideration (Cairns, 1986). Statistical methodology has re-directed the discipline in ways that have elevated methods to the status of theories (Gigerenzer, 1993) and led to the proliferation of pseudo-empirical research (Smedslund, 1995b). The "inference revolution" (dated approximately to 1940-1955 – Gigerenzer & Murray, 1987, Chapter 1) created a mono-vocal orthodoxy of the inferential techniques and introduced it as standard scientific practice in psychology.

One of the results of these social tendencies in mid-20th century psychology has been the loss of precision. This statement may seem paradoxical – given the multitude of numerical data presented in abundance in contemporary psychology journals. Yet precision is not in numbers but in what the numbers represent, and psychology's data have become largely unrepresentative of the phenomena they are derived from (Cairns, 1986). The result for knowledge construction is a conceptual dead-end street of contemporary psychology. It continues to be in a crisis – hence new areas of research – such as cultural psychology – may have a chance of restoring the phenomena <> data relationship for improved precision in our science.

Appendix

3.1. The self-constructed limitation of the social sciences

Above we have proven that sampling of specimens from population is based on premises that render the study of any structured systemic phenomena – of cultural and developmental kind – in principle impossible. Social sciences have moved into a dead-end street as they have, historically, tried to deal with the issue of multiple causality in phenomena. The roots of the notion of random sampling – uncontrollability of multiple assumed causes that operate within a population – creates the need for randomization of a sample selected from the population. It is based on the assumption of independence of the objects of sampling. In case of human populations the notion of randomness is misplaced – as it is applied to structurally interdependent human worlds (Shvyrkov & Persidsky, 1991).

4. Sampling in case of non-independent phenomena

The analysis above is still failing – we have not demonstrated how the philosophy of sampling of elements (of systemic units) also overlooks the autopoietic nature of the systems themselves. The systems are not "just there" to be found, and "collected" (Kindermann & Valsiner, 1989), but are self-organizing systems that develop in relation with the environment. Their survival depends upon that environment – and by their actions they change the environmental niche they inhabit (Odling-Smee et al., 2003). Hence an additional oversight is to treat the "sampling box" as if it is merely a "container" that keeps together the specimens to be sampled from (Figures A.1.1-A.1.5). Instead, the "box" is the environmental basis for survival and development (Figure A.1.6). It is the processes of development based on organism-environment relating that need to be sampled – not selected (and disconnected) surface outcome features of the specimens that have developed.

In the case depicted in Figure A.1.6, the traditional sampling – that would create a "sample" and later would make generalizing statements about "populations" – shows its fundamental misfit. The causal system that operates for the functioning

Appendix 1 Historically Structured Sampling (HSS)

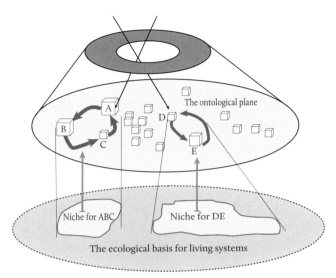

Figure A.1.6. An example of how traditional sampling bypasses the crucial feature of the living systems — interdependency with environments

and development of the discernible phenomena (A, B, C, D, E and others in Figures A.1.1-A.1.6) are not located at the plane of their ontological (manifest) level at all — but in-between the systemic organization (that can be detected at the manifest level) and the related plane of ecological basis for survival. Any analysis of the phenomena that transcends the immediate ontology of their being of some (or another) kind (category) needs to study (a) their systemic nature, together with (b) their functional relations with their ecological niches.

Living systems develop — and development entails creation of trails, life trajectories. So even Figure A.1.6 is limited — it shows the interdependency of the system and the ecological niche, *but not its history*. Yet it is the history that distinguishes the open-systemic phenomena from their closed-systemic or non-systemic counterparts. Thus, any study of human psychology (or sociology) is necessarily historical in its scope, if it is to maintain its focus on the issues the researchers declare to study.

We propose that the adequate sampling of the specimens of systems proceeds through the sampling of system-historical trajectories that include the past (retro-

Appendix

spective base), the present, and an analysis of the construction of the future trajectories. Any cultural system – be it personal or collective – can be understood only through its history.[5]

4.1. Systemic view: Axiomatic acceptance of interdependence

The interdependence of human psychological worlds is the axiom in cultural psychology – here sampling need not represent a population, but reflects the cultural histories of the cases studied. There is no value of taking any "random" set of individuals from population, since the individual cases are supposed to reflect the range of variation not in the population, but in the ways in which specific adaptations to concrete conditions exist. Thus, a new concept is proposed – *Historically Structured Sampling* (HSS). HSS utilizes the property of open-systemic phenomena – convergence at temporary equifinality points in their individual development.

5. Historically Structured Sampling (HSS): Selection by histories

The notion of HSS relies heavily upon the notion of equifinality that originated in the General Systems Theory (GST) of von Bertalanffy (von Bertalanffy, 1968). Von Bertalanffy pioneered the organismic conception of biology from which the GST developed. He regarded living organisms including human beings as not closed systems but open systems. Closed systems are considered not to depend upon their environments for their functioning. If phenomena in a particular science can be assumed to be of the kind of closed systems, the traditional sampling techniques (Figures A.1.1-A.1.2. above) would be sufficient and there would be no need for developing an alternative like HSS is. Yet no biological, psychological, or social system can be reasonably conceived as closed – hence the need for HSS.[6]

On the other hand, open systems receive information and interact dynamically or exchange with their environment. Taking the concept of the open system into his theory, von Bertalanffy (1968) outlined the principle of the equifinality as crucial for

Appendix 1   Historically Structured Sampling (HSS)

the open systems:

> In any closed system, the final state is unequivocally determined by the initial condition
> e.g., the motion in a planetary system where the positions of the planets at a time t are
> unequivocally determined by their positions at a time t_0 ... If either the initial conditions
> and or the process are altered, the final state will also be changed. This is not so in open
> systems. Here same final state may be reached from initial conditions and in different
> ways. This is what is called equifinality, and it has a significant meaning for the phenome-
> na of biological regulation. (von Bertalanffy, 1968, p 40)

The open-systemic nature of social and psychological phenomena has led to the need to consider complex events in their history. Sociologists' efforts at "event histo-ry analysis" (Blossfeld et al., 1989; Yamaguchi, 1991) and developmental psychology's look at person-context analysis (Cairns et al., 1996) are some of the existing recent ef-forts to move beyond the myopia for open-systemic nature in the traditional research habits.

5.1. Equifinality

Equifinality means that the same state may be reached from different initial conditions and in different ways in the course of time. We propose to call the trajec-tory model such a Figure A.1.7 as an Trajectory Equifinality Model. Equifinality is a general property of open systems. In the minimal case, the open systems dynamics entails the notion of individual trajectories (A and B) that may converge (at Equifi-nality Points; EFP), as in the Figure A.1.7. They may diverge after passing through the equifinality point – leading to further multifinality (see multifinality points in the Figure A.1.7).

It is important to emphasize that equifinality does not imply sameness – which is an impossible condition in any historical system. Rather, it entails a region of sim-ilarity in the temporal courses of different trajectories. It is only by our conventional use of language that we easily consider similarity to be sameness (Sovran, 1992) – a

Appendix

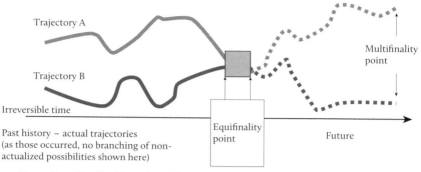

Figure A.1.7. **Equifinality point within irreversible time (past-to-future movement)**

move in language use that is unproblematic in the sciences where history is not relevant. In biology, psychology, sociology and beyond we only operate on the basis of functional similarities.

There are only two fundamentally general equifinality points in each human life that are universally shared by all (birth, death). But in most psychological studies, these two points may be not investigated too often. There is, of course, the possibility of looking at the pre-natal developmental trajectories as the antecedents towards the varied trajectories of post-natal development as an example of utilization of the equifinality point of birth for developmental research (see Hepper, 2003). Similar uses of the second universal equifinality points in psychological research is limited only to the trajectories of arrival at the equifinality point – the biological realities set severe limits on any further speculations.

The equifinality point is a "point in-between" – it is *both* a place for temporary similarity in the life courses of the systems, and a bifurcation point for further development. It plays the *central role in the selection of cases* of developing systems in case of HSS. Any psychological states and/or life events in what researchers have interest are structured historically. Of course the equifinality point is defined by specific parameters on what the investigator focuses. The researcher decides which aspects of the historically organized system are the objects of investigation – the EFP becomes a part of the conceptual scheme in the researchers' thinking.

Appendix 1   Historically Structured Sampling (HSS)

An example of equifinality point in human development is the case of infants'
beginning to walk independently. The usual – textbook – depiction of such deve-
opment is that of a linear sequence – infants begin to creep and crawl, then stand up
and begin to walk. However, this picture simplifies the complex reality of open systems – that develop by non-linear trajectories. The usual trajectory of development
of locomotion, it's not the only one (Valsiner, 2001b). As the work of Trettien (1900)
showed, there exists another (less frequently) trajectory. Some infants never creep
or crawl, but move from the sitting position to standing position, and from there –
to independent walking. And after beginning to walk, infants learn and acquire the
many way of locomotion. So independent walking becomes the equifinality point
en route to becoming an adult – both "crawling babies" and "sitting position babies"
will equally get their licenses to drive car – where sitting position suffices.

5.2. Obligatory passage points in the Trajectory Equifinality Model

There exist some additional basic concepts to depict this model. The model is
based on the assumption that all historical phenomena move in time on their unique
trajectories that at times converge at equifinality points. History occurs in *irreversible
time* and the varied trajectories may entail *Obligatory Passage Points* (OPP) – depicted
in Figure A.1.8. Irreversible time is the characteristic of real time never to repeat any
happening of the previous time period. Time flows from an infinite past towards an
infinite future (Valsiner, 2001b). Yet human being exist as finite organisms – living
from birth to death and creating their own personal lives through cultural means.

To understand the diversity of trajectory of development, it is important to
examine the passage points that lead to EFP. Then another concept is needed to understand the trajectory – passage points. Before reaching the EFP, people experience
many events and things. We call them passage points. Passage points are important
events for subjects (or informants). And they are always – not anytime – Bifurcation
Points (BFPs).

In this figure "the rectangle I" is the supposed EFP on what researchers focus in
their researches. For this EFP, there are many pathways to pass. "Ellipses B thorough

Appendix

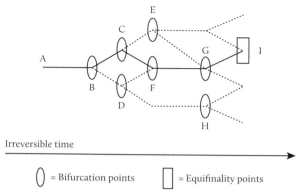

Figure A.1.8. Depicting the Trajectory Equifinality Model (modified after Valsiner, 2001b)

H" are BFPs in this TEM. We can call them passage points. Of course, many passage points are both EFP and BFP, but main EFP should be focused along researches' interests. Researchers can find many passage points. But no matter how many points we can find, the natures of all points are not equal. Some points are trivial, and the others are crucial. Some are inevitable, others suggested as if these were inevitable.

5.3. Obligatory Passage Points (OPP)

Latour (1988) came up with that concept in the context of the sociology of science. In our course of development there are two types of OPP, indigenous one and exogenous one. The former includes species-specific biological transition points – such as cutting of teeth in infancy, menarche, or menopause. The exogenous set up by the environment and/or custom. The cessation of menstruation in women at times of hardship ("war-time amenorrhea") is a result of environmentally produced transition phase. Adolescent initiation rituals that exist in many societies are culturally set exogenous OPPs. So is the obligatory formal schooling – children are sent to school as a socially set OPP that lasts for years.

By focusing the research theme, some points other than birth and/or death are found to be essential. For example, in the research of life course of infertility woman, hetero-marriage (whether legal or de-facto) is an OPP. Someone who never wants to

Appendix 1   Historically Structured Sampling (HSS)

make his/her own new family, infertility is a negative blocking biological factor that
disallows the move through species-specific (reproductive) OPP.

5.4. The practice of sampling: HSS

Up to now we have outlined the theoretical landscape for making sense of
cultural-psychological phenomena as open-systemic, multi-trajectory historical
processes. This only sets the stage for defining a fitting way to solve the problem of
sampling. Starting from the analysis of past trajectories of the personal life trajectories and their contextual structures at every EFP and BFP – seeing what OPP kinds of
demands existed at the bifurcation points – the researcher moves to select the participants on the basis of theoretically meaningful past histories. Note that all the persons singled out for study *are at the given moment in a similar state* (EFP), what makes
the difference is their past histories and their concrete organization (see contrast of
Trajectory A and Trajectory B in Figure A.1.7, above). Using various methods, these
past trajectories are analyzed for all potential participants in the investigation. Triangulation of methods is necessary. Preliminary open-ended questionnaire, intensive
interview data, historical knowledge, theoretical knowledge and even common sense
are all useful for empirical elaboration of the TEM as the basis for HSS.

Thus, OPP is the basic structure and/or canalization system of life trajectories
upon which our sampling technique – HSS – is set up. The act of HSS entails

(a) locating the relevant equifinality point (EFP) – as well as all relevant OPPs –
in the generic map of trajectories necessarily present for the generic system of
the processes under investigation (theoretically based activity),

(b) empirical mapping out all particular cases – systems open to study that move
through these points, and

(c) comparison of different actual trajectories as these approach to the equifinality point by superimposing onto each trajectory a pattern of theoretically
meaningful "range measure" – derived from (a) – that specifies whether the
given trajectory fits into the realm of selectable cases.

HSS thus maps the individual histories of particular systems onto the wider

Appendix

general system of possible trajectories of arrival at the equifinality point. HSS sets up contrasts between different trajectories – and between the same trajectory and its possible future under new OPPs beyond the EFP. It calls for an analysis of the sets of possibilities for the given system to proceed through, and sampling of that particular set out of all that are known, for further sampling of individual cases which have reached that selected point.

Such sampling of the cases – based on the past historic trajectory differences *that are currently absent* (all systems are in the same equifinality area at the time of sampling) is the opposite of traditional sampling of contrasting groups based on outcome data. In HSS the traditional notion of "experimental" versus "control" *groups* is not applicable. Instead, all the cases selected through HSS – who are currently in a specified similar EFP – can be contrasted with one (or more) *Virtual Comparison Condition* (VCC) – conditions which *clearly are absent now*, but which *could have been realistic had the persons involved at relevant BFPs in the past moved in different directions* than they actually did (see the example of coping with infertility, below). It is the personal history of not reaching the VCC state – contrastive state to the current actual EFP – that is relevant for the researcher who uses HSS. HSS operates with focusing on the contrast of what historically did happen, and what potentially could have happened – but did not.

HSS is thus capitalizing on the "life courses" of the objects of our investigation by selecting various cases on the basis of their movement through relations with environments. Yet it is not another label for life history – it is a technique of sampling for the study of some other – prospective – processes of cultural development that have not yet emerged. HSS may set the stage for prospective longitudinal observation of what would emerge in "natural contexts," or for a micro-genetic intervention experiment. Likewise HSS can be the basis for social intervention in a community (based on the HSS verified past movements in the community), and in clinical settings. HSS is a tool for researchers that replaces the reliance on the axiomatically accepted notion of "random sampling" in particular (as there is no "randomness" in history, but move from uncertainty to certainty) as well as the notion of "sample" as a

190

set out of a bigger set ("population"). HSS is based on different axioms than the ideology of "random sampling" – systemic and autopoietic nature of cultural phenomena, unique construction of life experiences in irreversible time, and relative structure of the landscape of life course (by structure of OPPs, and EFPs/BFPs).

6. Possible applications of HSS in research practices

Given the needs of cultural psychology, it is useful to understand the three levels of the process on the irreversible time; i.e., history, life course development and decision making. Three levels of organization of phenomena at which HSS is applicable are:

1. macro-genetic level – history of a society or social group, or institution
2. meso-genetic level – human individual life course development (ontogeny)
3. micro-genetic level – decision making in semiotically over-determined everyday life situations.

The application of HSS unites different levels. Thus, sampling by HSS takes place at one level, while the study to be conducted occurs at another. Thus, by selecting persons within a society that undergoes dramatic change (*macro*-genetic level HSS) it becomes possible to study ongoing *meso*-genetic (ontogenetic) level changes. Likewise, if HSS is made at the *meso*-genetic level (e.g., selecting persons of different life course trajectories, who have all reached the given equifinality point, e.g., have all reached a school, or an adolescent transition ritual place) the door is opened to the *micro*-genetic study of the relevant processes. The HSS *always occurs at one level more general than the actual study* for which the sampling is done, is to be conducted.

If one is to compare HSS with the traditional sampling procedures, the difference is in the acceptance of directionality of development in case of HSS. Different systems may be selected as examples of basically opposite movement at the more general (macro- or meso-genetic level) in order to test the properties of their further development at one level lower. Figure A.1.9 provides a generic example.

Appendix

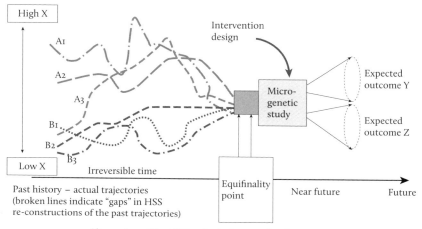

Figure A.1.9. The HSS as basis for a study of emergence

HSS leads to the selection if two sets of individual systems by their similar trajectories (A1, A2, A3 and B1, B2, B3) that all at the present time are located in the equifinality zone. All of these cases have been analyzed as to their past trajectories – and any reconstruction of this kind is uneven in its access to the life course as it actually happened. Yet it is documented how their ontogentic life courses fluctuated over time, on the dimension HIGH X <> LOW X. Even if the specific reconstructions of the past are vulnerable to selective recall and constructive confabulation, its directions between different BFPs can be ascertained.

Based on HSS, each of the selected systemic cases is subjected to a micro-genetic intervention procedure, the result of which is expected to be further life course trajectories in directions Y and Z. Such study entails the setting of new kinds of hypotheses of the kind – "GIVEN HISTORY {range A} and INTERVENTION Z the individual cases are expected to proceed in direction Z (or Y) with specifiable ranges of X." Note that what is absent in such hypotheses building is any notion of "control group" – since all hypotheses are to be tested within a single case, the trajectories discovered in the course of HSS operate as "control conditions." This orientation is analogous to behavioral single-case designs.

Appendix 1   Historically Structured Sampling (HSS)

7. How trajectories are made: The landscape model

Trajectories are possible only in models where time it retained. A point has no direction, a sequence of two points forms a line – which can be interpreted as having a direction – and becomes a trajectory. Not surprisingly, it is in the realm of developmental sciences – biology or psychology – that the notion of trajectories is theoretically important.

Trajectories can be posited without (see Figure A.1.9, above) depicting their generative context – or with it (see Figure A.1.6 above). The latter entail a field model where directional vectors (trajectories) are depicted within the context of a field parts of which they are. Perhaps the most widely known example of the latter is Waddington's (1956) classic epigenetic landscape model of the linking of genetic and environmental factors in development. In Waddington's own words,

> One can make a mental picture ... of development of a particular part of an egg as a ball running down a valley. It will, of course, tend to run down to the bottom of the valley, and if something temporarily pushes it up to one side, it will again have a tendency to run down to the bottom and finally finish up in its normal place. If one thinks of all the different parts of the egg, developing into wings, eyes, legs, and so on, one would have to represent the whole system by a series of different valleys, all starting out from the fertilized egg but gradually diverging and finishing up at a number of different adult organs. (Waddington, 1966, p. 49)

Waddington's interest was in the explanation of how biological organisms' morphogenesis takes place. After considerable search for a visual representation of that process (see Gilbert (1991), for a detailed history of his schemes), he ended up with a model as depicted in Figure A.1.10.

This model describes the nature of trajectories as diverging – the whole landscape broadens toward the end. This fits the biological differentiation of morphological structures (e.g., where the finally formed body parts do not "grow into" one

Appendix

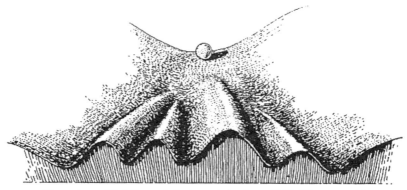

Figure A.1.10. Waddington's "epigenetic landscape" (Waddington, 1966)

another). From the viewpoint of HSS this landscape model is limited as it fails to include equifinality points (while being rich in bifurcation points).

If psychology or other social sciences were to consider an analog of his "landscape," both bifurcation and equifinality points need to be included. Furthermore, if the "ball" is the equivalent of the developing system in an open-systemic way, its relations with the landscape are not those of mere direction, but include mutually active role of both – the "ball" is "digging its way" thus making the valleys, while the system of existing valleys resists, and acts upon the "ball" attempting to direct it actively towards one or another location of "digging."

Given the absence of EFPs in Waddington's model, it represents only one example of trajectory-based theoretical thought in history of biology. Waddington's model serves merely as a reminder of a class of models that include the idea of trajectory but has no unification point for the sake of selection of developing systems for their baseline contemporary similarity.

8. Examples of empirical projects where HSS could be appropriate

Comparison of persons from different societies acquires a new meaning with

Appendix 1   Historically Structured Sampling (HSS)

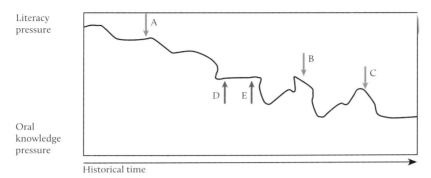

Figure A.1.11. Socio-historical pressures (arrows) upon the proportional prevalence of written (versus oral) transfer of cultural knowledge

the adoption of HSS. In terms of cultural histories, we look at the transition from the oral to the written literature traditions in the histories of two societies – Japan and Persia. Both – by the present time – have reached the equifinality point of the focus on the written literature in the formal schooling, yet by different historical trajectories if we take a historical view of a time frame of something like 2000 years.

Yet the different histories of the two societies lead individual persons of the current generation – while similar in their selected equifinality point (focus on written texts in formal education) – to different personal histories of arriving at that point, and different potentials for moving further ahead. In Figure A.1.11, the up arrow points the alleged position of the Japanese condition. In Japan, written literature prevails. But for example, present condition of Iran is different from Japan. Young adults (e.g., 30 year olds) in Iran can be expected to be much more familiar with oral literature (the down arrow) that their counterparts in Japan. This inter-societies difference can be found from looking at the cultural histories of each country prior to any study of any person in each. The continuity of the generic focus on oral <> written communication interchange in the histories of the societies sets up the expectations for what kinds of foci one can find within the persons of the current generation. However, the point of HSS is not to demonstrate that history of a society determines the mentality of its people. That would amount to linguistic/cultural determinism that

Appendix

has governed the thinking of social minds in the Occident (Valsiner & van der Veer, 2000).

The scheme (Figure A.1.11) shows how a society at different periods of time may prioritize the reliance of its members on written or oral communication of knowledge. This macro-sociological history can be plotted as to the proportions of oral/written transfer at different periods, with pressures towards increase in either the share of literacy (arrows A, B, C) or that of oral transfer (arrows D, E) at different times. For example, in the historical periods where main communication means were those of writing (and exchanging) paper-based documents, the pressures towards increased reliance on writing and reading can be observed. Thus, in the pre-Gutenberg era Europe, the majority of communication was based on oral communication channels. Together with the invention of the printing press that changed – and the additional social change of Lutheran Reformation delegating to the individual persons the most important communication task (i.e., that of communion with the God through reading the Bible by oneself) increased the pressure of the literacy to take over the dominant role from the oral knowledge transfer. Similarly, one may wonder if a reverse process is going on now in the 21st century – the age of cellular telephones, music-TVs, shredding machines, and saving knowledge in the virtual rather than physically tangible forms. Reading and writing becomes replaced by mouse-clicking, and relevant information on computer screens is no longer organized for reading, just for detection and reaction to pre-given choices.

Figure A.1.11 gives us a macro-historical background for HSS. Different persons within a society at the given time occupy different social role positions in relation to the oral/written literature relation – some (scholars) operate primarily within the written tradition, others (bards) – within the oral tradition. This would be similar for example both in Japan and in Iran in our time. Where the differences in the histories begin to play a major role is at the transition from the dominance of one to that of the other. Children entering formal education systems move from the dominance of one to the other. Their personal trajectories of the past encounters with the written and oral literatures can be found out from interviewing their caregivers when the

Appendix 1   Historically Structured Sampling (HSS)

children enter school. The results of such interviews will let the researcher chart out the systemic trajectories up to the selected equifinality point. So, here the HSS procedure makes use of two levels – macro-genetic (societies' histories) and ontogenetic (individual children's developmental trajectories). The study of the making of the future can now proceed at the micro-genetic level – as a kind of teaching/learning experiment in the classrooms. It is expected that the children – in the context of new literacy task – will bring their past personal-cultural histories to function as tools to adapt to the educational setting. For many of the Iranian children it may mean the need to confabulate – create oral "story" around a writing task. For many Japanese children, the way to handle the micro-genetic task may reflect their pasts.

Yet children do not just follow the guidance of the past – they re-construct it, and do it largely by acting in some form of contrast to their pasts. Resistance to learning can lead to learning (Poddiakov, 2001), or – work on one's deficiencies can leads to over-compensational excellence in precisely those areas. Hence the HSS leads to the possibility to study individual cases whose personal histories differ cardinally from the others in the same category. For instance, some children in Japan may have "Iranian-like" personal-cultural histories when it comes to the uses of literacy texts, and some Iranian children would have histories similar to those of Japanese children. These single cases – let us call them "cross-over cases" – are identified by HSS and can be studied in the micro-genetic procedure.

From the individual's perspective, we can consider two historical trajectories in different societies. We – human beings – cannot choose the birthplace. It's very first point, any baby enters the realm of oral communication – people around him or her making speech sounds that only slowly begin to make any sense. But, suppose that one baby is in the "oral transfer of knowledge" dominant society and another is in the "written transfer of knowledge" dominant society. So, babies in the former society tend to be in the oral communication culture and babies in the latter society tend to be in the oral communication culture. It's important for us to recognize that both oral and literal societies are equally equivalent for babies. We should not order the two societies – sure, in Figure A.1.11 we depicted the literal society might be superior

197

Appendix

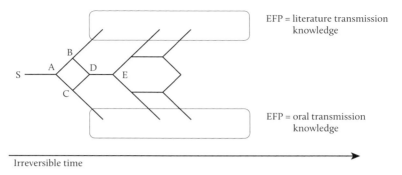

Figure A.1.12. **The system of polarized EFP for the case of people in-between the Oral and Written texts-dependence context – and the system of trajectories**

than oral society, but it reflect the developing order of two ways of communication. If one baby is born in the perfect oral communication society and is not promoted to study literacy, it doesn't mean his/her inferiority. We can set up the EFPs on the communication style such as oral and literary in our theoretical schemes, but these are both usable by people in their everyday lives. We may also call them as *Polarized Equifinality Points* (P-EFP). P-EFPs operate in "doubles" – they unite the opposites between which the developmental or historical processes proceed – guided by the promotional field one level more general that the phenomena under investigation.

Obviously, babies are not ready for written communication right after their birth. At the first bifurcation point "A," some go up to "B" where "written transfer of knowledge" dominates in the society, and the others go down to "C" where "oral transfer of knowledge" is dominant. In the former, children may start to learn reading and writing even at the kindergarten. In the other, they might start it late – if at all. After all, human cultural transfer occurred in pre-literate societies as well as literate ones – albeit with different role played by memory functions (Vygotsky & Luria, 1993, Chapter 2).

In Figure A.1.12, "D" is the supposed Obligatory Passage Point (OPP) of entering elementary school. Many societies today force children to go to elementary school. "E" is another BFP. One child may quit to study at school in "written transfer of

Appendix 1   Historically Structured Sampling (HSS)

knowledge" dominant society because of one's health problem. And another child in "oral transfer of knowledge" dominant society should quit the studying because of one's gender. For instance, girls have been underrepresented in formal schooling contexts in many societies – while women's role in the informal education context in any society has been central.

8.1. Re-considering ontogeny of tactile contact

We can consider a classic "intervention design" known in child psychology – the role of extra tactile contact between mothers and newborns in further development of the infants. In the usual habit of psychology, studies in child psychology have focused on something considered as "independent variable" at time t_0 as "having an effect" on some "dependent variable" at t_1. For example, Klaus & Kennell (1976) were pioneers of claiming the importance of early mother-baby tactile contact for later development. Yet such selection of "independent" and "dependent" variables denies the systemic organization of development both before the earlier antecedent condition (increased tactile contact) and from the experiences within the interval until the "dependent variables" were investigated. The act of giving mothers and newborns more time (than U.S. pediatric wards allowed in early 1970s) to sleep with one another cannot in itself operate as any "independent variable" to which causal properties can be attributed. Instead, it is a newly introduced life course event – a short period of stability of contact – that is part of the history of the life course – an equifinality point (or period) – for all the mothers and babies included in the Klaus & Kennell research program. Correlational analysis of finding relations between the "earlier" and the "later" indicators at the level of the sample do not represent the life course processes that are taking place. The "effects" of neonatal tactile contact are of systemic kind – instead of one form of such possible "effects" there are at least five possible ones (see Blossfeld & Rohwer, 1997, p. 368). Any correlational (or regression)-analytic finding of "an effect" is completely blind to which of these 5 (or other possible) forms of these "effects" might be in place. The early mother-child bonding hypothesis is one of many mythical hypotheses that proliferate in psychology – sup-

Appendix

ported by the common sense ideology that guides psychologists' thinking. Actually, Klaus & Kennell's early bonding hypothesis had not been borne out by subsequent research. So they changed their view (Schaeffer, 1998) – instead of assuming a single process (tactile contact –> future positive development) they accepted the dynamic and systemic nature of the "tactile effects."

How would the Kennel & Klaus research tradition fare from the perspective of HSS? Their intervention – provision of extra tactile mother/baby contact opportunity – introduced an EFP to all of the participants in the "experimental groups." In contrast, the "control groups" – mother-baby pairs without such event – did not share any pointedly similar experience. The personal life histories of each mother and her baby – if analyzed in terms of the trajectory through pregnancy and birth process – would be the basis for our HSS effort. The follow-up of each mother/baby pair after the extra tactile contact would entail an analysis of other relevant life course episodes in the subsequent lives of the mothers and babies: processes of breast-feeding, processes of exploration of the environment in toddlerhood, etc. The comparisons between individual cases would be made based on the distinctions of their HSS trajectory histories (see Figure A.1.9, above). The "control group" – where mothers and babies were *not* subjected to the extra tactile contact – would be irrelevant for the analysis of the construction of further trajectories *given* the EFP experience. Through HSS, the differences of the life histories that led to EFP are expected to make further difference – not the presence *versus* absence of the EFP at the given time.

Our example here illuminates a more important general point. In the strategy of conventional psychology tends to regard *attributes* of subjects (or informants) as important for the generalization of results. "Controlling" the variables such as nationality, sex, age – and many others – is expected to guarantee the objectivity and/or validity of the research. Yet no researcher can actually "control" psychological "variables" since those have auto-regulatory properties – the person acts in ways that neutralize or resist the efforts of the researcher to systematically vary the "variables." Some of the features referred to as "variables" in psychology are merely indices of

Appendix 1   Historically Structured Sampling (HSS)

fixed *status quo* – so, gender (male/female) is not controllable by way of experimenter's intervention, but only in a manner of speaking (recognizing existing gender differences). Interestingly, the notion of "controllable variables" is easily generalized in the minds of researchers – these "variables" become freed from their contextual dependencies, and of the time.

Using the HSS, wartime can be the point of sampling and we can see the diversity of trajectories which subjects experienced at this equifinality point with unraveling the interaction between human and environment. Here we can see the covariation pattern or configuration of cultural variables (Kojima, 1997 p. 318). Such covariation does not reveal causes of development (which are systemic) but allows for an overview of the high variety of forms in organism-environment relations.

Contemporary life-course sociology provides examples of equifinality points in the social domain (economic depression, war) that are inevitable for people (especially young people) to move through in their development. Because of human beings as an open system interact with their environments, sometimes almost all people in same environment were affected one big event such as a war and disaster. The experiences of such an equifinality point are similar (not same) in almost all people, but the influences tended to be different (not similar). As Shanahan et al. (1997) pointed out that, in biology and psychology, interest in time had been limited to a concern for development as "temporal accretion" or "critical periods." If we use the concept of equifinality to describe the interaction of people in any age with social events, it is possible to understand diversities in people in any age. Essentially, equifinality point is also a bifurcation point – for anything that is to come in the move from the present to the future (e.g., through interventions – Figure A.1.9, above).

8.2. Same event – different personal experiences

It is also an example of meso-genetic HSS that the different levels of ontogenetic development can operate as "trajectories" of entrance to the same life experience – but from different perspectives on the life-world. Lev Vygotsky's example – from his clinical experience – of the same episodic event (mother's drunken state) being

Appendix

experienced by her three sons is an example of how HSS can be used in the system of interrelated systems (within a family):

The essential circumstances were very straightforward. The mother drinks and, as a result, apparently suffers from several nervous and psychological disorders. The children find themselves in a very difficult situation. When drunk, and during these breakdowns, the mother had once attempted to throw one of the children out of the window and she regularly beat them or threw them onto the floor. In a word, the children are living in conditions of dread and fear due to these circumstances.

The three children are brought to our clinic, but each of them presents a completely different picture of disrupted development, caused by the same situation. The same circumstances result in an entirely different picture for the three children.

As far as the youngest of these children is concerned, what we find is the commonly encountered picture in such cases among the younger age group. He reacts to the situation by developing a number of neurotic symptoms, i.e. symptoms of defensive nature. He is simply overwhelmed by the horror of what is happening to him. As a result, he develops attacks of terror, enuresis and he develops a stammer, sometimes being unable to speak at all as he loses his voice. In other words, the child's reaction amounts to a state of complete depression and helplessness in the face of this situation.

The second child is developing an extremely agonizing condition, what is called a state of inner conflict, which is a condition frequently found in certain cases when contrasting emotional attitudes towards the mother make their appearance ... ambivalent attitude. On the one hand, from the child's point of view, the mother is an object of painful attachment, and on the other, she represents a source of all kinds of terrors and terrible emotional experiences ... The second child is brought to us with this kind of deeply pronounced conflict and sharply colliding internal contradiction expressed in a simultaneously positive and negative attitude towards the mother, a terrible attachment to her and an equally terrible hate for her, combined with terribly contradictory behaviour. He asked to be sent home immediately, but expressed terror when the subject of his going home was brought up.

... the third and the eldest child presented us with a completely unexpected picture. This child had a limited mental ability but, at the same time, showed signs of precautious maturity, seriousness, and solicitude. He already understood the situation. He understood

Appendix 1 Historically Structured Sampling (HSS)

that their mother was ill and pitied her. He could see that the younger children found themselves in danger when the mother was in one of her states of frenzy. And he had a special role. He must calm his mother down, make certain that she is prevented from harming the little ones and comfort them. Quite simply, he has become the senior member of the family, the only one whose duty it was to look after everyone else. (Vygotsky, 1994, pp. 340-341)

While Vygotsky himself found the situation of all three children traumatic (which it obviously was), here we can look at the example as an extension of the usefulness of meso-genetic HSS. By sampling of families of multiple members – children, or other adults (in extended families) – the researcher can investigate the contrasts between mutually connected parts of the social organism (system), where the personal histories of each member are known. Life course sociology does not maintain this kind of systemic unit, but separates the persons of different backgrounds into traditional "samples" that go through similar experiences. However, in terms of cultural psychology, these experiences are personally constructed – on the basis of the shared social history.

8.3. An example at the micro-genetic level

HSS is useful for using the decision making process of the subject in the life course in the past to study the re-construction of the future. Yet the HSS perspective transcends the decision-theoretic legacy of psychology in two ways. First – most of psychological works treat the "one shot" decision only. Even if process is being emphasized – such as in Cognitive Dissonance Theory (Festinger, 1957) – the decision making process remains a "one shot" deal, not a trajectory of decisions in a sequence.

The reason why dissonance *after* a decision has been made should be focused upon is needed as we look at the life processes at large that cannot be reduced to the episodes that Cognitive Dissonance Theory covers. So people after decision must cope with cognitive dissonance, but actually in daily life situation, not so little people try to re-make the previous decisions. Everyday life situation is under redundant

Appendix

control mechanism (Valsiner, 2001b), so decision making tends to be semiotically over-determined. In addition, we have many things to decide to do or don't – everyday decisions are of the kind of a sequence of ill-defined problems one feeding into the next. They are not independent, discrete problems that have simple solutions – each solution feeds forward to the emergence of a new problem.

Ironically, the stronger the exogenous settings (institution, custom and so on) are, the weaker people feel the pressure to make decisions. Entering to primary school is one of the examples. Contemporary citizens never bother whether they make children enter the primary school or not. But in everyday life situation, we have some kind of "degree of freedom" for decision making – "do or don't? If do, when and how?" For example, mothers may bother that when do they start to give pocket money to their children.

9. Culture and personal life trajectories

Our introduction of HSS as a tool for investigation leads to selecting persons who face sequential, interdependent decisions – such as young women's decisions how to wear makeup. The act of changing the appearance of the face has long history in culturally symbolic body painting and the making of ritual masks. These cultural-historical forms set the stage for our contemporary cosmetics use practices that function for beautification purposes.

Here it would be fitting to mention recent studies using the HSS and the equifinality trajectories idea (Sato, Yasuda et al., 2004). Yasuda (2004) approached the infertile experiences of married women in Japan looking at their reconstructed histories of moving between the P-FEP containing FERTILITY and INFERTILITY as the two opposites within the same whole. Because it's very difficult for graduate students to recruit such participants, all but one were recruited at the internet BBS of an association of adoption. The restriction of participants recruit method is not considered a "sampling error," but a part of the HSS that is determined by the partic-

Appendix 1   Historically Structured Sampling (HSS)

ipants themselves (their motivation to participate in the study on the topic of their life course desire – getting children).

First, Yasuda (2004) ambiguously treated the infertile experiences as the EFP. But the restriction of participants made her to focus on the two polarized results of infertile experiences, i.e., couple with children and couple with out children. In this study, equifinality point is not necessary defined a one single point. If a researcher tries to investigate the married women's TEM by HSS, both having children and having no children should be considered as equivalent equifinality points. And there are different trajectories for equivalent equifinality points. We again call such equifinality points as equivalent and/or polarized equifinality points. EFP depends on the researchers focus. If one wants to investigate the stability of marital couple's life, the presence or absence of children is only one of the passage points and other EFP should be set.

After setting up the polarized EFP for her study, Yasuda (2004) highlighted different OPPs in the field. The first OPP is the point when infertility treatments couple be aware of the adoption system as a solution that they could use. Yet that is an exclusive option – persons who expect to adopt must quit the infertility treatments in Japan. So this is the second OPP. The association of adoption recommends the couples to give up the infertility treatments before engaging in the adoption procedure. So the stopping the infertility treatments are "institutionalized" OPP for adoption.

Here, EFPs and OPPs were hypothetical ones. She conducted the semi-structured interview with participants. Participants were nine cases (six females and three couples). After writing down the transcripts of 9 records, Yasuda analyzed the transcripts of the oral narratives that were obtained by the interview. So she could get the 9 life stories about the women with infertility treatments. She struggled to map the events and psychological status of 9 participants with irreversible time. The network of trajectories for all nine cases are in Figure A.1.13. Even though medical definition of infertility is rather difficult to prove – it is a diagnosis based on documented non-happening of something expected (pregnancy), once people are conscious about that label, they usually reflect upon it through two options – "Let it be" or "try infer-

Appendix

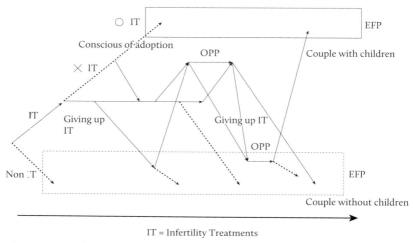

Figure A.1.13. Observed trajectories in 9 women moving towards the EFP of having children in contrast to not having children

tility treatments." So they see it as a bifurcation point for their life course.

This look at the multitude of possible and actualized trajectories makes it possible to understand the trajectory of infertile experiences from the viewpoint of persons who chose the infertile treatments and took the adoption into consideration. Both "being conscious of infertility" and "taking the adoption into consideration" are not only personal experience but historically structured ones. Actually, this figure looks different from deductively derivable formal models of trajectories unfolding within the field of P-EFP {FERTILITY <> INFERTILITY}. Yet it reflects the real trajectories of movement of the women who were involved in the study. In this figure, solid lines express the possible and real courses. And dashed lines expressed possible (supposed) but not captured this research.

If the picture in Figure A.1.13 – depicting different ontogenetic trajectories of the Trajectory Equifinality Model – is used as a basis for HSS, one could study women of different trajectories – those of direct and repeated efforts towards arriving at fertility (repeated infertility treatments), and others with "up-and-down" trajectories (still ending up in efforts of child-bearing). It would be reasonable to expect that any

206

Appendix 1   Historically Structured Sampling (HSS)

micro-genetic next event in their life course – for instance, their personal ways of relating to next episode of infertility treatment – would be organized differently by way of their personal cultures (Valsiner, 2000).

10. General conclusion

In any psychological research effort, sampling is inevitable. Actually, many kind of sampling methods are used in psychology. We have expanded the notion of sam-pling to include its historical-developmental version – HSS. It is an alternative to the usual way of random sampling.

The difficulty of random sampling had been elaborated in this appendix. Its reliance on the assumed "randomness" of the singular acts of selection of persons from population into "samples," and its in-built overlook of the person-environment interaction (Figure A.1.6, above) are sufficient reasons to refrain from using such sampling techniques in cultural psychology. However, after demonstrating the misfit of the traditional technique we needed to develop a more promising alternative – and our notion of Historically Structured Sampling (HSS) is meant as such. Aside from being open to history and uniqueness of the life course, it is also an example of theoretically based sampling. Psychology at large has moved away from theory-based empirical efforts – much to its epistemological detriment. Our hope is that HSS in cultural psychology will restore the centrality of theory.

There are also practical matters. In any real – life situation where the investiga-tor operates, access to the phenomena is institutionally constrained. The researcher may be in a position of not just being unable to choose the participants – but even not choose the institution where the potential participants are socially embedded. If researcher wants to enter one high school, it is not the researcher but the high school administrator – teacher or director – who makes the decision. The strategy of HSS may render this obstacle less dangerous to research – even if one high school rejects the research; another school may help the researchers to study. Sampling like this is

Appendix

not random, but not capricious. From the perspective of HSS, any school of similar background constitutes a EFP. So it's worth studying whenever the access is possible. Contrasting such study with a study involving a large number of college student questionnaire responses is not worthwhile. Sampling such large study is convenient and capricious – and far from the unreachable traditional ideal of "randomness."

Furthermore – a person is not the pile of traits, or an automation that provides answers to vaguely formed items of personality questionnaires and surveys. A human being – or a social group, or community – as an open system lives with cultural historical events. In its history different potential events might happen (at bifurcation points), but are either made not to happen, or they just do not happen. The focus on HSS brings into our empirical research practices a contrast much discussed by philosophers, but not implemented in empirical research – between potential events and actual events. HSS is based on the contrast of the real (what did happen, in the past) and the functional non-real (what could have happened at the particular bifurcation points, but did not – White, 1972).

How will cultural psychology's knowledge base be improved by use of HSS? We think HSS will have a couple of implications like as Freud's theory has at least three implications to psychiatry, psychology and our life – aetiology of mental disease, therapeutic method and the theory of human development. The HSS should be the theory for sampling in psychology – by integrating the three levels of historicity, i.e., macro-, meso-, and micro-geneses. It lives up to the general claim that psychological systems can be studied only through the history of their emergence and trajectories to the present state. Depicting the TEM makes us possible to grasp the trajectory with irreversible time.

Lastly the HSS – based on TEM trajectories – helps the researcher to identify the persons who are involved in important life decisions. Consider the sorrow and/or trouble of a mother of mildly mentally handicapped children. She could select the "normal" class or "special" classrooms as her EFP for the child's education. She may have selected the latter, but has been worrying about ever since. The HSS based research helps psychologists to advise such mother to mitigate her sorrow and/or trou-

Appendix 1   Historically Structured Sampling (HSS)

ble. Because, either "normal" or "special" classroom ought to lead anyone to same equifinality points later on. HSS allows to see different historical opportunities for further development beyond each EFP. Similarly to the service to parents, HSS based knowledge would support the special education teachers to arrange the environment differently for children of unusual pasts at the equifinality points.

The HSS trajectory need not assume linearity and/or uni-dimensional nature of the life course. Although the HSS started from the criticism to sampling method of developmental psychology, the developmental theory derived from the HSS have a power to change the epistemology of developmental psychology. HSS restores the central role of time – duration of life forms – to the study of social and psychological systems. Behavior of such systems – in the widest sense – is only understandable as the history of such systems – a point made in the 1920s by the Russian paedologist Pavel Blonskii that fascinated Lev Vygotsky but failed to gain ground in psychology in subsequent decades. Perhaps we are now in an OPP for the social sciences to consider the historicity of the phenomena we study in an internally coherent way – rather than follow the preaching of missionaries for the "right methods" in science. The latter are normative claims – basically power assertions – which may lead psychology astray in its complicated efforts to make sense of human beings.

Acknowledgments

The authors are grateful to the Ritsumeikan Uiniversity for bringing the first author to Kyoto in February 2004 for a series of seminars in cultural psychology, within which the idea of HSS was collectively conceived. Discussions in the "kitchen seminar" at Clark on October, 20, 2004, and feedback from Wolfram Fischer, Alexander Poddiakov, Emily Abbey, Roger Bibace, Tania Zittoun, and Nandita Chaudhary is gratefully acknowledged.

Notes

1) Randomness of series of numbers can be mathematically determined – but statements about randomness (or non-randomness) of each single number in the series cannot (see Chaitin, 1975). Social scientists' sampling efforts are necessarily single decisions – take X rather than Y or Z at time t, and thus cannot be random, even

Appendix

if "randomization machines" like tossing coins, using random number generators, etc. are practically used in the sampling process.

2) The traditional statistical inference philosophy recognizes the unknowability of the "hypothetically infinite population" but *considers it to be stable in its infinity*. That legitimizes the notion of getting to know it through random sampling techniques (Gigerenzer & Murray, 1987, p. 15) and the reliance on the "law of large numbers." In contrast, *if the infinite nature of population is assumed to entail any form of change of the whole population*, random sampling would lead to creation of systematic artifacts.

3) The ideas of sampling do not consider the prerogatives of sampled subjects to refuse to participate, or to undermine the investigation by way of self-presentational or any other intentional goal.

4) Note the attribution error in this way of phrasing the issue – the language use implies some property that is inherent in *each* of the marbles, while the actual outcome of being selected (or not) depends fully on the interaction of the selected marble and the field.

5) Here we paraphrase the point emphasized by Lev Vygotski – after his fellow paedologist Pavel Blonski – behavior can be understood only as history of behavior (van der Veer & Valsiner, 1991).

6) It is important to note that the decisions whether a given system is "open" or "closed" is an axiomatic one – where the centrality of the basic assumptions and phenomena connection in the methodology cycle (see Branco & Valsiner, 1997) is crucial.

Appendix 2

Brief Practice for Using Trajectory Equifinality Model (TEM)

As a General Tool for Understanding the Human Life Course within Irreversible Time

Keywords

Trajectory Equifinality Model (TEM), Equifinality Point (EFP), Historically Structured Inviting (HSI), Bifurcation Point (BFP), Polarized EFP (P-EFP), Obligatory Passage Point (OPP), Social Direction (SD), Social Guidance (SG), Dialogical Self (DS), Irreversible time, Second EFP, Second P-EFP, TEM saturation

Trajectory Equifinality Model (TEM) is a part of the broad scheme of the Trajectory Equifinality Approach (TEA). In appendix 2, we focus on brief advice for using TEM (not TEA) as a methodological tool for understanding the human life course, as TEM is a promising method to better elucidate the process (not structure) of human life experience within irreversible time.

TEM is a method to describe the life course of individuals within irreversible time. Through this method, researchers decide which important events in the life course are Equifinality Points (EFPs) *for researches*. At the beginning of a study, an EFP is conceptualized as a focused question in which the researchers have interest. TEM is a kind of innovation that allows for the expansion of research themes in psychology. Anything of interest can be chosen for pursuit (e.g., entering/dropping higher education, infertility experience of married women, decision about abortion

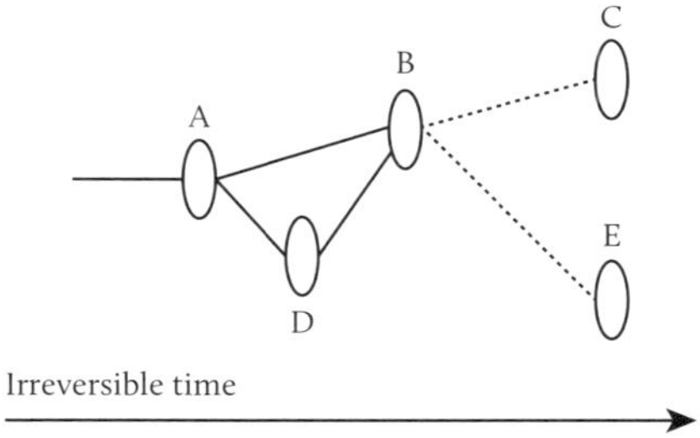

Appendix

C
B
A
E
D

Irreversible time

A = BFP; finishing middle education
B = EFP; entering higher education
C = finishing higher education in future
D = working after middle education
E = drop out from higher education

Figure A.2.1. Bifurcation and equifinality in educational trajectories

made by high school students, an occasion for authentic reflection by a delinquent adolescent, decision to study abroad, etc.).

After determining the EFP of focus, individuals who have experienced the specific EFP are invited to participate in the study, which is a procedure termed Historically Structured Inviting (HSI). EFPs can be thought of as a kind of research focus and viewpoint of *inviting research participants*. Following invitation, participants construe their life courses with selecting one possible option from other available options. For example, after completion of middle education, some individuals may wish to enter higher education, and others may desire employment (Figure A.2.1). After entering college, some may drop out. Conversely, those that worked directly after middle education may decide to enter the university after five years of employment. In such imaginary cases, personal will should be regarded as a cultural phenomenon, not as an individual or rational phenomenon. Higher education should have many trajectories ultimately leading to entrance. Using the conceptual tools of TEM, completion of middle education would be considered a Bifurcation Point (BFP), and entering higher education would be set as an Equifinality Point (EFP).

When describing the TEM, Polarized EFPs (P-EFP) should be set so that the model avoids evaluation of the life course. The dimension of EFPs (EFP and P-EFP)

212

Appendix 2 Brief Practice for Using Trajectory Equifinality Model (TEM)

Figure A.2.2. Describing life trajectories in 2 dimensions: EFP and P-EFP construct another dimension

is practically useful for setting the orthogonal dimension within irreversible time (Figure A.2.2).

1. Research using TEM: Simple practice on TEM

TEM is a kind of collaborative framework, similar to Linux. It can be used without permission *with reference* to create new researches. The most important thing is to "Use two dimensions dynamically!" Researchers should consider complimentary classes when considering EFPs of focus. P-EFPs is the preferred method for treating complimentary classes of EFPs. Both EFP and P-EFP can create a vertical dimension within TEM.

Research practice utilizing TEM is an adventure into the synthesis of ideas within the field of cultural psychology. TEM is not a "technique" for research, but rather a series of activities to observe and understand the interactions between the individual and outer world. Hearing and observing one's life with his/her chronotope (time and place) is important, and understanding and describing the uniqueness of his/her life with using the basic notions of TEM is important. Below, the simple version of TEM practice is outlined.

Appendix

2. Steps in using TEM for single case example

1) Define a relevant EFP, and think about its complementary set as a P-EFP. Invite individuals that have experienced the EFP.
2) Find the "turning point" experience, activated by the promoter sign. This can be considered an "aha" experience.
3) Record some important experiences (turning points) relative to the EFP sequentially on a timeline. Here it is not necessary for two dimensions to be used.

Figure A.2.3. Putting events on one dimensional time line

4) Explore the historical trajectory relative to the EFP, using the vertical dimension. Find the one important contingent event, and assume it as the starting point.

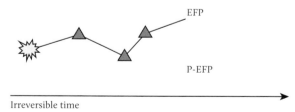

Figure A.2.4. Using vertical dimension for creating a trajectory

5) Redefine the experiences as Bifurcation Points (BFP) and draw dotted lines, if possible.

Appendix 2   Brief Practice for Using Trajectory Equifinality Model (TEM)

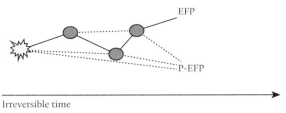

Irreversible time

Figure A.2.5. Visualizing possible and impossible trajectories

6) Identify the Obligatory Passage Point (OPP) in the map of trajectories of the process.

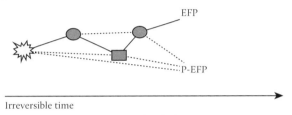

Irreversible time

Figure A.2.6. Identifying OPP

7) Analyze the relationships at each point with using "Social Direction (SD)," "Social Guidance (SG)," and "Dialogical Self (DS)."

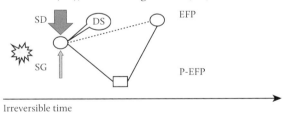

Irreversible time

Figure A.2.7. Focusing a BFP: Finding social direction, social guidance, and dialogical self

8) Personal experience is now drawn as a TEM figure, with many concept-tools, such as EFP, P-EFP, BFP, OPP, SD, SG, and DS, within irreversible time.

215

Appendix

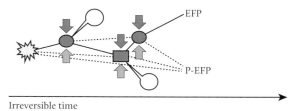

Figure A.2.8. Setting up the locations for social direction and social guidance

3. Toward a saturation of TEM: The second EFP

We need to emphasize that the TEA is an enduring innovation that will be useful for many years to come. Everyone can take part in using TEA, making it richer. In other words, TEA is a generic and systemic framework for understanding the human life course from the perspective of cultural psychology. In the tentative concluding remarks, we are happy to discuss the innovative idea of the second EFP to readers.

From the perspective of methodology, the EFP is regarded as having two connotations for TEA. First, the EFP is regarded as a research focus in which researchers have interest (e.g., entering higher education, infertility experience of married women, an occasion for authentic reflection of a delinquent adolescent, decision to study abroad etc.). Additionally, the EFP plays guidance function for inviting individuals to take part in the research (i.e., HSI). However, we should consider that the EFP set by the researcher is a reflection of a misleading assumption. We re-name it as the first EFP within this context. It is the participants him/herself who is the first-person. Therefore, we should try to understand the EFP of participants themselves.

Then, the second EFP as a future aim of participants is highly needed. The first EFP is set by researcher and he/she invites the individuals who have experienced the EFP. This is the procedure of HSI. Even though the researcher is interested in the EFP, time has passed after the EFP for participants. *So, each participant might have his/her own EFP.*

Here, the P-EFP for the second EFP is also needed (Figure A.2.9). This is the no-

Appendix 2   Brief Practice for Using Trajectory Equifinality Model (TEM)

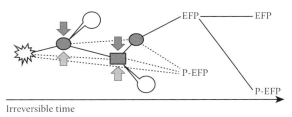

Irreversible time

Figure A.2.9. Second EFP and P-EFP: Full picture of TEM

tion for treating a complimentary class within the second EFP. Both the second EFP and the P-EFP for the second EFP create a vertical dimension of TEM. If researchers can reach the dimension of the second EFP and P-EFP, then it could be said that the researcher and the participants can reach the kind of saturation, or a "TEM saturation."

References

Abbey, E. (2007). Perpetual uncertainty of cultural life: Becoming reality. In J. Valsiner & E. Rosa (Eds.), *The Cambridge handbook of sociocultural psychology* (pp. 362-372). New York: Cambridge University Press.

Abbey, E., & Valsiner, J. (2005). Emergence of meanings through ambivalence. *FQS: Forum Qualitative Sozialforschung / Forum: Qualitative Social Research*, **6**(1), Article 23.

Aeschleman, S. R., & Schladenhauffen, J. (1984). Acquisition, generalization and maintenance of grocery shopping skills by severely mentally retarded adolescents. *Applied Research in Mental Retardation*, **5**, 245-258.

Akasaka, M. (2009). Process of living with chronic inflammatory bowel disease and role of clinical psychologists in caring for patients. Master thesis of Human Sciences, Ritsumeikan University, Kyoto, Japan.

Anisov, A. (2001). Svoistva vremeni [features of time]. *Logical Studies*, **6**, 1-22.

Anisov, A. (2005). Time as a computation process. In A. N. Pavlenko (Ed.), *Zamysel Boga v teoriakh fiziki kosmologii* (pp. 72-88). Vremia.

Arai, T. (1912). *Mental fatigue*. N. Y. Teachers' College Columbia University.

Arakawa, A., & Takada, S. (2006). Choosing abortion and its effect on one's life based on a TEM (trajectory equifinality model) analysis. Poster for ISSBD meeting, Melbourne, Australia, July.

Armstrong-Dailey, A., & Zarbock, S. (Eds.) (2001). *Hospice care for children* (2nd ed.). New York: Oxford University Press.

Bakhtin, M. M. (1984). *Problems of Dostoevsky's poetics*. Minneapolis: University of Minnesota Press.

Bakhtin, M. M. (1986). *Speech genres and other late essays*. Austin, TX: University of Texas Press.

Baldwin, J. M. (1906). *Thought and things: A study of the development and meaning of thought, or genetic logic (Vol. 1.: Functional logic, or genetic theory of knowledge)*. London: Swan Sonnenschein & Co.

Baldwin, J. M. (1908a). *Thought and things: A study of the development and meaning of thought, or genetic logic (Vol. 2: Experimental logic, or genetic theory of thought)*. London: Swan

Sonnenschein & Co.

Baldwin, J. M. (1908b). Knowledge and imagination. *Psychological Review*, **15**, 181-196.

Baldwin, J. M. (1930). James Mark Baldwin. In C. Murchison (Ed.), *A history of psychology in autobiography* (*Vol. 1*, pp. 1-30). New York: Russell & Russell.

Baltes, P. B., Staudinger, U. M., & Lindenberger, U. (1999). Lifespan psychology: Theory and application to intellectual functioning. *Annual Review of Psychology*, **50**, 471-507.

Benedict, R. (1946). *Chrysanthemum and the sword: Patterns of Japanese culture*. Boston: Houghton Mifflin.

Benetka, G. (1995). *Psychologie in Wien: Sozial- und Theoriegeschichte des Wiener Psychologischen Instituts 1922-1938*. Wien: WUV-Universitätsverlag.

Bergold, J. B. (2000). The affinity between qualitative methods and community psychology. *FQS: Forum Qualitative Sozialforschung / Forum: Qualitative Social Research*, **1**(2). Article 28.

Bergson, H. (1907/1945). *L'évolution créatrice*. Genève: Éditions Albert Skira.

Bergson, H. (1911). *Creative evolution*. Translated by Arthur Mitchell. New York: Henry Holt and Company.

Berti, A. E., & Bombi, A. S. (1988). *The child's construction of economics*. Cambridge: Cambridge University Press.

Blossfeld, H.-P., Hamerle, A., & Mayer, K. U. (Eds.) (1989). *Event history analysis: Statistical theory and application in the social sciences*. Hillsdale, NJ: Erlbaum.

Blossfeld, H.-P., & Rohwer, G. (1997). Causal inference, time and observation plans in the social sciences. *Quality & Quantity*, **31**, 361-384.

Branco, A. U., & Valsiner, J. (1997). Changing methodologies: A co-constructivist study of goal orientations in social interactions. *Psychology and Developing Societies*, **9**, 35-64.

Bruner, J. (1986). *Actual minds, possible worlds (The Jerusalem-Harvard Lectures)*. Cambridge, MA: Harvard University Press.

Brunswik, E. (1947). *Systematic and representative design of psychological experiments: With results in physical and social perception*. Berkeley: University of California Press.

Burton, C. R. (2000). Re-thinking stroke rehabilitation: The Corbin and Strauss chronic illness trajectory framework. *Journal of Advanced Nursing*, **32**, 595-602.

Cairns, R. B. (1986). Phenomena lost. In J. Valsiner (Ed.), *The individual subject and scientific psychology* (pp. 97-111). New York: Plenum.

Cairns, R. B. (1998). The making of developmental psychology. In W. Damon & R. M. Lerner (Eds.), *Handbook of child psychology* (*Vol. 1. Theoretical models of human development*, 5th ed., pp. 25-105). New York: John Wiley and Sons.

References

Cairns, R. B., Elder, G. H. J., & Costello, E. J. (Eds.) (1996). *Developmental science*. New York: Cambridge University Press.

Callero, P. L. (2003). The sociology of the self. *Annual Review of Sociology*, **29**, 115-133.

Chaitin, G. J. (1975). Randomness and mathematical proof. *Scientific American*, **232**(5), 47-52.

Chappel, T. J. H. (1974). The Yoruba cult of twins in historical perspective. *Africa*, **49**, 250-265.

Cochran, W. G. (1963). *Sampling techniques* (2nd ed.). New York: John Wiley and Sons.

Cole, M. (1996). *Cultural psychology: A once and future discipline*. Cambridge, MA: Harvard University Press.

Corbin, J. M., & Strauss, A. (1988). *Unending work and care: Managing chronic illness at home*. San Francisco: Jossey-Bass.

Corbin, J. M., & Strauss, A. (1991). A nursing model for chronic illness management based upon the trajectory framework. *Scholarly Inquiry for Nursing Practice*, **5**, 155-174.

Corbin, J. M., & Strauss, A. (1992). A nursing model for chronic illness management based upon the trajectory framework. In P. Woog (Ed.), *The chronic illness trajectory framework: The Corbin & Strauss nursing model* (pp. 9-28). New York: Springer.

Cortés, M. (2008). A dialogical self – Trajectory equifinality model for higher education first year persistence/abandon study. Paper presented at the 5th International Conference of Dialogical Self.

Cortés, M., & Londoño, S. (2009). What sense can the sense-making perspective make for economics? *Integrative Psychological & Behavioral Science*, **43**, 178-184.

Cressey, P. G. (1932). *The taxi-dance hall: A sociological study in commercialized recreation and city life*. New York: Greenwood Press.

Daaleman, T. P., & Elder, G. H., Jr. (2007). Family medicine and the life course paradigm. *Journal of the American Board of Family Medicine*, **20**, 85-92.

Danziger, K. (1990). *Constructing the subject: Historical origins of psychological research*. New York: Cambridge University Press.

Danziger, K. (1997). *Naming the mind: How psychology found its language*. London: Sage.

Darwin, C. (1877). A biographical sketch of an infant. *Mind*, **2**, 285-294.

Desrosières, A. (1993). *La politique des grands nombres*. Paris: Editions La Decouverte.

Diriwächter, R. (2004). Völkerpsychologie: The synthesis that never was. *Culture & Psychology*, **10**, 85-109.

D'Onofrio, M. J., & Gendron, M. S. (2001). Technology assisted research methodologies: A historical perspective of technology-based data collection methods. Paper presented at the Internet Global Summit: A Net Odyssey. Mobility and the Internet. The 11th Annual

Internet Society Conference, Stockholm Sweden.

Driesch, H. (1908). *The science and philosophy of the organism*. London: Adam and Charles Black.

Driesch, H. (1914). *The history and theory of vitalism*. London: Macmillan.

Eisenberg, L. (1977). Disease and illness: Distinctions between professional and popular ideas of sickness. *Culture, Medicine and Psychiatry*, **1**, 9-23.

Elder, G. H., Jr. (Ed.) (1985). *Life course dynamics: Trajectories and transitions*. Ithaca, NY: Cornell University Press.

Elder, G. H., Jr. (1998). The life course and human development. In R. M. Lerner (Ed.), *Handbook of child psychology* (*Vol. 1: Theoretical modxels of human development*, 5th ed., pp. 939-991). New York: Wiley.

Escobar, A. (1995). *Encountering development: The making and unmaking of the Third World*. Princeton, NJ: Princeton University Press.

Fayers, P. M., & Machin, D. (2007). *Quality of life: The assessment, analysis and interpretation of potient-reported outcomes* (2nd ed). Chichester, England: Wiley.

Festinger, L. (1957). *A theory of cognitive dissonance*. Stanford, CA: Stanford University Press.

Fetterman, D. M. (2008). Ethnography. In L. M. Given (Ed.), *The Sage encyclopedia of qualitative research methods*. Sage.

Fogel, A. (2006). Dynamic systems research on interindividual communication: The transformation of meaning-making. *Journal of Developmental Processes*, **1**, 7-30.

Frank, A. W. (1995). *The wounded storyteller: Body, illness, and ethics*. Chicago: University of Chicago Press.

Frank, L. K. (1939). Time perspective. *Journal of Social Philosophy*, **4**, 293-312.

Freier. M. (2006). Chronos and Kairos: Intoxication and the quest for transcendence.

Furnham, A. (1999). Economic socialization: A study of adults' perceptions and uses of allowances (pocket money) to educate children. *British Journal of Developmental Psychology*, **17**, 585-604.

Gesell, A. (1940). *The first five years of life: A guide to the study of the preschool child*. London: Methuen.

Gigerenzer, G. (1993). The superego, the ego, and the id in statistical reasoning. In G. Keren & C. Lewis (Eds.), *A handbook for data analysis in the behavioral sciences: Methodological issues* (pp. 311-339). Hillsdale, NJ: Lawrence Erlbaum Associates.

Gigerenzer, G., & Murray, D. J. (1987). *Cognition as intuitive statistics*. Hillsdale, NJ: Lawrence Erlbaum Associates.

References

Gigerenzer, G., Swijtink, Z., Porter, T., Daston, L. J., Beatty, J., & Krüger, L. (1989). *The empire of chance: How probability changed science and everyday life*. Cambridge, UK: Cambridge University Press.

Gilbert, S. F. (1991). Epigenetic landscaping: Waddington's use of cell fate bifurcation diagrams. *Biology & Philosophy*, **6**, 135-154.

Ginsburg, S., & Jablonka, E. (2007). The transition to experiencing. I. Limited learning and limited experiencing. *Biological Theory*, **2**, 218-230.

Glaser, B. G., & Strauss, A. L. (1967). *The discovery of grounded theory: Strategies for qualitative research*. Chicago: Aldine.

Goldberg, L. R. (1990). An alternative "description of personality": The Big-Five factor structure. *Journal of Personality and Social Psychology*, **59**, 1216-1229.

Gubrium, J. F., & Holstein, J. A. (2001). From the individual interview to the interview society. In J. F. Gubrium & J. A. Holstein (Eds.), *Handbook of interview research: Context & method* (pp. 3-32). Thousand Oaks, CA: Sage.

Günther, I. A. (1998). Contacting subjects: The untold story. *Culture & Psychology*, **4**, 65-74.

Hammond, K. R. (1948). Subject and object sampling: A note. *Psychological Bulletin*, **45**, 530-533.

Handwerker, W. P. (2004). Sample design. In K. Kempf-Leonard (Editor-in-chief), *Encyclopedia of social measurement* (pp. 429-436). San Diego, CA: Academic Press.

Hatfield, G. (1992). Empirical, rational, and transcendental psychology: Psychology as science and as philosophy. In P. Guyer (Ed.), *The Cambridge companion to Kant* (pp. 200-227) Cambridge University Press.

Hepper, P. (2003). Prenatal psychological and behavioural development. In J. Valsiner & K. J. Connolly (Eds.), *Handbook of developmental psychology* (pp. 91-113). London: Sage.

Herbst, D. P. (1995). What happens when we make a distinction: An elementary introduction to co-genetic logic. In T. Kindermann & J. Valsiner (Eds.), *Development of person-context relations* (pp. 67-79). Hillsdale, NJ: Erlbaum.

Hermans, H. J. M. (1999). Self-narratives as meaning construction: The dynamics of self-investigation. *Journal of Clinical Psychology*, **55**, 1193-1211.

Hermans, H. J. M. (2001). The dialogical self: Toward a theory of personal and cultural positioning. *Culture & Psychology*, **7**, 243-281.

Hermans, H. J. M. (Ed.) (2002). Special issue on dialogical self. *Theory & Psychology*, **12**, 147-280.

Hermans, H. I. M. (2008). The dialogical self: State of the art. Keynote speech at the 5th international conference on the dialogical self. Cambridge, UK.

Hermans, H. J. M., & Bonarius H. (1991). The person as co-investigator in personality research.

European Journal of Personality, **5**, 199-216.

Hermans, H. J. M., & Dimaggio, G. (2007). Self, identity, and globalization in times of uncertainty: A dialogical analysis. *Review of General Psychology*, **11**, 31-61.

Hermans, H. J. M., & Kempen, H. J. G. (1993). *The dialogical self: Meaning as movement.* San Diego: Academic Press.

Hidaka, T. (2010). Transformation process of the meanings of disease – Life ethnography of multilayered support for ALS patients in home care. Paper presented at the 6th International Conference on Dialogical Self, Athens, Greece, October.

Higashi, M., Hashimoto, N., Kato, T., & Fujimoto, T. (1994). The structure of university students' concepts of psychology. *The Bulletin of Faculty of letters (Ohtemon university)*, **2**, 1-7 [in Japanese].

Hood, K. E. (2006). Times of life and timing in developmental psychology. *Culture & Psychology*, **12**, 230-244.

Josephs, I. (1998). Constructing one's self in the city of the silent: Dialogue, symbols, and the role of "as if" in self-development. *Human Development*, **41**, 180-195.

Kabinga, M., & Banda, S. S. (2008). A conceptual review of the demands of chronic care and the preparedness of nurses trained with the general nursing council of Zambia curriculum. *Medical Journal of Zambia*, **35**, 105-109.

Kant, I. (1786). *Metaphysical foundations of natural science.* Konigsberg [in German].

Kawakita, J. (1986). *The KJ Method: Seeking order out of chaos.* Tokyo: Chuokoron-sha [In Japanese].

Keith, R. A., Granger, C. V., Hamilton, B. B., & Sherwin, F. S. (1987). The functional independence measure: A new tool for rehabilitation. *Advances in Clinical Rehabilitation*, **1**, 6-18.

Kelly, G. A. (1955). *The psychology of personal constructs.* New York: Norton.

Kennell, J. H., Jerauld, R., Wolfe, H., et al. (1974). Maternal behavior one year after early and extended post-partum contact. *Developmental Medicine & Child Neurololgy*, **16**, 172-179.

Kharlamov, N. A. (2012). The city as a sign: A developmental-experiential approach to spatial life. In J. Valsiner (Ed.), *The Oxford handbook of culture and psychology* (pp. 277-302). New York, NY: Oxford University Press.

Kido, A. (2006). The TEM (trajectory equifinality model) of the transition of cosmetic use by Japanese women in the United States. Poster for ISSBD Australia.

Kido, A. (2011). Makeup behavior of the use by adolescent female students in the females in different cultural situation settings – Qualitative analysis of subjects in Japan and the USA – Qualitative analysis of interview Japan and U.S. *Japanese Journal of Qualitative Psychology*,

10, 79-96 [in Japanese].

Kindermann, T., & Valsiner, J. (1989). Strategies for empirical research in context-inclusive developmental psychology. In J. Valsiner (Ed.), *Cultural context and child development* (pp. 13-50). Toronto-Göttingen-Bern: C. J. Hogrefe and H. Huber.

Klaus, M. H., & Kennell, J. H. (1976). *Maternal-infant bonding*. St. Louis, MO: Mosby.

Kleinman, A. (1980). *Patients and healers in the context of culture: An exploration of the border-land between anthropology, medicine and psychiatry*. Berkley, CA: University of California Press.

Kleinman, A. (1988). *The illness narratives: Suffering, healing and the human condition*. New York: Basic Books.

Kojima, H. (1997). Problems of comparison: Methodology, the art of storytelling, and implicit models. In J. Tudge, M. J. Shanahan & J. Valsiner (Eds.), *Comparisons in human development: Understanding time and context* (pp. 318-333). New York: Cambridge University Press.

Kourilsky, M. L., & Graff, E. (1986). Children's use of cost-benefit analysis: Developmental or non-existent. In S. Hodkinson & D. Whitehead (Eds.), *Economic education: Research and development issues* (pp. 127-139). Kansas City, Missouri: Longman.

Kuklick, H. (1991). *The savage within: The social history of British anthropology, 1885-1945* Cambridge, MA: Cambridge University Press.

Kullasepp, K. (2006). Identity construction of psychology students: Professional role in the making. *European Journal of School Psychology*, **4**, 251-280.

Latour, B. (1987). *Science in action*. Philadelphia: Open University Press.

Latour, B. (1988). *The pasteurization of France*. Cambridge, MA: Harvard University Press.

Latour, B., & Woolgar, S. (1979). *Laboratory life: The social construction of scientific facts*. Los Angeles: Sage.

Leary, D. E. (1982). Immanuel Kant and the development of modern psychiatry. In W. R. Woodward & M. G. Ash (Eds.), *The problematic science: Psychology in nineteenth-century thought* (pp. 17-42). New York: Praeger.

LeCompte, M. D., & Preissle, J. (1993). *Ethnography and qualitative design in educational research* (2nd ed.). San Diego, CA: Academic Press.

Lerner, R. M., & Busch-Rossnagel, N. A. (Eds.) (1981). *Individuals as producers of their development: A life-span perspective*. New York: Academic Press.

Lewin, K. (1939). Field theory and experiment in social psychology: Concepts and methods. *American Journal of Sociology*, **44**, 868-896.

Lewin, K. (1943). Defining the "field at a given time." *Psychological Review*, **50**, 292-310. (Republished in *Resolving social conflicts & field theory in social science*, Washington, DC: American Psychological Association, 1997)

Lewin, K. (1952). *Field theory in social sciences: Selected thoretical papers*. London: Tavistock.

Macmillan, R., & Eliason, S. (2003). Characterizing the life course as role configurations and pathways: A latent structure approach. In J. T. Mortimer & M. J. Shanahan (Eds.), *Handbook of the life course* (pp. 529-554). New York: Kluwer Academic/Plenum Publishers.

Malinowski, B. (1922). *Argonauts of the Western Pacific*. London: Routledge and Kegan Paul.

March, J. G. (1994). *A primer on decision making: How decisions happen*. New York: Free Press.

Marks, E. S. (1947). Selective sampling in psychological research. *Psychological Bulletin*, **44**, 267-275.

Maslow, A. H. (1943). A theory of human motivation. *Psychological Review*, **50**, 370-396.

Matsuzawa, T., Biro, D., Humle, T., Inoue-Nakamura, N., Tonooka, R., & Yamakoshi, G. (2001). Emergence of culture in wild chimpanzees: Education by master-apprenticeship. In T. Matsuzawa (Ed.), *Primate origins of human cognition and behavior* (pp. 557-574). Tokyo: Springer.

McAdams, D. P., & Pals, J. L. (2006). A new Big Five: Fundamental principles for an integrative science of personality. *American Psychologist*, **61**, 204-217.

McCrae, R. R., & Costa, P. T., Jr. (1996). Toward a new generation of personality theories: Theoretical contexts for the five-factor model. In J. S. Wiggins (Ed.), *The five-factor model of personality: Theoretical perspectives* (pp. 51-87). New York: Guilford.

McGee, H. M., O'Boyle, C. A., Hickey, A., O'malley, K., & Joyce, C. R. (1991). Assessing the quality of life of the individual: The SEIQoL with a healthy and a gastroenterology unit population. *Psychological Medicine*, **21**, 749-759.

McNemar, Q. (1940). Sampling in psychological research. *Psychological Bulletin*, **37**, 331-365.

McQuellon, R. P., Russell, G. B., Rambo, T. D., Craven, B. L., Radford, J., Perry, J. J., et al. (1998). Quality of life and psychological distress of bone marrow transplant recipients: The 'time trajectory' to recovery over the first year. *Bone Marrow Transplantation*, **21**, 477-486.

Mischel, W. (1968). *Personality and assessment*. New York: Wiley.

Mitchell, C., Kaufman, C., & Beals, J. (2004). Equifinality and multifinality as guides for preventive interventions: HIV risk/protection among American Indian young adults. *Journal of Primary Prevention*, **25**, 491-510.

Mizuki, S., & Minami, H. (2010). How children perceived their hometown from the viewpoint of local environmental interaction. *Ritsumeikan Journal of Human Sciences*, **20**, 65-77.

Molenaar, P. C. M. (2004). A manifesto on psychology as idiographic science: Bringing the person back into scientific psychology, this time forever. *Measurement: Interdisciplinary Research and Perspectives*, **2**, 201-218.

Molenaar, P. C. M. (2007). Psychological methodology will change profoundly due to the necessity to focus on intra-individual variation. *Integrative Psychological and Behavioral Science*, **41**, 35-40.

Molenaar, P. C. M., Huizinga, H. M., & Nesselroade, J. R. (2002). The relationship between the structure of inter-individual and intra-individual variability. In U. Staudinger & U. Lindenberger (Eds.), *Understanding human development* (pp. 339-360). Dordrecht: Klüwer.

Molenaar, P. C. M., & Valsiner, J. (2005). How generalization works through the single case: A simple idiographic process analysis of an individual psychotherapy case. *International Journal of Idiographic Science*, **1**, 1-13.

Mori, N. (2009). Methodological issues on two types of TEM study; retrospective and prospective. In T. Sato (Ed.), *Starting qualitative study using the TEM as a new method* (pp.153-157). Tokyo: Seishin-Shobo [in Japanese].

Morioka, M. (2008). Voices of the self in the therapeutic chronotope: *Utushi* and *ma*. *International Journal for Dialogical Science*, **3**, 93-108.

Moro, Y. (1999). The expanded dialogic sphere: Writing activity and authoring of self in Japanese classroom. In Y. Engestrom, R. Miettinen & R.-P. Punamaki (Eds.), *Perspectives on activity theory* (pp. 165-182). Cambridge, MA: Cambridge University Press.

Müller, U., & Giesbrecht, G. F. (2006). Psychological models of time: Arrows, cycles and spirals. *Culture & Psychology*, **12**, 221-229.

Murray, H. A. (1938). *Explorations in personality*. New York: Oxford University Press.

Nerlich, B. (2004). Coming full (hermeneutic) circle: The controversy about psychological methods. In Z. Todd, B. Nerlich, S. McKeown & D. D. Clarke (Eds.), *Mixing methods in psychology: The integration of qualitative and quantitative methods in theory and practice* (pp. 17-36). East Sussex: Psychology Press.

Neyman, J. (1934). On the two different aspects of the representative method: The method of stratified sampling and the method of purposive selection. *Journal of the Royal Statistical Society*, **97**, 558-606.

Nishida, M. (2010). Communication deficiencies and misunderstandings in home care services for patients with severe progressive diseases who live alone: A case study of an Amyotrophic Lateral Sclerosis (ALS) patient. *Core Ethics*, **6**, 311-321 [in Japanese].

Nozoe, S., Minami, M., & Mochizuki, A. (2004). Teaching retrieval skills using the mail function of the cell phone to a student with developmental and hearing disabilities. *Ritsumeikan*

Journal of Human Sciences, **7**, 181-191 [In Japanese with English abstract].

Nuttin, J., & Lens, W. (1985). *Future time perspective and motivation: Theory and research method.* Mahwah, NJ: Lawrence Erlbaum Associates.

O'Boyle, C. A. (1994). The Schedule for the Evaluation of Individual Quality of Life (SEIQoL). *International Journal of Mental Health*, **23**(3), 3-23.

O'Boyle, C. A., McGee, H., Hickey, A., Joyce, C. R., Browne, J. P., & O'malley, K. (1995). *The Schedule for the Evaluation of Individual Quality of Life (SEIQoL): Administration manual.* Dublin: Royal College of Surgeons in Ireland.

O'Boyle, C. A., McGee, H., Hickey, A., O'malley, K., & Joyce, C. R. (1992). Individual quality of life in patients undergoing hip replacement. *Lancet*, **339**(8801), 1088-1091.

Odling-Smee F. J., Lakland, K. N., & Feldman, M. W. (2003). *Niche construction: The neglected process in evolution.* Princeton, NJ: Princeton University Press.

Oh, S. A. (2005). Giving and exchange: typology of 'Ogori (treating)' in Korea. First ISCAR (International Society for Cultural and Activity Research) Congress. Seville, Spain. p. 267.

Oh, S. A., Pian, C., Yamamoto, T., Takahashi, N., Sato, T., Takeo, K., et al. (2005). Money and the life worlds of children in Korea-Examining the Phenomenon of *Ogori* (Treating) from cultural psychological perspectives. *Bulletin of Maebashi Kyoai Gakuen College*, **5**, 73-88.

Omi, Y. (1997). History of use of data analyses in psychology in Japan. In T. Sato & H. Mizoguchi (Eds.), *History of psychology in Japan* (pp. 444-461). Kyoto: Kitaoji-Shobo [in Japanese].

Omi, Y. (1998). Some questions to psychological research using "scales." In T. Sato (Ed.), *Psychology for personality* (pp. 221-227). Tokyo: Shibundo [in Japanese].

Omi Y. (2006). During the historical course toward the acceptance of "fieldwork" and the establishment of "qualitative research." In T. Yoshida (Ed.), *A new framework of psychological research methods* (pp. 195-217). Tokyo: Seishin-Shobo [in Japanese].

Omi, Y., & Kawano, K. (1994). Criteria of convincedness: What do psychologists work? *The Bulletin of Faculty of Social sciences and Humanities (Tokyo Metropolitan University)*, **269**, 31-45 [in Japanese].

Oyama, T., Sato, T., & Suzuki, Y. (2002). Shaping of scientific psychology in Japan. *International Journal of Psychology*, **36**, 396-406.

Parsons, T. (1951a). *The social system.* New York: The Free Press.

Parsons, T. (1951b). Social structure and dynamic process: The case of modern medical practice. In *The social system* (pp. 288-322). New York: The Free Press.

Patton, M. Q. (2002). *Qualitative research and evaluation methods* (3rd ed.). Thousand Oakes, CA: Sage.

References

Peirce, C. S. (1892/1923). The law of mind. In C. Peirce (Ed.), *Chance, love and logic* (pp. 202-237). London: Kegan Paul, Trench, Trubner & Co.

Peirce, C. S. (1896/1957). The principal lessons of the history of science. In *Essays in the philosophy of Science*. Indianapolis.

Peirce, C. S. (1908). *Collected papers of Charles Sanders Peirce*. Edited by C. Hartshorne, P. Weiss & A. W. Burks. Cambridge, MA: Harvard University Press.

Phipps W. J., Monahan F. D., Sands J. K., Marek J. F., & Neighbors M. (2003). *Medical-surgical nursing: Health and illness perspectives* (7th ed.). St. Louis, MO: Mosby.

Poddiakov, A. N. (2001). Counteraction as a crucial factor of learning, education and development: Opposition to help. *FQS: Forum Qualitative Sozialforschung / Forum: Qualitative Social Research*, **2**(3), Article 15.

Popple, A. V., & Levi, D. M. (2000). Wundt versus Galton – two approaches to gathering psychophysical measurements. *Perception*, **29**, 379-381.

Preyer, W. T. (1882). *Die Seele des Kindes*. Leipzig: Grieben.

Prigogine, I. (1978). Time, structure, and fluctuations. *Science*, **201**(4358), 777-785.

Prigogine, I. (1987). Exploring complexity. *European Journal of Operational Research*, **30**, 97-103.

Radaev, V. V. (2005). *Ekonomicheskaya sotsiologia [Economic sociology]*. Moscow: Izdatel'skii Dom GU-VShE.

Rosa, A. (2007). Acts of Psyche: Actuations as synthesis of semiosis and action. In J. Valsiner & A. Rosa (Eds.), *The Cambridge handbook of sociocultural psychology* (pp. 205-237). New York: Cambridge University Press.

Rudolph, L. (2006). The fullness of time. *Culture & Psychology*, **12**, 169-204.

Salgado, J., & Goncalves, M. (2010). Dialogical self dynamics within frames. Paper presented at the 6th International Conference of Dialogical Self, October.

Salvatore, S., Dananzati, G. F., Poti, S., & Ruggieri, R. (2009). Mainstream economics and sense-making. *Integrative Psychological & Behavioral Science*, **43**, 158-177.

Sato, T. (2002). *Acceptance and development of psychology in Japan*. Kyoto: Kitaoji-Shobo [In Japanese].

Sato, T. (2003). History of psychology in Japan. In T. Sato & M. Takasuna, *Readings the history of psychology* (pp. 131-159). Tokyo: Yuhikaku [In Japanese].

Sato, T. (2005). *The history of applied psychology in Japan. The Rits Reports for Human Services*, **9**, 76-90.

Sato, T. (2007). Development, change or transformation: How can psychology conceive and depict professional identify construction? *European Journal of School Psychology*, **4**, 321-334.

Sato, T. (Ed.) (2009). *Starting qualitative study using the TEM as a new method.* Tokyo: Seishin-Shobo [in Japanese].

Sato, T., Hidaka, T., & Fukuda, M. (2009). Depicting the dynamics of living the life: The Trajectory Equifinality Model. In J. Valsiner, P. C. M. Molenaar, M. C. D. P. Lyra & N. Chaudhary (Eds.), *Dynamic process methodology in the social and developmental sciences* (pp. 217-240). New York: Springer.

Sato, T., Mori, N., & Valsiner, J. (Eds.) (2016). *Making of the future: The Trajectory Equifinality Approach in cultural psychology.* Charlotte, NC: Information Age Publishing.

Sato, T., Namiki, H., Ando, J., & Hatano, G. (2004). Japanese conception and research on human intelligence. In R. J. Sternberg (Ed.), *International handbook of intelligence* (pp. 302-324). New York: Cambridge University Press.

Sato, T., & Sato, T. (2005). The early 20th century: Shaping the discipline of psychology in Japan. *Japanese Psychological Research,* **47**, 52-62.

Sato, T., & Valsiner, J. (2006). Historically Structured Sampling (HSS) and Trajectory Equifinality Model (TEM): New methodologies for cultural historical approach. Poster symposium for ISSBD, Melbourne, Australia, July.

Sato, T., & Valsiner, J. (2010). Time in life and life in time: Between experiencing and accounting. *Ritsumeikan Journal of Human Sciences,* **20**, 79-92.

Sato, T., Watanabe, Y., & Omi, Y. (2000). *The birth of psychology studies: Fieldwork of 'psychology.'* Kyoto: Kitaohji-Shobo [in Japanese].

Sato, T., Watanabe, Y., & Omi, Y. (2007). Beyond dichotomy: Towards creative synthesis. *Integrative Psychological & Behavioral Science,* **41**, 50-59.

Sato,T., Yasuda, Y., & Kido, A. (2004). Historically Structured Sampling (HSS) Model: A contribution from cultural psychology. Paper presented at the 28th International Congress of Psychology, Beijing, China, August 12.

Sato, T., Yasuda, Y., Kido, A., Arakawa, A., Mizoguchi, H., & Valsiner, J. (2007). Sampling reconsidered: Idiographic science and the analyses of personal life trajectories. In J. Valsiner & A. Rosa (Eds.), *The Cambridge handbook of sociocultural psychology* (pp. 82-106). New York: Cambridge University Press.

Schaffer, H. R. (1998). *Making decisions about children: Psychological questions and answers* (2nd ed.). Oxford, UK: Blackwell.

Schug, M. C. (1983). The development of economic thinking in children and adolescents. *Social Education,* **47**, 141-145.

Scupin, R. (1997). The KJ method: A technique for analyzing data derived from Japanese ethnology. *Human Organization*, **56**, 233-237.

Sen, A. (1992). *Inequality Reexamined*. New Delhi: Oxford University Press.

Sen, A. (1999). *Development as freedom*. Oxford, UK: Oxford University Press.

Shanahan, M. J., Valsiner, J., & Gottlieb, G. (1997). Developmental concepts across disciplines. In J. Tudge, M. J. Shanahan & J. Valsiner (Eds.), *Comparisons in human development: Understanding time and context* (pp. 34-71), New York: Cambridge University Press.

Sherif, M. (1936). *The psychology of social norms*. New York: Harper Collins.

Shvyrkov, V., & Persidsky, A. (1991). The importance of being earnest in statistics. *Quality & Quantity*, **25**, 19-28.

Simon, H. (1999). Karl Duncker and cognitive science. *From Past to Future*, **1**(2), 1-11.

Smedslund, J. (1995a). Auxiliary versus theoretical hypotheses and ordinary versus scientific language. *Human Development*, **38**, 174-178.

Smedslund, J. (1995b). Psychologic: Common sense and the pseudoempirical. In J. A. Smith, R. Harré & L. van Langenhove (Eds.), *Rethinking psychology* (pp. 196-206). London: Sage.

Smith, T. M. F. (1976). The foundations of survey sampling: A review. *Journal of the Royal Statistical Society, Series A*, **139**, 183-204.

Sovran, T. (1992). Between similarity and sameness. *Journal of Pragmatics*, **18**, 329-344.

Stevens, S. S. (1946). On the theory of scales of measurement. *Science*, **103**(2684), 677-680.

Stevens, S. S. (1951). Mathematics, measurement and psychophysics. In S. S. Stevens (Ed.), *Handbook of experimental psychology* (pp. 1-49). New York: Wiley.

Strauss, A. (1952). The development and transformation of monetary meaning in the child. *American Sociological Review*, **17**, 275-286.

Swanson, B. M. (2005). *Careers in health care* (5th ed.). New York: McGraw-Hill.

Taine, H. (1876). Note sur l'acquisition du langage chez les enfants et dans l'espèce humaine. *Revue philosophique*, **1**, 5-23.

Takasuna, M. (2007). Proliferation of Western methodological thought in psychology in Japan: Ways of objectification. *Integrative Psychological and Behavioral Science*, **41**, 83-92.

Takasuna, M., & Sato, T. (2004). Felix Krueger and Ganzheitspsychologie in Japanese psychology. *From Past to Future*, **5**, 17-23.

Takeo, K., Takahashi, N., Yamamoto, T., Sato, T., Pian C., & Oh, S. A. (2009). Developmental changes of parent-child relationships as mediation by money as a cultural tool. *The Japanese Journal of Developmental Psychology*, **20**, 406-418 [in Japanese].

Tanimura, S., Sato, T., & Tsuchida, N. (2008). Gender role consciousness of the parents which let daughters aim at "The Normal Marriage (a full-time homemaker)": From the talk of the women who married in 1980's. *Ritsumeikan Journal of Human Sciences*, **17**, 61-74 [in Japanese with English abstract].

Toomela, A. (2007). Culture of science: Strange history of the methodological thinking in psychology. *Integrative Psychological & Behavioral Science*, **41**, 6-20.

Toomela, A. (2008). Variables in psychology: A critique of quantitative psychology. *Integrative Psychological & Behavioral Science*, **42**, 245-265.

Toomela, A. (2009). How methodology became a toolbox – and how it escapes from that box. In J. Valsiner, P. C. M. Molenaar, M. C. D. P. Lyra & N. Chaudhary (Eds.), *Dynamic process methodology in the social and developmental sciences* (pp. 45-66). New York: Springer.

Trettien, A. (1900). Creeping and walking. *American Journal of Psychology*, **12**, 1-57.

Uzawa, H. (1989). *Perspective of economics*. Tokyo: Iwanami Shoten [in Japanese].

Valsiner, J. (1984). Two alternative epistemological frameworks in psychology: The typological and variational modes of thinking. *The Journal of Mind and Behavior*, **5**, 449-470.

Valsiner, J. (1986a). Sequence-structure analysis: Study of serial order within unique sequences of psychological phenomena. In J. Valsiner (Ed.), *The individual subject and scientific psychology* (pp. 347-389). New York: Plenum.

Valsiner, J. (1986b). Between groups and individuals: Psychologists' and laypersons' interpretations of correlational findings. In J. Valsiner (Ed.), *The individual subject and scientific psychology* (pp. 113-152). New York: Plenum.

Valsiner, J. (Ed.) (1986c). *The individual subject and scientific psychology*. New York: Plenum.

Valsiner, J. (1997). *Culture and the development of children's action: A theory of human development* (2nd ed.). New York: John Wiley and Sons.

Valsiner, J. (2000). *Culture and human development*. London: Sage.

Valsiner, J. (2001a). The first six years: Culture's adventures in psychology. *Culture & Psychology*, **7**, 5-48.

Valsiner, J. (2001b). *Comparative study of human cultural development*. Madrid: Fundación Infancia y Aprendizaje.

Valsiner, J. (2002). Irreversibility of time and ontopotentiality of signs. *Estudios de Psicología*, **23**(1), 49-59.

Valsiner, J. (2003a). Culture and its transfer: Ways of creating general knowledge through the study of cultural particulars. In W. J. Lonner, D. L. Dinnel, S. A. Hayes & D. N. Sattler (Eds.), *Online readings in psychology and culture* (Unit 2, Chapter 12), Center for Cross-Cultural Research, Western Washington University, Bellingham, Washington, USA.

Valsiner, J. (2003b). Beyond social representations: A theory of enablement. *Papers on Social representations*, **12**, 7.1-7.16.

Valsiner, J. (2004). Semiotic autoregulation: Dynamic sign hierarchies constraining the stream of consciousness. Seminar Presentation at the Seminar on Symbolic Forms Ecole Normale Supérieure, Paris, February, 6.

Valsiner, J. (2005). Transformation and flexible form: Where qualitative psychology begins. *Qualitative Research in Psychology*, **4**, 39-57.

Valsiner, J. (2006). Developmental epistemology and implications for methodology. In R. M. Lerner (Ec.), *Handbook of child psychology* (*Vol. 1: Theoretical models of human development*. 6th ed., pp. 166-209). New York: John Wiley and Sons.

Valsiner, J. (2007). *Culture in minds and societies*. New Delhi: Sage.

Valsiner, J. (2008). Baldwin's quest: A universal logic of development. In J. W. Clegg (Ed.), *The observation of human systems: Lessons from the history of anti-reductionistic empirical psychology* (pp. 45-82). New Brunswick, NJ: Transaction Publishers.

Valsiner, J. (2009). Persistent innovator: James Mark Baldwin rediscovered. In J. Valsiner (Introduction), James Mark Baldwin, *Genetic theory of reality* (pp. xv-lix). New Brunswick, NJ: Transaction Publishers.

Valsiner, J., & Connolly, K. J. (2003a). The nature of development: The continuing dialogue of processes and outcomes. In J. Valsiner & K. J. Connolly (Eds.), *Handbook of developmental psychology* (pp. ix-xviii). London: Sage.

Valsiner, J., & Connolly, K. J. (Eds.) (2003b). *Handbook of developmental psychology*. London: Sage.

Valsiner, J., & Diriwächter, R. (2005). Qualitative Forschungsmethoden in historischen und epistemologischen Kontexten. In G. Mey (Ed.), *Handbuch Qualitative Entwicklungspsychologie* (pp. 35-55). Köln: Kölner Studien Verlag.

Valsiner, J., Diriwächter, R., & Sauck, C. (2004). Diversity in unity: Standard questions and non-standard interpretations. In R. Bibace, J. Laird, K. Noller & J. Valsiner (Eds.), *Science and medicine in dialogue: Thinking through particulars and universals* (pp. 289-307). Stamford, CT: Greenwood Press.

Valsiner, J., & Rosa, A. (Eds.) (2007a). *The Cambridge handbook of sociocultural psychology*. New York: Cambridge University Press.

Valsiner, J., & Rosa, A. (2007b). General conclusions: Socio-cultural psychology on the move: Semiotic methodology in the making. In J. Valsiner & A. Rosa (Eds.), *The Cambridge handbook of sociocultural psychology* (pp. 692-708). New York: Cambridge University Press.

Valsiner, J., & Sato, T. (2006). Historically Structured Sampling (HSS): How can psychology's methodology become tuned in to the reality of the historical nature of cultural psychology? In J. Straub, D. Weidemann, C. Kölbl & B. Zielke (Eds.), *Pursuit of meaning: Advances in cultural and cross-cultural psychology* (pp. 215-251). Bielefeld: Transcript.

Valsiner, J., & van der Veer, R. (2000). *The social mind: Construction of the idea.* New York: Cambridge University Press.

van der Veer, R., & Valsiner, J. (1991). *Understanding Vygotsky: A quest for synthesis.* Oxford, UK: Basil Blackwell.

van der Veer, R., & Valsiner, J. (Eds.) (1994). *The Vygotsky reader.* Oxford, UK: Blackwell.

van Drunen, P., & Jansz, J. (2004). Child-rearing and education. In J. Jansz & P. van Drunen (Eds.), *A social history of psychology* (pp. 45-92). Malden, MA: Blackwell.

von Bertalanffy, L. (1950). The theory of open systems in physics and biology. *Science*, **111**(2872), 23-29.

von Bertalanffy, L. (1955). An essay on the relativity of categories. *Philosophy of Science*, **22**, 243-263.

von Bertalanffy, L. (1968). *General systems theory: Foundations, development, applications.* New York: George Braziller.

Vygotsky, L. (1930). Socialisticheskaja peredelka cheloveka. *VARNITSO*, the journal of the All-Union Association of Workers in Science and Technics for the Furthering of the Socialist Edification in the USSR.

Vygotsky, L. S. (1978). *Mind in society: The development of higher mental processes.* Cambridge, MA: Harvard University Press.

Vygotsky, L. S. (1994). The problem of the environment. In R. van der Veer & J. Valsiner (Eds.), *The Vygotsky reader* (pp. 338-354). Oxford, UK: Blackwell.

Vygotsky, L. S., & Luria, A. R. (1993). *Etiudy po istorii povedenia: Obezjana, primitiv, rebenok [Studies in the history of behavior: ape, primitive, and child].* Moscow: Pedagogika-Press.

Waddington, C. H. (1956). *Principles of embryology.* New York: MacMillan.

Waddington, C. H. (1966). *Principles of development and differentiation.* New York: MacMillan.

Watson, G. (1934). Psychology in Germany and Austria. *Psychological Bulletin*, **31**, 755-776.

Weber, M. (1949). *The methodology of the social sciences.* Translated and edited by E. A. Shils & H. A. Finch. NewYork: Free Press.

Wheaton, B., & Gotlib, I. H. (1997). Trajectories and turning points over the life course: Concepts of themes. In I. H. Gotlib & B. Wheaton (Eds.), *Stress and adversity over the life course: Trajectories and turning points* (pp. 1-25). New York: Springer.

White, M. (1972). On what could have happened. In R. Rudner & I. Scheffler (Eds.), *Logic & art:*

Essays in honor of Nelson Goodman (pp. 310-325). Indianapolis: Bobbs-Merrill.

Whyte, W. F. (1943). *Street corner society: The social structure of an Italian slum*. Chicago: University of Chicago Press.

Wieland, W. (1985). Prologomena zum Zeitbegriff. In H. Schipperges (Ed.), *Pathogenese: Grundzüge und Perspektiven einer Theoretischen Pathologie* (pp. 7-31). Berlin: Springer-Verlag. Leipzig: Wilhelm Engelmann.

Wirth, U. (1997). Abduction and comic in the sign of the three: Peirce, Freud, Eco. In I. Rauch & G. F. Carr (Eds.), *Semiotics around the world: Synthesis in diversity* (pp. 895-898). Berlin: Mouton de Gruyter.

Wozniak, R. H. (1998). *Classics in psychology, 1855-1914: Historical Essays*. Bristol: Thoemmes Press.

Wundt, W. (1896/1897). *Outlines of psychology*. Translated by C. H. Judd. Leipzig: Wilhelm Engelmann; first published in German as Wundt, W. (1896). *Grundriss der Psychologie*. Leipzig: Wilhelm Engelmann.

Yamada, Y., & Kato, Y. (2006). Images of circular time and spiral repetition: The Generative Life Cycle Model. *Culture & Psychology*, **12**, 143-160.

Yamaguchi, K. (1991). *Event history analysis*. Newbury Park, CA: Sage.

Yamamoto, T., & Pian, C. (2000). Culture as pocket money, or "how to foster 'true' wizard." *Journal of Home Economics of Japan*, **51**, 1169-1174 [in Japanese].

Yamamoto, T., & Takahashi, N. (2007). Money as a cultural tool mediating personal relationships: Child development of exchange and possession. In J. Valsiner & A. Rosa (Eds.), *The Cambridge handbook of sociocultural psychology* (pp. 484-507). New York: Cambridge University Press.

Yamamoto, T., Takahashi, N., Sato, T., Pian, C., Oh, S., & Kim, S. (2003). Children's money and their life-world in Jeju Island: A field research from cultural psychological perspectives. *Bulletin of Maebashi Kyoai Gakuen College*, **3**, 13-28 [in Japanese].

Yasuda, Y. (2004). The processes of reminiscing themselves through experiences of being infertility. Unpublished Master's thesis, Ritsumeikan University [In Japanese].

Yasuda, Y. (2005). Self-reassessment following infertility: Branching selection by couples unable to have children after infertility treatment. *Qualitative Research in Psychology*, **4**, 201-226 [In Japanese with English abstract].

Yasuda, Y. (2006). A trial to describe the diversity of infertility treatments with development of the Trajectory Equifinality Model (TEM). Poster presentation for ISSBD Australia, July.

Yasuda, Y., Arakawa, A., Takada, S., Kido, A., & Sato, T. (2008). Young women's abortion experiences: The influence of social expectation and relationships with others. *Qualitative*

Research in Psychology, **7**, 181-203 [in Japanese with English abstract].

Yin, R. K. (2003). *Case study research: Design and methods* (3rd ed.). Thousand Oaks, CA: Sage.

Young, A. (1995). *The harmony of illusions: Inventing post-traumatic stress disorder*. Princeton, NJ: Princeton University Press.

Yule, G. U. (1929). *An introduction to the theory of statistics* (9th ed.). London: C. Griffin.

Subject index

A

abduction 126
abortion 108
Activities of Daily Living
  (ADL) 160
addressivity 152
adoption 102, 206
AIDS 97, 130
Amyotrophic Lateral Sclerosis
  (ALS) 97, 156, 160
analytical generalization 94
anthropology 147
armchair anthropology 147

B

Barthel Index (BI) 160
Bifurcation Point (BFP) 18,
  35, 100, 127, 130, 154, 187,
  189, 212, 214
Big Five 122
Bone Marrow Transplanta-
  tion (BMT) 117
broom of time 13

C

Chicago school 148
Child Life Specialist (CLS) 153
child psychology 78, 199
child study 78
chronic illness trajectory
  model 146, 151
chronogenesis 9, 12
chronotope 11, 150
Classifying Science (CS) 76

clinical psychology 121
clock time 4, 9
Cognitive Dissonance Theory
  52, 203
contingent experience 97
control 59
control condition 192
correlational coefficients 122
cosmetics 106
cosmic time 7
cross situational consistency
  122
cultural attribution error 31
cultural histories 195
cultural psychology 26, 48,
  53, 92, 144, 150, 168, 174
culture 176

D

decision making 56, 136, 203
dependent variable 199
developmental psychology
  48, 50, 78, 121
Dialogical Self (DS) 52, 133,
  139, 158, 167, 215
Dialogical Self Theory 52, 139
disease 144
dropout 135
durée 19
dynamic of living with disease
  167
dynamics of the living 114,
  123

E

ecological niche 183
epigenetic landscape model
  193
equifinality 48, 98, 127, 129,
  145, 185
Equifinality Point (EFP) 18,
  35, 47, 68, 99, 127, 135,
  153, 185, 189, 211, 212
Erikson's developmental
  stage theory of learning
  self-esteem and trust 115
error 61, 128
ethnography 146, 147
event history analysis 185
experimental methodology
  77

F

fertility treatment 102
field psychology 123
fieldwork 146
Freud's psychosexual stage
  theory 115
Functional Independence
  Measure (FIM) 161

G

General Systems Theory
  (GST) 98, 127, 145, 184
generalization 58, 74, 93
Generative Life Cycle Model
  (GLCM) 7
genetic logic 15

German – Austrian method-
ology (thought) 57, 62
Gestalt psychology 64

H

hierarchy of needs model 116
historical psychology 176
Historically Structured Inviting (HSI) 212
Historically Structured Sampling (HSS) 45, 48, 51, 53,
67, 98, 128, 153, 174, 177,
184, 189, 191
history 56
homogeneity 82

I

Idiographic Science (IS) 75
illness 144
independent variable 199
inference revolution 62
infertility 101, 204
Inflammatory Bowel Disease
(IBD) 155
interdependency 183
intervention design 199
I-position 52, 133, 139
irreversible time 18, 56, 130,
187, 191, 211

K

kairos 19
KJ method 107, 136
Kohlberg's stage theory of
moral values 115

L

life course 6, 190, 211
life course development 56

life course developmental
psychology 47
life course paradigm 114
life course studies 117
life ethnography 149, 150
life stage theory 114
life trajectory 41, 118, 153, 183
Life with Illness (LWI) 144
lifetime 6
lived time 5, 9

M

macro-genetic level 56, 139,
191
makeup 106, 135, 204
medical anthropology 150
medical sociology 146
meso-genetic level 56, 139,
191, 201
methodology 18, 60
methodology of rating scale
114
Michikusa 5, 9
micro-ethnography 147, 150
microgenesis 48, 139, 176
micro-genetic level 56, 139,
150, 191, 197
MMPI 61
money 23
Money and Child research
project 29
multifinality 48, 130, 167, 185

N

natural context 190
neo-Galtonian research paradigm 63
new Big Five 123
non-experimental methodol-

ogy 77
North American psycho-
logical methodology
(thought) 57, 61

O

Obligatory Passage Point
(OPP) 18, 50, 100, 130,
135, 187-189, 198, 215
OCEAN Model 122
Ogori 31, 33
open system 37, 40, 46, 68,
95, 132, 145, 154, 184
oral transfer of knowledge
198
over time stability 122

P

personality psychology 120
person-context analysis 185
person-situation debate 121
Piaget's stage theory of a
child's thinking 115
Pocket Money (PM) 27, 30,
32, 40
point model 123
point-scale measurement 123
Polarized Equifinality Point
(P-EFP) 52, 101, 129, 135,
154, 198, 212
population 60, 74, 81, 94, 177,
191
promoter sign 139, 167, 214
psychology in Japan 63

Q

qualitative psychology 69
Quality of Life (QoL) 160

Subject index

R

random sampling 46, 59, 128, 174, 190
randomization 83
rating scale 120
relationalistic view 67

S

sample 74, 190
sampling 46, 73, 80, 89, 174
saturation 217
scale 119
Schedule for the Evaluation Individual QoL (SEIQoL) 163, 168
second EFP 216
sick role concept 161
sign 68, 94, 169
single case 34, 49, 75, 92, 192, 214
snow rabbit 10, 13
snowball method 90, 175
Social Directions (SD) 19, 50, 131, 137, 154, 215
Social Guidance (SG) 19, 131, 137, 154, 215

socio-cultural experience 97
socio-cultural psychology 68, 94
specimen 74, 81
stage model 115
statistical generalization 94
Structural Equation Models (SEM) 118
Stunde 11, 20
subjects 66
Synthesized Personal Orientation (SPO) 19, 137, 154
systemic view 67

T

TEM saturation 217
Three Layers Model of Genesis (TLMG) 138, 139
time 3
traditional sampling 179
trajectory 49, 117, 129, 145, 193
Trajectory Equifinality Approach (TEA) 211
Trajectory (and) Equifinality Model (TEM) 18, 29, 34,

45, 68, 99, 114, 126, 141, 145, 153, 157, 167, 174, 185, 206, 211
trajectory model 123
transformation 53, 132
true value 61, 128

U

urban sociology 148

V

variables 128
vector model 123
Virtual Comparison Condition (VCC) 190

W

Winnicott's development stages 115
written transfer of knowledge 198

Z

Zeit 11, 20
Zone of Finality (ZoF) 131, 137, 159

Name index

A

Abbey, E. 96, 123
Aeschleman, S. R. 29
Akasaka, M. 155
Anisov, A. 13, 14, 16
Arai, T. 51, 138, 139
Arakawa, A. 108, 109
Armstrong-Dailey, A. 153

B

Bakhtin, M. M. 12, 150, 152, 153
Baldwin, J. M. 9, 14, 15, 94
Baltes, P. B. 47
Banda, S. S. 151
Bekhterev, V. M. 67, 84
Benedict, R. 148
Benetka, G. 88
Bergold, J. B. 77
Bergson, H. 4, 16, 17, 130
Berti, A. E. 25
Binet, A. 78
Blonskii, P. 209
Blossfeld, H.-P. 185, 199
Bombi, A. S. 25
Bonarius, H. 121, 163
Branco, A. U. 177, 210
Bruner, J. 50, 56, 126
Brunswik, E. 88
Bühler, K. 92
Burton, C. R. 151, 152
Busch-Rossnagel, N. A. 118

C

Cairns, R. B. 78, 95, 181, 185
Callero, P. L. 119, 120
Chaitin, G. J. 209
Chappel, T. J. H. 7
Cochran, W. G. 73
Cole, M. 26, 27, 176
Connolly, K. J. 16, 78, 95, 98
Corbin, J. M. 146, 151, 152
Cortés, M. 23, 24, 42, 133
Costa, P. T., Jr. 122
Cressey, P. G. 148
Crick, F. 80

D

Daaleman, T. P. 117
Danziger, K. 47, 61, 66, 79, 85
Darwin, C. 77
Desrosières, A. 94
Dimaggio, G. 158
Diriwächter, R. 89, 93, 94, 177
D'Onofrio, M. J. 85
Driesch, H. 10, 11, 39, 98, 165, 166

E

Ebbinghaus, H. 60
Eisenberg, L. 144, 145
Elder, G. H., Jr. 117
Eliason, S. 117
Erikson, E. H. 115
Escobar, A. 96

F

Fayers, P. M. 160
Fechner, G. T. 60, 76, 94
Festinger, L. 52, 203
Fetterman, D. M. 146
Fisher, R. A. 83
Fogel, A. 157
Frank, A. W. 96
Frank, L. K. 124
Freier, M. 18
Freud, S. 115
Furnham, A. 30

G

Galton, F. 62, 118
Gendron, M. S. 85
Gesell, A. 78, 79
Giesbrecht, G. F. 6
Gigerenzer, G. 10, 62, 63, 86, 181, 210
Gilbert, S. F. 193
Ginsburg, S. 144
Glaser, B. G. 110
Goldberg, L. R. 122
Goncalves, M. 157
Gotlib, I. H. 118
Graff, E. 25
Gubrium, J. F. 67
Günther, J. A. 91

H

Hall, G. S. 63, 78
Hammond, K. R. 88
Handwerker, W. P. 110

Name index

Hatfield, G. 60
Hepper, P. 186
Herbart, J. F. 76
Herbst, D. P. 15
Hermans, H. J. M. 45, 52, 67, 82, 121, 133, 139, 158, 163, 168
Hidaka, T. 156, 157
Higashi, M. 54, 55
Holstein, J. A. 67
Hood, K. E. 7
Hubble, E. 8

J

Jablonka, E. 144
James, W. 139
Jansz, J. 77
Josephs, I. 7

K

Kabinga, M. 151
KAMO-no-Chomei 113
Kant, I. 60
Kato, Y. 6, 7, 10, 114
Kawakita, J. 107, 136
Kawano, K. 58
Keith, R. A. 161
Kelly, G. A. 163
Kempen, H. J. G. 67, 139, 163
Kennell, J. H. 199, 200
Kharlamov, N. A. 148
Kido, A. 50, 106, 107, 108, 135, 136
Kindermann, T. 182
Klaus, M. H. 199, 200
Kleinman, A. 144, 150
Kofka, K. 64
Kohlberg, L. 115
Köhler, W. 64

Kojima, H. 201
Kourilsky, M. L. 25
Kuklick, H. 148
Kullasepp, K. 45, 51-54, 133
Külpe, O. 67, 84, 94

L

Latour, B. 100, 130, 148, 188
Leary, D. E. 77
LeCompte, M. D. 146
Lens, W. 124
Lerner, R. M. 118
Levi, D. M. 62
Lewin, K. 5, 6, 64, 123, 124
Londoño, S. 23, 24, 42
Luria, A. R. 198

M

Machin, D. 160
Macmillan, R. 117
Malinowski, B. 147
March, J. G. 42
Marks, E. S. 86
Maslow, A. H. 116
McAdams, D. P. 122, 123
McCrae, R. R. 122
McGee, H. M. 163
McNemar, Q. 86, 128
McQuellon, R. P. 117
Mendel, M. 80
Minami, H. 5
Mischel, W. 121, 122
Mitchell, C. 130
Mizuki, S. 5
Molenaar, P. C. M. 62, 67, 68, 74, 92, 98
Mori, N. 136
Morioka, M. 12
Moro, Y. 152

Motora, Y. 63
Müller, U. 6
Murray, H. A. 62, 86, 113, 182, 210

N

Namiki, H. 65
Nerlich, B. 94
Neyman, J. 85, 86
Nishida, M. 156
Nozoe, S. 29
Nuttin, J. 124

O

O'Boyle, C. A. 163, 164
Odling-Smee, F. J. 182
Oh, S. A. 30-32
Omi, Y. 58, 65, 66
Onoshima, U. 64
Oyama, T. 65

P

Pals, J. L. 122, 123
Parsons, T. 146, 161, 162, 167
Patton, M. Q. 89
Pavlov, I. P. 67, 84
Pearson, K. 118
Peirce, C. S. 41, 82, 126, 136, 144
Persidsky, A. 182
Phipps, W. J. 151
Piaget, J. 115
Pian, C. 24, 28, 30
Poddiakov, A. N. 197
Popple, A. V. 62
Preissle, J. 146
Preyer, W. T. 77
Prigogine, I. 179

R

Radaev, V. V. 96
Rohwer, G. 199
Rosa, A. 15, 68, 80, 83, 92, 94, 111, 168
Roux, W. 10, 11
Rudolph, L. 6, 10

S

Sakuma, K. 64
Salgado, J. 157
Salvatore, S. 23, 24, 28, 41, 42
Sato, T. ii, 10, 16, 18, 19, 29, 39, 43, 45, 46, 48, 51-53, 60, 63-65, 67, 91, 93, 99, 101, 103, 106, 127, 128, 133, 135, 136, 138, 145, 153, 154, 157, 204
Schaeffer, H. R. 200
Schladenhauffen, J. 29
Schug, M. C. 25
Scupin, R. 136
Sen, A. 56, 110
Shanahan, M. J. 201
Sherif, M. 27
Shvyrkov, V. 182
Simon, H. 94
Skinner, B. F. 67, 84, 94
Smedslund, J. 15, 181
Smith, T. M. F. 86
Sovran, T. 185
Stevens, S. S. 119
Strauss, A. 25, 110, 146, 151, 152
Swanson, B. M. 153

T

Taine, H. 77
Takada, S. 108, 109
Takahashi, N. 24, 27, 30
Takasuna, M. 63, 64
Takeo, K. 37
Tanimura, S. 133
Thorndike, E. L. 51, 138
Titchener, E. B. 56
Toomela, A. 10, 15, 47, 57, 58, 63-66, 68
Trettien, A. 187

U

Uzawa, H. 24

V

Valsiner, J. ii, 7, 10, 11, 15, 16, 18, 26, 27, 29, 38, 43, 45, 46, 48-53, 59, 74, 76, 78, 80, 82, 88, 89, 91-95, 98, 99, 101, 111, 121, 123, 127, 128, 130, 133, 135, 139, 144, 145, 153, 154, 157, 168, 174, 176, 177, 179, 181, 182, 187, 196, 204, 207, 210
van der Veer, R. 92, 181, 196, 210
van Drunen, P. 77
von Bertalanffy, L. 34, 35, 47, 98, 99, 127, 129, 145, 166, 184, 185
Vygotsky, L. S. 67, 84, 92, 141, 144, 169, 198, 201, 203, 209

W

Waddington, C. H. 164, 165, 193, 194
Watanabe, Y. 128
Watson, G. 57, 58, 63, 66
Watson, J. 80
Watson, J. B. 67, 84
Weber, E. H. 60
Weber, M. 176
Werner, H. 92, 139, 150
Wertheimer, M. 64
Wheaton, B. 118
White, M. 208
Whyte, W. F. 148
Wieland, W. 15
Wirth, U. 83
Woolgar, S. 148
Wozniak, R. H. 76
Wundt, W. 60, 67, 76, 77, 84, 94, 95

Y

Yamada, Y. 6, 7, 10, 114
Yamaguchi, K. 185
Yamamoto, T. 24, 26-28, 30
Yasuda, Y. ii, 18, 29, 39, 43, 45, 47, 48, 67, 102, 104-106, 127-129, 133, 135, 136, 145, 153, 154, 157, 204, 205
Yin, R. K. 93, 94
Young, A. 150
Yule, G. U. 86

Z

Zarbock, S. 153

TATSUYA SATO is professor in the College of Comprehensive Psychology at Ritsumeikan University. Executive director of the Division of General Planning and Development at the Ritsumeikan Trust. Ph.D. (Tohoku University, 2002).

He has recently published *Psychology as the science of human being: The Yokohama Manifesto* (Springer, 2015, co-editor), *Making of the future: The Trajectory Equifinality Approach in cultural psychology* (Information Age Publishing, 2016, co-editor), History of "history of psychology" in Japan (*Japanese Psychological Research*, **58**(SP1), 110–128, 2006, co-author), Influence of G. Stanley Hall on Yuzero Motora as the first psychology professor in Japan: How the kymograph powered Motora's career in psychology (*American Journal of Psychology*, **125**, 395-407, 2012, co-author) etc.

Collected Papers on
Trajectory Equifinality Approach

2017 年 3 月 31 日　第 1 刷発行

著　者	Tatsuya Sato
発行者	櫻 井 堂 雄
発行所	株式会社ちとせプレス（Chitose Press Inc.）
	〒 154-0001
	東京都世田谷区池尻 2-31-20　清水ビル 5F
	電話　03-4285-0214
	http://chitosepress.com
装　幀	山 影 麻 奈
印刷・製本	大日本法令印刷株式会社

© 2017, Tatsuya Sato. Printed in Japan
　ISBN 978-4-908736-03-2　C3011

価格はカバーに表示してあります。
乱丁，落丁の場合はお取り替えいたします。